The publisher gratefully acknowledges the generous
contribution to this book provided by the Pacific Basin
Institute and by the Tokio Marine Kagami Memorial
Foundation through the Association for
100 Japanese Books.

The costs of this book have been defrayed in part
by the 1998 Hiromi Arisawa Memorial Awards
from the Books on Japan Fund with respect to
Marketing the Menacing Fetus in Japan and *Japan's Total Empire*,
published by the University of California Press.
The Awards are financed by The Japan Foundation
from generous donations contributed by Japanese
individuals and companies.

HARUKOR

VOICES FROM ASIA

HARUKOR

AN AINU WOMAN'S TALE

HONDA KATSUICHI

Translated by
KYOKO SELDEN

with a Foreword by
David L. Howell

UNIVERSITY OF CALIFORNIA PRESS

Berkeley · Los Angeles · London

University of California Press
Berkeley and Los Angeles, California

University of California Press, Ltd.
London, England

Ainu Minzoku by Honda Katsuichi
Copyright © 1993 by Honda Katsuichi
Original Japanese edition published by Asahi Shimbun Publishing Co., Ltd.
English translation rights arranged with Honda Katsuichi through
Japan Foreign-Rights Centre
Translation © 2000 by the Regents of the University of California

Manufactured in the United States of America

17 16 15 14 13 12 11 10 09
10 9 8 7 6 5 4 3 2

The paper used in this publication meets the minimum require-
ments of ANSI/NISO Z39.48-1992 (R 1997) (*Permanence of Paper*).

Contents

Illustrations

MAPS

FIGURES

Foreword
David L. Howell

The author of this book, Honda Katsuichi, is one of Japan's leading journalists and writers. After a distinguished career at the
influential daily *Asahi Shinbun*, he turned to writing a series of
books and essays on controversial political and historical topics,
always with the aim of forcing the Japanese people to face un-
pleasant truths about their country's abuses of human rights and
degradation of the environment.[1] Honda is deeply committed to
the cause of justice, and he is not afraid to make his readers confront issues they might prefer to forget or to never even know
about in the first place.

What prompted an author like Honda to write about the culture and history of the Ainu people of Hokkaidō? And how
should the knowledge that he is an activist journalist affect the
way we read this book?

The answer to the first question is straightforward. Honda feels
that Japan has not treated its indigenous people fairly. He also
finds much to admire in a people and a culture that prized nature's bounty and sought to live in harmony with it. He sees the
expansion of the Japanese state (and of the people whose im-

1. For a representative sample of his writings in English, see Honda Katsuichi, *The Impoverished Spirit in Contemporary Japan: Selected Essays of Honda Katsuichi*, ed. John Lie, trans. Eri Fujieda, Masayuki Hamazaki, and John Lie (New
York: Monthly Review Press, 1993).

migration it sponsored) into the Ainu homeland since the mid–nineteenth century as an exploitative colonial enterprise, conducted with scant regard for the welfare of the people who had been living there for centuries. While the state never engaged in systematic physical violence against the Ainu, it stripped them of their land and denied them access to Hokkaidō's natural resources. Moreover, it has long subjected them to an aggressive policy of ethnic negation—that is, the state has consistently refused to recognize the preservation of Ainu culture as a legitimate alternative to assimilation into the general Japanese population. Writing this book was Honda's way of alerting the Japanese people to this injustice; its translation into English carries his message to a much broader readership.

The second question is more complex. As readers, we must recognize this book as an unabashedly partisan portrayal of the Ainu people's history. To make its central points, it constructs a history of the Ainu largely in isolation from their relations with the Japanese state, particularly from their role as agents in dealings with that state. Honda's Hokkaidō is an idyllic island in which the Ainu have attained a harmonious relationship with nature; he portrays Ainu culture as unchanging and the Ainu themselves as passive victims of Japanese aggression. In the paragraphs that follow I shall present a more detached—and certainly less impassioned—version of Ainu history. But before doing so, I should like to pause to offer a brief defense of Honda's approach.

This book serves an important purpose in contemporary discourse about indigenous peoples. As a writer dedicated to battling injustice, Honda's first concern is to undermine his readers' prejudices. By idealizing the Ainu, he forces his Japanese readers to examine their own past and confront their complicity in the government's policies toward their fellow citizens. For his non-Japanese readers as well, the message is clear: we all must face the reality that modern development has been achieved only through violence to the environment and to indigenous cultures. Writing a dispassionate study of the Ainu would have diluted the power of Honda's important message, for it would have allowed his readers to see the position of the Ainu in contemporary Japan as the inevitable result of impersonal historical processes; it might even have prompted some readers to see whatever hardships they now face as being the Ainu's own fault. In that sense, Honda's account can be read not only for what it says explicitly about the Ainu but also for its implicit critique of contemporary Japanese society and government, for Honda is by training and temperament above all a social critic.

Honda's story of the Ainu woman Harukor is a vivid and often moving portrait of daily life in the *Ainu moshir*, or the Land of Humans, as the island of Hokkaidō was known to its indigenous people. Harukor was not an actual person. Rather, she is an ethnographic reconstruction—a collage assembled from a wide variety of sources on Ainu life, including anthropology and archaeology, oral literature and history. Although Harukor was not a real person, the events recounted in her story are all thoroughly plausible, the sorts of experiences an Ainu woman living in southeastern Hokkaidō several centuries ago might well have had. Moreover, her attitudes toward those experiences, and toward her family and community, the natural world, and the world of the gods, were ones that the Ainu shared and to some extent continue to share today.

Honda's decision to write his story from a woman's perspective is quite significant, for in so doing he goes beyond the usual image of the Ainu as hunters—hunting was a male activity—and takes us instead into the Ainu community itself, where women's roles were central. It is an ingenious strategy, for the focus on women allows Honda to make the most of the available ethnographic sources, including traditional knowledge of midwifery, child-rearing, and other practices. His narrative strategy also allows him to highlight the work of the men and women who recited the *yukar* and other types of oral literature; these extraordinarily rich bardic tales are our main source of insight into the Ainu's view of themselves and their world before the late nineteenth century.

Honda wrote the story of Harukor not only to convey a sense of what it meant to be Ainu but equally to encourage his readers to reconsider what it means to be Japanese, for the Ainu today are every bit as "Japanese" as their majority neighbors. But this story gives us all an opportunity to consider how identities—as women and men, as children and adults, as members of a community and an ethnic group—are formed in the crucible of everyday life. Likewise its lessons about the relationship of a people to their natural environment have a relevance that extends well beyond the Japanese archipelago.

Until their lives were permanently transformed by contact with the Wajin (the majority Japanese)—a long and complex process, as I shall outline below—the Ainu supported themselves mainly through fishing, hunting, and gathering.[2] They supplemented these activities with farming and trading, both among themselves and with neighboring peoples, particularly the Wajin. Like other peoples whose lives depended on an intimate knowledge of the land and its bounty, as well as of its awesome power, the Ainu developed a belief system that reflected this intimacy. Animals and natural phenomena like fire were seen as gods, and the Ainu's relationship with them was systematized in elaborate ritual prac-

---

2. The term *Wajin* is a relatively recent (late-eighteenth-century) coinage that refers to the majority Japanese as an ethnic group. The Ainu usually called Wajin *shisam*, or neighbors; the Japanized form of this word, *shamo*, is often used interchangeably with Wajin. In Part 1, Honda refers to the Wajin as "Shisam Japanese."

tices, such as the owl-spirit-sending ceremony depicted in this book. For us as contemporary readers, it is this close relationship with nature that offers the most immediate lessons for own daily lives. By seeing ourselves as completely distinct from the natural world, we have learned to treat the environment as an adversary to be conquered and harnessed to our own needs; we have accordingly developed technologies that have created a world that is materially prosperous yet far more fragile and alienated from the environment than anything Harukor or her people could ever have imagined.

To the Ainu, there was no fundamental break between the human and natural realms: humankind was indistinguishable from nature as manifested in the gods and their activities. Ainu who respected nature and honored the gods that inhabited it were rewarded with bountiful catches of salmon, plentiful hunts of deer and bear, and abundant crops, while those who failed to do so were punished with hard times. In a sense, humankind was not so much a part of nature as nature was an extension of humanity, for the gods had human characters, with all of humanity's nobility and capriciousness. The Ainu thus always strove to maintain a balance with nature, to take what they needed from the land without jeopardizing its ability to sustain them in the future. A good example of this effort can be seen in their practice of waiting each autumn until most of the salmon running in the rivers near their settlements had had a chance to spawn before catching them, an ecologically sound fishing method that also gave them fish ideally suited to preservation for the long and cold Hokkaidō winters.[3]

Yet it would be a grave error to read Harukor's story simply

---

3. See Kayano Shigeru, *Our Land Was a Forest: An Ainu Memoir*, trans. Kyoko Selden and Lili Selden (Boulder, Colo.: Westview, 1994), pp. 58–59.

for its lessons about the relationship between humankind and nature. For one thing, it would be both misleading and a bit patronizing to see the Ainu as being completely one with nature, for that suggests they were passively at its mercy. In fact, the Ainu, like Native Americans and other indigenous peoples throughout the world, actively manipulated their environment to meet their subsistence needs through such means as farming, damming rivers, and selective hunting.[4] Moreover, seeing the Ainu only in terms of their relationship to nature minimizes their historicity—that is, this perspective plays down the fact that Ainu culture was the product of specific historical developments and that it changed considerably over time. Such a static view of Ainu culture tends to negate their importance for an understanding of contemporary Japan, inasmuch as for a hundred years or more no Ainu have lived as Harukor did. In fact, Ainu culture is very much alive today, though the content of that culture is quite different from the one portrayed in this book. To appreciate this point, we must pause here and briefly examine the historical development of the Ainu people, especially their relationship with the majority population of the Japanese archipelago.[5]

Until quite recently, the Ainu had no recognized history, at least in the conventional sense of an autonomous story of cultural, economic, and political development. Beginning with the

4. See William Cronin, *Changes in the Land: Indians, Colonists, and the Ecology of New England* (New York: Hill and Wang, 1983), for a case study of the American Indians' manipulation of their physical environment.

5. In the following paragraphs I shall limit my discussion to the Hokkaidō Ainu; other groups of Ainu lived in Sakhalin and the Kurile Islands, but their cultures and histories differed significantly from those of their far more numerous Hokkaidō neighbors, on whom Honda concentrates. In the notes below I cite a number of recent works on the Ainu, focusing especially on materials available in English. A good place to start is Richard Siddle's excellent study of Japanese discourse about the Ainu and Ainu social and political movements in the twentieth century: *Race, Resistance, and the Ainu of Japan* (London: Routledge,

Chronicle of Japan (*Nihon shoki*) of 720 C.E., the ancestors of today's Ainu appeared in Japanese records only as the object of conquest. They were known variously as the Ebisu, Emishi, or Ezo, names given to the unassimilated peoples of the northeastern part of Honshū and Hokkaidō that all meant "eastern barbarians." Even after Hokkaidō was formally absorbed into the modern Japanese state in 1868, the Ainu were referred to in official documents and much public discourse as *kyūdojin,* or "former aborigines," a label that survived well into the twentieth century. As these names suggest, the Ainu were treated as the objects, but not the subjects, of historical development. Fortunately, scholars and activists have recently embarked on an effort to rectify this situation. By making use of the material remains available to archaeologists, oral traditions, and a sensitive rereading of the documentary record, they have at last begun to produce a new and much more nuanced picture of Ainu history.

Ainu culture as we know it is the product of history. Until about the fourteenth century C.E. the ancestors of the Ainu people lived in two quite distinct cultural zones, the Satsumon and Okhotsk. The Satsumon culture of northeastern Honshū and southern and central Hokkaidō is named after the pottery its bearers produced. Archaeologists have traced its origins to the Neolithic Jōmon culture that once encompassed the entire Japanese archipelago from the Ryūkyū Islands in the south to Hokkaidō in the north. Evidence suggests that the Jōmon people were the ancestors not only of the Ainu but of the rest of the Japanese population as well. The Okhotsk culture spread southward from Sakhalin to northern Hokkaidō and the Kurile Islands. Its bearers were a maritime people who hunted sea mam-

---

1996); see also Siddle, "Ainu: Japan's Indigenous People," in *Japan's Minorities: The Illusion of Homogeneity,* ed. Michael Weiner (London: Routledge, 1997), pp. 17–49. A standard ethnography is Hitoshi Watanabe, *The Ainu Ecosystem: Environment and Group Structure* (Seattle: University of Washington Press, 1972).

mals and also produced a distinctive style of pottery. Eventually—
we still do not know how or precisely when—the Satsumon and
Okhotsk cultures merged into what we know as Ainu culture.[6]
Although Ainu culture shares much with its predecessors—
the Satsumon and Okhotsk people also were fishers, hunters, and
gatherers—it differs in significant ways, too. Most strikingly, the
Ainu stopped making pottery and eventually lost the knowledge
of its manufacture. Their loss of such an important and obviously
useful technology seems odd until we consider the reason: iron.
The availability of iron utensils, particularly cooking pots and
swords, through trade with the Wajin to the south made pottery
manufacture obsolete, and so the Ainu abandoned it. The Ainu
obtained many other commodities from the Wajin as well, including rice, cloth, lacquerware, and even pottery, which by the
fourteenth century was being mass-produced in central Honshū
and traded all along the Japan Sea coast.

The metamorphosis of the pottery-making Satsumon and
Okhotsk cultures into the iron-using Ainu culture reveals that
the Ainu were traders as well as fishers, hunters, and gatherers.
Without trade, the Ainu would never have had access to iron,
and without iron, the distinctive Ainu culture of the archaeological and historical record would never have existed.

Seeing the Ainu as traders forces us to reconsider the place of
the Ainu homeland of Hokkaidō in Japanese and East Asian history. Today, Hokkaidō is seen as the frontier of Japan, and this image makes sense from the perspective of the Japanese state, which
has always been centered at least six hundred miles away. But in
the period in which Ainu culture developed—roughly the four-

6. See Kikuchi Toshihiko, "Continental Culture and Hokkaido," in *Windows on the Japanese Past*, ed. Richard J. Pearson (Ann Arbor: Center for Japanese Studies, University of Michigan, 1986), pp. 149–62; Hanihara Kazurō, ed.,
International Symposium on Japanese as a Member of the Asian and Pacific Populations
(Kyoto: International Research Center for Japanese Studies, 1992).

teenth through mid–sixteenth centuries—Hokkaidō and northernmost Honshū constituted a center in their own right, the focus of trade routes that extended along the Japan Sea coast from
central Honshū to Hokkaidō, Sakhalin, and the Amur River basin
of northeastern China, and across the sea to Korea. Military
strongmen based in Tosaminato, a port on the Tsugaru peninsula
at the northern tip of Honshū, sent a diplomatic mission to the
Korean court in 1482. Merchants in southern Hokkaidō amassed
great wealth, as evidenced by a cache of hundreds of thousands
of Chinese copper coins discovered in a fortress near the modern
city of Hakodate. The ethnic identities of these strongmen and
merchants are unclear but in any case probably irrelevant, as there
is no reason to believe they thought in terms of a sharp distinction between essentially different Wajin and Ainu cultures.

Northernmost Honshū and southern Hokkaidō ceased to be
an autonomous trading and diplomatic center during the era of
Japan's reunification as a centralized state in the sixteenth century. The establishment of the Tokugawa shogunate in 1603 completed this process of reunification and left a clear boundary between Japan and the realm of the Ainu—nominally autonomous
yet clearly subordinated to the Japanese state—in southern
Hokkaidō.[7] Over the course of the seventeenth century the Ainu
gradually lost access to Honshū. Although they continued to trade
with their neighbors to the north and east in Sakhalin and the
Kuriles, their world became much more insular as a result of this
process of state building in Japan.

7. On the Ainu during the Tokugawa period, see David L. Howell, "Ainu
Ethnicity and the Boundaries of the Early Modern Japanese State," *Past and
Present,* no. 142 (February 1994): 69–93; Howell, *Capitalism from Within: Economy, Society, and the State in a Japanese Fishery* (Berkeley: University of California Press, 1995); and Brett L. Walker, "Reappraising the *Sakoku* Paradigm: The
Ezo Trade and the Extension of Tokugawa Political Space into Hokkaidō," *Journal of Asian History* 30.2 (1996): 169–92.

The Ainu did not accept this new geopolitical reality without a struggle. Indeed, the period between the mid–fifteenth and late seventeenth centuries was marked by almost continuous warfare in southern Hokkaidō, culminating in Shakushain's War of 1669, the last significant armed conflict between the Ainu and their Wajin overlords. Shakushain was a chieftain based in the Hidaka region of western Hokkaidō. He led an alliance of Ainu in battle against the Matsumae domain, a Wajin foothold on the southern tip of the island, in an attempt to gain better trade terms, but he was beaten after several months of fierce fighting. His defeat left the Ainu more dependent on the Matsumae domain and its agents: they continued to need Japanese commodities but were no longer able to dictate the terms of trade.

Over the course of the next two centuries, increasing numbers of Wajin came to Hokkaidō to trade and particularly to fish. At first the inflow was quite small, but by the beginning of the nineteenth century the entire coast of the island was dotted with commercial fishing stations, which employed both Ainu and Wajin labor. Wage labor at these fishing stations gradually replaced trade as the Ainu's main source of iron, cloth, rice, lacquerware, and other needed commodities.

During the Tokugawa period (1603–1868), the Ainu were in many respects an embattled people. Their dependence on imports forced them to submit to Wajin control at the fishing stations for several months of every year. The Wajin took advantage of their dominant position by mistreating Ainu workers, appropriating Ainu women as concubines, and breaking up Ainu families. Moreover, smallpox, measles, and other epidemic diseases introduced from the south repeatedly decimated Ainu communities. Although we do not have precise data, it is generally accepted that as a result of mistreatment and disease the Ainu population fell steadily from a peak of perhaps 40,000 before finally leveling off at about 17,000 in the middle of the nineteenth century.

The Ainu could do little to fight this onslaught other than engage in individual acts of resistance, such as flight, or, much more rarely, join to rise in protest against especially egregious outrages. But so long as the balance of power so heavily favored the Wajin they had no way to change the fundamental state of affairs. Ainu culture remained extremely vibrant, despite the loss of political and economic autonomy. For example, the bear *iyomante*, which some scholars consider to be the defining feature of early modern Ainu culture, developed in its present form only after the late eighteenth century.[8] It was an elaborate ceremony in which the spirit of a bear cub that had been raised in an Ainu settlement was sent back to the realm of the gods laden with gifts. The *iyomante* was the most important religious ritual of the Ainu, and it gave geographically dispersed lineage groups an opportunity to gather and reaffirm their sense of community. Having lost the ability to form meaningful political units, the Ainu compensated by creating a ritual framework to assert their independence from Wajin domination.

The position of the Ainu changed radically after 1868, when the modern Japanese state included Hokkaidō within its boundaries and began sending agricultural colonists into the interior of the island.[9] Unlike the Tokugawa regime, which was generally content to let the Ainu maintain a distinct identity, the mod-

---

8. For a discussion of the importance of the *iyomante* in Ainu culture, see Watanabe, *Ainu Ecosystem*; on Ainu social organization more generally, see Takashi Irimoto, "Ainu Territoriality," *Hoppō bunka kenkyū* 21 (1992): 67–81. On the historical development of the *iyomante*, see Sasaki Toshikazu, "Iomante kō: Shamo ni yoru Ainu bunka rikai no kōsatsu" (On the Iyomante: A consideration of Shamo understandings of Ainu culture), *Rekishigaku kenkyū*, no. 613 (November 1990): 111–20, and Utagawa Hiroshi, *Iomante no kōkogaku* (Archaeology of the *iyomante*) (Tokyo: University of Tokyo Press, 1989).

9. See David L. Howell, "The Meiji State and the Logic of Ainu 'Protection,'" in *New Directions in the Study of Meiji Japan: Proceedings of the Meiji Studies Conference*, ed. Helen Hardacre (Leiden: Brill, 1997), pp. 815–47.

ern state launched an assault against Ainu culture and society—particularly after 1899, when it implemented the Former Hokkaidō Aborigine Protection Act (Hokkaidō Kyūdojin Hogohō), which sought to transform the Ainu into farmers. Universal education in Japanese undermined the Ainu language, and the influx of hundreds of thousands of Wajin immigrants into Hokkaidō left the Ainu dispossessed of their land and unable to support themselves through fishing and hunting. The state validated the immigrants' assault on the Ainu economy by imposing laws that criminalized the very activities that had sustained them for centuries. Moreover, as a result of intermarriage with Wajin, the number of people of unmixed Ainu ancestry dwindled rapidly. By the beginning of the twentieth century the Ainu culture of Harukor's time was a thing of the past.

Unlike the indigenous peoples of North America, the Ainu were never placed in reservations or otherwise isolated from the rest of Japanese society. Instead, the government treated them at least superficially like other subjects and assumed that they would find their own way in modern Japan. The Ainu "protection" act of 1899 made small plots of land available to them to farm, the idea being that their traditional way of life was incompatible with their new status as modern Japanese. Some Ainu successfully made the transition to farming, while others turned to full-time wage labor to support themselves; still others developed new livelihoods, such as handicraft production for the tourist trade. In general, however, modernity was hard on the Ainu, as few of them had the resources or training to succeed in the new order. Their difficulties were compounded by the cultural insensitivity and persistent discrimination they faced from officials and immigrants. Even such well-intended policies as the systematic replacement of Ainu dwellings (*chise*) with wooden houses had unforeseen deleterious effects, such as rendering the Ainu more vulnerable to tuberculosis and other debilitating ailments.

Yet Ainu culture did not die. Despite the strong desire of many officials to see the Ainu assimilate completely into Wajin society, the Ainu—by now a small minority within their own homeland— retained their distinctive identity even though they were mostly monolingual in Japanese, farmed or worked for wages, and maintained few elements of their historic culture. During the first half of the twentieth century, a number of Ainu, such as the poet Iboshi Hokuto and the Christian activist Nukishio Hōmaku, sought to find a place for a non-Wajin identity within a rapidly industrializing and thoroughly modern Japanese society. Although they failed to influence government policy, their activities are significant nonetheless. They embraced their status as subjects of the Japanese emperor and hence as citizens of Japan, while at the same time asserting the validity of their own Ainu identity. That is, they argued that one could be both Ainu and Japanese, thereby opening the door to the possibility of a multiethnic society within the Japanese archipelago. At the time this was a radical proposal, for it ran counter to the officially prescribed ideology of a homogeneous Japanese people united under the emperor.

After Japan's defeat in World War II, the government abandoned its most heavy-handed assimilation policies toward the Ainu, though it retained the fundamental notion that Japan is and ought to be a culturally and ethnically homogeneous nation.[10] During the past decade or two a number of activists have responded by asserting the Ainu's fundamental difference from the

10. On the Ainu in contemporary Japan, see Siddle, *Race, Resistance, and the Ainu*, pp. 147–89; Fred C. C. Peng and Peter Geiser, eds., *The Ainu: The Past in the Present* (Hiroshima: Bunka Hyōron, 1977); Katarina Sjöberg, "Practicing Ethnicity in a Hierarchical Culture: The Ainu Case," in *Indigenous Peoples of Asia*, ed. R. H. Barnes, Andrew Gray, and Benedict Kingsbury (Ann Arbor, Mich.: Association for Asian Studies, 1995), pp. 373–88; and David L. Howell, "Ethnicity and Culture in Contemporary Japan," *Journal of Contemporary History* 31.1 (1996): 171–90.

Wajin, stressing instead their status as an indigenous people who have been victimized by centuries of Wajin aggression and domination. In this context, they have called for a measure of Ainu political autonomy and have attempted to revive the Ainu language and cultural practices; these efforts, which have drawn public attention to the Ainu's situation, have encouraged many Ainu to take pride in their identity. In 1997 the government responded by replacing the "protection" law of 1899 with a new measure that guarantees support for Ainu cultural activities but does not grant political autonomy. In the meantime, however, the number of people intimately familiar with the historic Ainu culture has steadily declined—indeed, no one now speaks the Ainu language in daily life, and ritual practices such as performances of oral literature and the *iyomante* have been transformed from private, local expressions of community solidarity into highly visible, self-conscious assertions of Ainu ethnic identity.

Preserving Ainu culture does not mean maintaining it like a relic in a museum for scholars to study. Doing so would be tantamount to admitting that it no longer survives and that the Ainu as a people are extinct (or nearly so). Throughout the modern period, Wajin writers have often called the Ainu a "dying people" (*horobiyuku minzoku*), a tag that has seemed unproblematic to them in light of the undeniable decline of historic Ainu cultural practices.[11] The struggle against that imagery is one of the few links between the pre–World War II Ainu movement and its contemporary counterpart. After all, admitting to the Ainu's imminent extinction would render their efforts at cultural revival meaningless.

---

11. This picture of the Ainu has made its way into Western-language discourse as well. See, for example, Mary Inez Hilger, *Together with the Ainu: A Vanishing People* (Norman: University of Oklahoma Press, 1971), a well-meaning but quite condescending portrait of Ainu life in the 1960s.

Ainu culture survives, and self-aware communities of Ainu continue to negotiate a place for themselves in Japanese society. One way the activists among them do this is by emphasizing the contribution of Ainu culture to Japan's (and the world's) response to environmental crises. Ainu culture must be preserved, they say, because it offers a model that we can all learn from. As many Wajin and non-Japanese have themselves been seeking just such a model, the strategy has been successful; indeed, this book is a by-product of those efforts. Another strategy has been to forge ties with other indigenous peoples around the world, thereby contributing to Japan's "internationalization" in a way that contrasts sharply with the usual realms of trade and diplomacy. This effort, too, has been successful because of the worldwide concern over the environment and the symbolic importance of all indigenous peoples as its guardians. Finally, many Ainu activists have argued that their culture ought to be nurtured out of a simple concern for fairness: the Ainu were in Hokkaidō for centuries before their culture and society were subjected to the onslaught of the Wajin, and so they have a fundamental right to preserve their lifeways in the contemporary world.[12] Wajin concerned with making modern Japan a more just society have responded enthusiastically to this argument; Honda Katsuichi is one such person.

Most of the 30,000 or so Ainu in contemporary Japan are not activists, of course. Whatever their feelings about the movement to preserve their people's historic culture, they are more immediately concerned with the daily struggle to support their families and make lives for themselves within Japanese society. Since the most visible emblems of Ainu identity—things like the per-

---

12. See Richard Siddle, "Deprivation and Resistance: Ainu Movements in Modern Japan," in *Diversity in Japanese Culture and Language*, ed. John C. Maher and Gaynor Macdonald (London: Kegan Paul International, 1995), pp. 147–59.

formance of the *iyomante* and traditional fishing, hunting, and gathering techniques—have never been at the center of their daily lives (or even of their parents' lives, for that matter), "Ainu culture" as it is usually perceived has little to do with their everyday needs. Indeed, asserting one's Ainu identity too aggressively makes it difficult to get by in what is still a very insular Japanese society.

To such people, being Ainu means facing every day the possibility of discrimination at school, in the workplace, and in marriage. It means combating resilient stereotypes about their culture. It means being seen as primitive in a society that aggressively strives to assert its modernity, both to itself and to the outside world. But they are not somehow less authentically Ainu than their activist neighbors or their ancestors. Rather, their sense of being Ainu reveals that their identity has been transformed from a distinctive set of cultural practices into a sense of community, of connection to Hokkaidō as their homeland and to their neighbors as people who share that connection.

As Hokkaidō has changed and the relationship of its people to the outside world has changed, the Ainu have adapted and will continue to adapt. We should not see the Ainu only as the object of Wajin aggression, nor should we make light of their victimization at the hands of the Japanese state. Trade, dependence, and colonization were all part of the history of the Ainu people, and all therefore contributed to the development of Ainu culture. The first step that we as non-Ainu must take to appreciate the challenges that face the contemporary Ainu is abandoning the conceit that there existed in the past an unchanging, pristine, "true" Ainu culture that can only be perceived in isolation from contact with Wajin.

This book can help us in that task. For although it is set centuries ago and therefore appears to portray a culture frozen in time, in fact it encourages us to look at Ainu culture as a living entity, formed and re-formed through the mundane experiences of an individual woman. "Ainu culture" to Harukor was not an abstract concept: it was nothing other than the sum of her daily endeavors and the worldview that guided her in them. Harukor's efforts to contribute to her family's well-being were no different from our own: as she used the knowledge passed down to her by her forebears and the materials at hand, her primary concern was always to get through life as best she could. That is the most we can expect of anyone, for everyday life is the arena in which culture is produced.

Translator's Note

This translation project began in the summer of 1994, but my personal interest in the Ainu people goes back a long way. Kindaichi Kyōsuke, the pioneer linguist who collaborated with Ainu bards to study and preserve Ainu oral literature in written form, lived in my neighborhood when I was a child. Not only did Kindaichi live around the corner in Higashitamachi in Suginami-ku, Tokyo, but I grew up in the house the Kindaichis had previously lived in. I remember being inspired when I learned that our western-style room, with its large desk and many bookshelves, was the study where Kindaichi had written his first book on Ainu epic poetry.

Decades later when I read Kayano Shigeru's *Ainu no ishibumi* (1980, translated as *Our Land Was a Forest*, 1994), I learned that Kayano had assisted Kindaichi in the early sixties and visited his Higashitamachi house several times. Had I not left Tokyo in 1959, I might even have seen Kayano on the narrow neighborhood street where I often saw Kindaichi.

I have another memory that keeps returning to me. I first met Ainu people during a school trip to Hokkaidō in the mid-fifties. We traveled by train along the southwest coastline, and by bus in central Hokkaidō, across grassy fields covered with yellow and light purple wildflowers, then through dark forests of age-old trees with gigantic trunks and roots. There was one especially unforgettable occasion when we visited a settlement in the southwest. After the village head's solemn ceremonial greeting in a voice that seemed to come from the depths of the earth, a small group of villagers danced in a circle, surrounded by all two hundred fifty of us in the sunny, open space. The village head beat the time with his staff. The dancers were silent and expressionless. I felt as if we were watching a pantomime we were not meant to see. Perhaps I was sensing the discomfort of the villagers as they performed before tourists, especially before ignorant teenagers, playing the role of "display Ainu" in Kayano Shigeru's expression. The thought remains with me as I translate from Japanese writings about the Ainu.

The main portion of Honda Katsuichi's *Harukor: An Ainu Woman's Tale* is a first-person narrative of an Ainu woman who lived several centuries ago. Why did Honda, a contemporary Japanese male journalist and critic, choose to portray traditional Ainu life through the fictional account of an Ainu woman of long ago? Honda explains that his intention to reconstruct what Ainu village life must have been like in southeastern Hokkaidō several hundred years ago, a period for which few written records remain, led him to choose the vehicle of an Ainu prose narrative style, *uwepeker*. In choosing that style and interweaving it with other traditional forms, including epic, love song, and elegy, he also attempted something that distinguishes this work from that of Kindaichi Kyōsuke and other Japanese researchers. They had recorded and translated Ainu oral literature into Japanese, an act criticized by some today as one of fossilizing performance into printed words that are stripped of the performative and participatory circumstances, of emphasizing written documents over the words and songs of generations of people who transmitted the literature. In the first-person narration of Harukor's story, Honda attempts to engage, in his own way, in traditional Ainu story-making. It seems to me a return courtesy from Honda to the Ainu people who have allowed him to step into their lives in the decades since the 1950s, when he first went to Hokkaidō as a young reporter for the *Asahi Shimbun*. One challenge in preparing this translation was the handling of the abundance of Ainu terms with Japanese translations in parentheses. The Ainu expressions lend both beauty and authenticity to the text. However, in order to reduce distractions for English-language readers, the number of Ainu words in the text has been reduced. Where variants occur, one form alone is retained. For the three principal forms of oral literature, for example, Honda's original respects regional differences by using *yukar, kamui yukar,* and *uwepeker* in the general discussion in Part 1, and frequently applying their eastern equivalents *sakorpe, oina* or *matyukar,* and *tuitak* in the narrative in Part 2. Here, however, *yukar, kamui yukar,* and *uwepeker* are used throughout.

Ainu and Japanese words are italicized without distinction in the text, but Japanese words are so indicated in the glossary. Japanese names of Japanese and Ainu individuals are given in the Japanese style, with family names first. In Aoki Aiko, for example, Aoki is the family name, Aiko the personal name.

Lili Selden and Christopher Ahn have been my constant collaborators. From Ann Arbor, Tokyo, Matsumoto, and Ithaca, they have contributed at every stage of the translation. Fumiko Ikawa-Smith and Jane Marie Law read the first chapter and made helpful suggestions. Honda Katsuichi was invariably punctilious in providing detailed answers to my persistent questions, and generous in providing materials, including his own photos. David Howell provided a historian's perspective on critical issues of Ainu life and Ainu-Japanese relations. Alice Falk's careful reading enhanced the quality of the translation. First Laura Driussi, then Sue Heinemann, editors at the University of California Press, provided invaluable assistance not only with language and style but also with the organization of the English edition. Among many others to whom I am indebted, I would like to express my appreciation to Sōma Junko, who introduced me, during my visit to Hokkaidō in the summer of 1998, to a variety of northern plants that appear in this book, and Sassa Chikako, who helped me with English botanical names.

Kyoko Selden
Ithaca, New York

Preface

At about the same time that Europeans entered the North American continent in large numbers, mainland Japanese began to encroach on Hokkaidō, resulting in several centuries of aggression that led to the subjugation of the indigenous people and the destruction of their way of life. The present volume introduces the society and culture of the Ainu people prior to that aggression.

I first came in contact with the Ainu on a trip to Hokkaidō when I was nineteen, in 1951. However, my perspective at the time was not unlike that of a tourist. I was far from understanding their situation. In 1959, posted to Hokkaidō as a reporter for the *Asahi Shinbun*, I had another chance for contact with the Ainu. But even then, my contacts did not take me beyond visiting the Ainu *kotan* (village) to report, for example, on the traditional hunting dog of the Ainu. To the extent that the Ainu themselves at that time forswore the name *Ainu*, viewing it as discriminatory, their pride and awareness of themselves as a nation and a people were suppressed. This atmosphere made me hesitate to report on them.

The motivation to seriously address Ainu issues came from my visit to the United States. In 1969 I reported on Black Power, then in its ascendance. I also looked into the conditions of Native Americans in New Mexico. Reporting on the awakening of Blacks as an oppressed people led me to reflect on the Ainu. Likewise, reporting on Native Americans led me to think about Japan's indigenous people. Native Americans also soon entered a time of rebellion highlighted by the 1973 clash with federal authorities at Wounded Knee, South Dakota. The resurgence of Red Power in the United States clearly influenced the Ainu, and Ainu claims of what we may call "Ainu Power" emerged at this time.

My interest in these issues predated my 1969 U.S. trip, however. I reported on the Inuit in Canada in 1963, on Highlanders in New Guinea in 1964, on Bedouins in Saudi Arabia in 1965, and on Montagnards in Vietnam in 1967–68. The experience of reporting on indigenous peoples throughout the world intensified my concern for Japan's indigenous people. I began serious research on the Ainu in the 1970s.

My plan was to divide this work into three sections: first, Ainu society prior to Japanese aggression; second, the period of aggression in the century up to the Meiji Restoration of 1868; and, finally, the present situation of the Ainu. Regrettably, I have yet to write the second and third parts. This volume presents Ainu society of several hundred years ago.

The problem of treating the Ainu prior to Japanese encroachment is a challenging one. Since the Ainu had no written language, no documentary record remains from those days. I was at first at a loss about how to write about this period. In preparing a journalist's report rather than a scholar's thesis, one must find a different means to draw readers into the subject. To convey a sense of Ainu society several hundred years ago, I drew inspiration from the voluminous oral traditions, songs, and epics that constitute the rich legacy of this people. I also learned from surviving elders—or *ekashi,* as they are called in Ainu—and drew on the research of Ainu and other scholars. In particular, I borrowed *uwepeker,* one important form of oral tradition, to convey something akin to an Ainu perspective on culture and society. My hope is that telling the story through this Ainu form will help the reader to bridge the gap of time, space, and culture.

I have been fortunate to have the cooperation of many Ainu

and Japanese researchers. I cannot mention all their names, but I would like to acknowledge those who have been particularly helpful. First is Kayano Shigeru, whose book *Our Land Was a Forest: An Ainu Memoir* is available in English translation. Kayano, who is a writer, folklorist, collector, and translator of important Ainu oral texts, became the first Ainu member of the Japanese Diet. Next, I thank Fujimura Hisakazu, who is not an Ainu but who studied Ainu language and culture with an *ekashi* and mastered them. Katayama Tatsumine provided the romanization of Ainu words. Finally, I thank Kyoko and Mark Selden, who gave me a chance to introduce the world of the Ainu people to English-language readers, including Americans.

Honda Katsuichi

PART ONE

AINU MOSHIR

With thirty-two thousand square miles, Hokkaidō, the north-ernmost island of the Japanese archipelago, is one-fifth of the entire area of Japan and twice as large as Switzerland. Before the Meiji era (1868–1912), it was a land of abundant resources.

The oldest site uncovered in Japan dates from twenty to thirty thousand years ago, during the Paleolithic period, which is also known in Japan as the Preceramic period. At this time, in the middle of the Würm glaciation, Hokkaidō was connected by land to the continent and still inhabited by mammoths. The glacial period ended approximately ten thousand years ago, during the late Paleolithic period.

It is difficult to ascertain whether the people who shaped the culture of that period are the direct ancestors of the Ainu. If we hypothesize that the Ainu today are completely unrelated to the Paleolithic people, then the Ainu's ancestors (a Neolithic people) must have driven out or killed the former inhabitants in the course of a mass migration, or they must have moved in after their predecessors had left or become extinct. There is, however, no evidence from archaeology or oral tradition to suggest such large shifts in population. It makes more sense to assume some relationship between the two groups. Our best hypothesis is either that the Ainu descended directly from the Paleolithic people or that the Paleolithic inhabitants mixed with another people and the Ainu descended from that combination.

The Neolithic, or Jōmon, period was ushered in seven or eight thousand years ago in Hokkaidō when pottery making began to be practiced there. This period lasted five or six thousand years. Approximately two thousand years ago, small amounts of iron

3

Hokkaidō

were introduced from either southern Japan or the continent, inaugurating a new age, customarily called the Epi-Jōmon period, characterized by the simultaneous use of metal and stone.[1] The

1. "Epi-Jōmon" refers to the surviving Jōmon-like stage in Hokkaidō, in which the remnants of the Jōmon tradition persisted until the Satsumon culture developed in the eighth century.

A fully dressed Kunashiri Ainu, drawn by Maeno
Chōhatsu, from an 1898 publication.

inhabitants of Hokkaidō from at least that time forward are
considered to be direct ancestors of the Ainu.[2] Until we find
sufficient positive evidence to judge otherwise, it seems most rea-

2. Of the many reference materials on the maturation of Ainu culture, see
esp. Enomoto Morie, *Hokkaidō no rekishi* (A history of Hokkaidō) (Hokkaidō
Shinbunsha, 1981).

sonable to assume that the Jōmon people had a close, if not direct, relationship with the Ainu.

A group more clearly recognizable as direct ancestors of the Ainu flourished from the eighth to the thirteenth century, when unique pottery called *Satsumon doki*, characterized by an exterior finished by scraping with wood, emerged in Hokkaidō and northern parts of Tōhoku, or northern Honshū. Genuine Ainu culture began after this period. Some scholars apply the term "proto-Ainu" to the approximately twelve hundred years of the Epi-Jōmon and Satsumon periods; others include the seven thousand years from the Jōmon through the Satsumon period.

Ainu culture—represented, for example, by voluminous verse epics called *yukar*—seems to have fully developed most of its distinctive characteristics after the Satsumon period, either around the Muromachi period (1336–1573) or during the three to four hundred years from late Kamakura to early Edo times (early fourteenth to early seventeenth century).[3] Iron tools had already been introduced, and millet and other grains were being raised in small amounts.[4] There was a fair amount of trade with the Japanese in the southernmost part of Hokkaidō and in northern Tōhoku. Similarly, the people of northern Hokkaidō were in contact with the continent.

3. *Yukar* (the accent falls on the first syllable) is epic poetry that is musically chanted. The form has various names—*sakorpe* in northeastern Hokkaidō, where the central story of this book is set; *sakorpe* and *hauki* in Sakhalin Ainu—but the term *yukar* will be used throughout the book. The genre is divided into divine *yukar* (*kamui yukar*) and human *yukar*.

4. Ainu in the southwest region of Hokkaidō appear to have been farming for one thousand years. See Hayashi Yoshishige, *Ainu no nōkō bunka* (The farming culture of the Ainu) (Keiyūsha, 1969). Recent excavations point to the possibility that the cultivation of buckwheat and mung beans goes back three thousand years.

In studies of the Ainu, two issues have often been disputed: whether the Ainu and the Ezo in the northeast of the mainland are the same people, and whether the origins of the Japanese and the Ainu (as well as the origins of the Japanese language and the Ainu language) are related. These debates engage archaeology, ethnology, anthropology, linguistics, history, geography, and other fields. Interpretations have been offered from the perspective of each area, but no decisive verification has been possible. What can be said with certainty is that for a long time Ainu people, or the bearers of Ainu culture, inhabited Honshū, the main Japanese island, as its indigenous people.

In the seventeenth century, Ainu was still spoken in northern Tōhoku—for example, in portions of Tsugaru province (now Aomori prefecture). Forty-three Ainu households, spread over fifteen villages, are said to have existed there. When Tsugaru province negotiated with a group of Ainu in Hokkaidō, members of these households accompanied Tsugaru officials as interpreters.[5] Their names were, of course, Ainu names.

In spacious Tōhoku, many places still have Ainu names today. The number increases in northern Tōhoku, north of the Akita-Yamagata and Iwate-Miyagi prefectural borders.[6] Farther south, the derivations of some place-names are disputed; nonetheless, a fair number in the central northeast probably reflect Ainu origin. Some experts point to place-names of Ainu origin in Shikoku and Kyūshū; others even detect Ainu names in Okinawa. Similarities in physical features between the Ainu and people in

---

5. Asai Tōru, "Ezogo no koto" (On the Ezo language), in *Ezo,* ed. 'Ōbayashi Taryō (Shakaishisōsha, 1979). Asai discusses "Emishi" as a language between Ainu and Japanese.

6. Yamada Hidezō, *Ainugo-shuzoku Kō* (On Ainu speakers) (Puyara Shinsho, 1972).

southern Kyūshū and the Ryūkyū Islands have been remarked upon as well.[7] Ever since the Meiji era, various debates have arisen between (1) those who hold that the aboriginal peoples who spread throughout Japan, especially the Jōmon people, shared their ancestral origins with the Ainu (that is, even if they mingled with later groups of inhabitants, people in today's Honshū, Kyūshū, Shikoku, and Okinawa are closely related to the Ainu) and (2) those who hold that the Ainu and their language are unrelated to and isolated from the groups that surround them. Still other scholars have located the Ainu between these two positions. The development of new research methods and the discovery of new materials in various fields demand reevaluation of this debate in anthropological, linguistic, and archaeological terms.

Toyooka Yukinori (Ainu name, Sanniyaino; 1946–) writes:

> In Shiranuka, where I was born, when I went to work at the house of an Ainu by the name of Shitaku Yae, now deceased, she told me without apparent motive: "Long, long ago, the Ainu and Shisam (mainland Japanese) were all brethren. The Ainu lived in Japan before the Shisam. Ainu married Shisam, who came over by boat. They had many offspring, and these are today's Japanese. So, in the old days, a lot of Ainu blood flowed in Shisam bodies. . . . Now, Japanese and Ainu are viewed as totally different languages, but today's Japanese, I'm sure, was formed by mixing the two languages."[8]

Such beliefs have been handed down among the Ainu. In any case, historically speaking, all of Hokkaidō at least belonged to

---

7. Toyooka Kiichi, *Yamataikoku o miru* (Looking at Yamataikoku) (author, 1976); *Ainu no yūkara konjaku* (Ainu Yukar now and long ago) (author, 1972).

8. Sannyoaino (Toyooka), "Ainugo—Nihongo ni osensareta gengo" (Ainu, a language polluted by Japanese), *Gengo* (Language), March 1982. On the Shisam, see below.

Vertical pit dwellings from 3,500 years ago (right) and 1,000
years ago, reproduced in the Shibetsu-Pō River Natural Park.

Lacquerware placed on *iyoikir* (treasure altar) and swords hung
on the wall. Photo by Nagai Hiroshi, at Nibutani Museum of
Ainu Cultural Resources.

The late bard Shitaku Yae.

the Ainu until relatively recently. In Ainu, Hokkaidō is *Ainu Moshir* (land of the Ainu). The word *ainu* means "human being."

AINU AND SHISAM

Many peoples have used their word for "human" to designate themselves. Among them are the Inuit (Eskimo), Koin (Hottentot), Sahme (Lapp), Nivf (Giriyak), Wilta (Orokko), Iterimen (Kamchadahl), Caescar (Arakalf), and Yamana (Yagan). The connotation of this word "human" differs somewhat from people to people, reflecting their various backgrounds.

In the case of *ainu*, the word is, first of all, contrasted to *kamui*, a word that designates the male and female gods who dwell in the spiritual world.[9] (As I shall explain more fully later, the Ainu concept of the gods is broad, including the spirits of the dead as well as good and evil deities and demons.) The word *ainu* refers, instead, to a living body—a being of the secular as opposed to the spiritual world. The word originally denoted humans in general, not just the Ainu people.

In contrast, the word *pito* (related to the Japanese *hito,* or "human"), which occurs in such classical poems as *yukar*, more often than not signifies humans who take on character traits of the spiritual world, demigods, and people fulfilling shamanistic roles. However, it can also be used as the antonym of *kamui* to denote human beings.

The word *ainu* is, of course, used for humans as opposed to animals; but depending on the context, it can mean "husband," as in the compound *kukorainu* (my man), or it can mean "man" as opposed to "woman," or "father" as opposed to "child."

Compared with the Japanese word *hito*, the word *ainu* carries a greater feeling of exaltation or elegance. The *huchi* (grandmother) and *hapo* (mother) of Kayano Shigeru (1926–) habitually said, "However poor we may be, *ainu neno an ainu e=ne p ne na* (you must become a humanlike human)."[10] "A humanlike hu-

9. Chiri Mashiho, *Bunrui Ainugo jiten: ningenhen* (Classified Ainu dictionary: Humanity) (Nihon Jōmin Bunka Kenkyūjo, 1945; Heibonsha, 1993). According to this dictionary, *ainu* may earlier have been *aino*. In some areas, *aino* or *airo* is used as a vocative without gender distinction.

10. *Translator's note:* An equal sign in this romanization system denotes the relationship between a noun or a verb and an affix indicating person and number;

man" here means a person of virtue with a far higher degree of perfection than the equivalent Japanese expression *hito no naka no hito* (a human among humans). To "become" such a person implied striving to approach the ideal image of a saint; how closely one could approach it was the measure of one's virtue. (The antithesis is a *wenpe*, a narrow-minded, ill-natured person.) A similar Ainu expression is based on the word *pito*. According to Fujimura Hisakazu,[11] when praising someone for a good deed people used to say, "*Eyaipitonere eyaikamuinere* (that makes you a human, makes you a god)."

Ainu can also be attached as an honorific suffix meaning "Mr." or "a person of." This usage is somewhat less respectful than the suffix *-kur*. For example, referring to a Saru region inhabitant as *Sarunkur* is more respectful than *Sarainu*. The latter broadly includes middle and lesser, or average, people. Sometimes, however, *-kur* is employed without the connotation of respect. Thus *wenkur* (a bad human) simply means the same thing as *wenpe*. In addition, *ainu* can be suffixed to a male name in a manner that corresponds to the Japanese *-rō* in Tarō, *-o* in Akio, or *-hito* in Hirohito. The ending of the names of the Ainu heroes Koshamain and Shakushain is considered to stem from *ainu*.[12]

---

thus *e=ne* is a word made of the second-person singular prefix *e-* and the verb *ne*, meaning "to become." Kayano discusses his mother's frequent use of this saying in his *Ainu no sato Nibutani ni ikite* (Living in Nibutani, an Ainu village) (Hokkaidō Shinbunsha, 1987), pp. 102–3, 126–28. See also *Kayano Shigeru's Ainugo jiten* (Kayano Shigeru's Ainu-Japanese dictionary) (Sanseidō, 1997), p. 4; Kayano Shigeru, *Our Land Was a Forest: An Ainu Memoir,* trans. Kyoko Selden and Lili Selden (Boulder, Colo.: Westview, 1994), p. 56.

11. Born in Sapporo (1940–), Fujimura is a professor of Hokkai Gakuen University specializing in Ainu language and culture. He learned the language from elderly men and women in eastern Hokkaidō. His books include *Ainu no rei no sekai* (The Ainu spiritual world) (Shōgakkan, 1983) and *Ainu, kamigami to ikiru hitobito* (Ainu, people who live with the gods) (Fukutake Shoten, 1985).

12. Koshamain (d. 1457) led the anti-Japanese rebellion of 1456–57. Shakushain (d. 1669) led the 1669 uprising.

I have given a rather lengthy explanation of the real meaning of *ainu* because this word, which originally signified humanity, tended to be used improperly as a pejorative term, especially in Ainu Moshir from the Meiji era onward. Although that tendency continues to a certain extent, in recent years increasing numbers of Ainu have taken pride in its original meaning and endorsed the appellation.

Given this background, it seems necessary to define *ainu* so as to clarify the Ainu people's relationship with non-Ainu around them. Ainu call Japanese *shisam*.[13] This word, from *shi* (one's) and *sam* (side or vicinity), means "neighbor." In this context, the word *ainu* is a self-appellation, the name of a people rather than of humanity in general.

Shisam, then, is the most accurate term differentiating mainland Japanese from the Ainu. *Nihonjin* (the Japanese) is a broad term inclusive of the Ainu and others and hence inappropriate for distinguishing Japanese from Ainu. The often-used expression *Wajin* (Yamato people) is associated with the ancient Chinese name for the Japanese as a whole. It is, therefore, logically contradictory to use *Wajin* as a term denoting mainland Japanese as opposed to Ainu. In addition, some feel that the term has derogatory connotations.[14]

There was once a time when "Ainu" could be used on the same level as "Japanese." Until the late Edo period (mid–nineteenth century), Hokkaidō, the Kurile Islands, and southern Sakhalin—which constituted Ainu Moshir—were not yet recognized as constituting Japanese territory. They were neither claimed by Japa-

13. Another name for Japanese is *shamo*, which is often used contemptuously. *Shamo* is said to come from *samor* (a neighboring place), or *samor-moshir* (a neighboring country, i.e., Honshū). *Samor* is a compound from *sam*, meaning "vicinity" (e.g., *shisam*), and *or*, meaning "place."

14. For example, see Yamakawa Tsutomu, *Ainu minzoku bunkashi e no shiron* (Essays toward a cultural history of the Ainu people) (Miraisha, 1980).

nese authorities nor recognized as Japanese under international law.[15] Thus, the Ainu were neither Japanese nationals nor, of course, Russian, but the Ainu people, or *Ainujin* in Japanese. The suffix *-jin* need not be ascribed only to a nation; it often means "a people," as with the Basques in Spain and the Cherokees in the United States. Thus, the term *Ainujin* is appropriate for denoting the Ainu people today.

In early Meiji times, through a one-sided procedure—annexation without mutual agreement or discussion with the Ainu people—major portions of Ainu Moshir, known until then to the Japanese as the Ezo islands, were designated as *Hokkaidō* (the north sea region). The spacious mountains and fields were taken without payment and turned into "state-owned land" or "imperial forests"; some portions were sold to the large financial conglomerate Mitsui and others became "privately owned forests." As a result, any Ainu who built a house with trees cut down from one of those places was committing the crime of stealing lumber. The Ainu became, or rather were forced to become, "Japanese." This can be compared to the relationship between the Ryūkyū kingdom and the Japanese state: *Ainu* and *Shisam* correspond to the Okinawan terms *Uchinanchū* and *Yamatonchū,* which mean "Okinawans" and "Japanese."[16]

If we search for something tantamount to an international treaty between the Ainu and the Japanese in Hokkaidō, we should note the 1550 peace treaty concluded between the Kakizaki do-

15. International law is nothing more than contractual relations based on power—contracts derived from the concept of the state according to the values of modern Western nations. Thus, it reflects neither the wishes nor the consciousness of nonmainstream peoples—e.g., aboriginal peoples in the Americas, Bretons in France, the Basques in Spain, Khmer and mountain dwellers in Vietnam, and Ainu in Japan.

16. Ryūkyū was a kingdom from the early fifteenth century to 1879, when the Meiji government appropriated it as Okinawa prefecture.

main (the later Matsumae province) and a powerful Ainu chieftain. At that time, as a result of the hundred-year conflict that had begun with the Koshamain War, the tip of Matsumae Peninsula to the south of the line connecting Tomonai and Kaminokuni became Japan's exclusive territory.

In sum, the Ainu are undoubtedly "Japanese" in terms of international law. But the term "Ainu Japanese" more accurately locates the Ainu among the Japanese. Similarly, among Americans (or, more precisely, citizens of the United States), there are "Japanese Americans," "French Americans," "Jewish Americans," and so forth. Note, too, that even though there is the concept of "Jews" as a people, there are no "Jews" as the people of a state; there are only "Israelis." To distinguish mainlanders from the Ainu Japanese, we can use the phrases "Shisam Japanese," "mainland Japanese,"[17] or "Yamato Japanese." Since the word "Yamato," in a narrow sense, has the flavor of the dynasty of conquest whose center was around Nara, those from outside the Nara area may feel uncomfortable with its use. I would like to use "Shisam" to denote mainland Japanese as distinct from the Ainu.

Those inhabitants who presently have Japanese citizenship include not only Shisam Japanese but Ryūkyūan Japanese, Korean Japanese, Ainu Japanese, and Chinese Japanese; although limited in number, there are also Uilta Japanese (the so-called Orokho), Russian Japanese, German Japanese, and others—perhaps even French-American Japanese. Shisam Japanese outnumber the rest, but Japan has never been a racially homogeneous nation. Shisam Japanese themselves can be divided into Izumo Japanese, Kumaso Japanese, Emishi Japanese, Shinano Japanese, Micronesian Japa-

17. This phrase, *naichikei Nihonjin* in Japanese, is used in, e.g., Chiri Mashiho, *Ainugo nyūmon* (Introduction to Ainu) (Hokkaidō Shuppan Kikaku Center, 1985).

nese, and many other subgroups.[18] It has, however, for a long time
become difficult to differentiate distinct characteristics, such as
linguistic ones, among these groups.

THE GREAT FORESTS

To draw a picture of traditional Ainu life, we should begin with
the great forests, which played a central role in that life. At least
until recently, there was considerable forest cover throughout
Japan, owing to climatic conditions, topography, and farming
practices that did not include animal grazing. As in Europe, the
old-growth broad-leaved evergreen forests of western Japan have
disappeared or been replaced with planted forests in the relatively
recent past. Some of the old-growth forests of eastern Japan existed even longer, composed mostly of varieties of Japanese beech
and Japanese oak. Vast forests endured longest on the island of
Hokkaidō.[19]

Until one hundred years ago, nearly all of Hokkaidō was covered with old-growth forests. These forests were quite different
from those of Honshū, and indeed resembled more closely the
forests of northern Europe or the borderlands between Canada
and the United States. Broad-leaved deciduous trees were inter-
spersed with patches of evergreens. In Hidaka district, for example, evergreens such as fir and silver fir grew together with deciduous trees such as *katsura, mizunara, Ezo itaya, ohyō (opiu* in

18. *Translator's note: Izumo* is an old name for present-day Shimane prefecture in Honshū and *Kumaso* for present-day Miyazaki and Kagoshima prefectures in southern Kyūshu.

19. According to environmental archaeologist Yasuda Yoshinori's article in
1981 edition of UNESCO's MAB (*Man and Biosphere*), old-growth forests disappeared early in western Japan; and in eastern Japan, too, they vanished in the
seventeenth century except in mountainous areas. See *Honda Katsuichi shū* (Collected works of Honda Katsuichi) (Asahi Shinbunsha, 1997), vol. 25, p. 207.

Deciduous forest in early spring near Shikotsu Lake
in eastern Hokkaidō.

Ainu), *yachidamo, kalopanax,* and *asada* (species, respectively, of
Japanese oak, maple, ash, and birch). Trees of each kind were often clustered within a certain area, as reflected in the large number of Ainu place-names based on the names of trees. From the
basin of the Saru, the longest river in Hidaka district, a survey by
Kayano Shigeru provides the following names of creeks and

Loading giant *katsura* trees at Hobetsu in Hidaka in the upper reaches of the Mu River. Photo provided by Kaizawa Ichitarō.

marshes in Nibutani in Biratori town alone: Okeneushi (where black alder grows by the marsh), Tunnitai (oak forest), Pinni (*yachidamo*), Yainitai (poplar forest), Ruwepero (thick *mizunara*). In Nioi, adjacent to Nibutani, is a marsh named Chisekarushnai, or "marsh that provides house wood."

Ranging in age from several hundred to several thousand years, these trees formed a sea of foliage that began on the slopes of the Hidaka mountain range, still heavily scarred by glaciers, and spread out onto the flat coastal land. Many documents from the Edo period (1600–1868) onward refer to these great forests. Taking the Saru region once again as an example, an 1856 travelogue titled *Kyōwa shieki* (A harmonious journey on a private mission), by Kubota Nezō, describes the shoreline road to the river mouth: "All I saw, after leaving Saru until my arrival here (over three miles), were oak forests. The oaks, of which there are tens of thousands, are colossal."[20] Even in the Meiji era, Isabella Bird recorded the following passages in her *Unbeaten Tracks in Japan*, the record of a journey she made in 1878:

We took three horses and a mounted Aino guide and found a beaten track the whole way. It turns into the forest at once on leaving Sarufuto [present-day Tomikawa], and goes through forest the entire distance, with an abundance of reedy grass higher than my hat on horseback along it, and, as it is only twelve inches broad and much overgrown, the horses were constantly pushing through leafage soaking from a night's rain, and I was soon wet up to my shoulders. The forest trees are almost solely the *Ailanthus glandulosus* and the *Zelkowa keaki*, often matted together with a white-flowered trailer of the Hydrangea genus. The undergrowth is simply hideous, consisting mainly of coarse reedy grass, monstrous docks, the large-leaved *Polygonum cuspitatum*, several umbelliferous plants, and a "ragweed" which, like most of its gawky fellows, grows from five to six feet high. The forest is dark and very silent, threaded by this narrow path, and by others as narrow, made by the hunters in search of game. . . .

There is something very gloomy in the solitude of this silent land, with its beast-haunted forests, its great patches of pas-

20. Akizuki Toshiyuki, formerly of Hokkaidō University, points out (letter to author, February 23, 1997) that in the introduction to his edition of *Kyō-wa shieki* in *Nihon shomin seikatsu shiryō shūsei* (Collected documents on the lives of common Japanese) (San'ichi Shobō, 1969), vol. 4, Takakura Shin'ichirō interprets the title as referring to a journey independent of an official governmental mission. Kubota Nezō, a samurai of Sakura province (now northern Chiba), and two others were dispatched to Hokkaidō in 1856 by the Sakura lord Hotta Masaatsu.

ture, the resort of wild animals which haunt the lower regions in search of food when the snow drives them down from the mountains.[21]

The trail Bird traversed is now a paved two-lane road surrounded by farms and pastures. Not a single massive tree reminiscent of the past, let alone the old-growth forest, is to be seen.

In the Meiji era, deciduous forests became a target of destruction for the first time. As new land was developed, wood was used to produce railroad ties and charcoal. In the later Meiji years, *mizunara,* a kind of oak, was exported to Europe to make quality furniture and coffins; evergreens were used for pulpwood and Western-style buildings. In wartime the deforestation intensified with military ship-building projects and the need for ties for the Manchurian Railroad. By the end of World War II, the majority of the great forests in the foothills had been completely destroyed. After the war old-growth forests in the interior also disappeared. All of the older men talk of the once vast numbers of huge trees. The older the men, the larger and denser the forests in their memories. One first-generation settler, who arrived to open up this area in 1907, reminisces in a town history of Hayakita:

> Around the time I settled in the farmland of the Eastern Shore, what is now a stretch of rice paddies was covered so densely with *yachidamo* and walnut trees, three to four feet in diameter, that it was dark even during the day. To open up this area, we just laid out the big trees, then burned them in a pile. After the railroad station was built, we cut up the trees and put them out as lumber and railroad ties. Timber for ships was mostly *katsura,* usually two to three feet square and four to five

21. Isabella Bird, *Unbeaten Tracks in Japan: An Account of Travels in the Interior Including Visits to the Aborigines of Yezo and the Shrine of Nikko* (London: John Murray, 1905), pp. 236–37.

yards long. Some huge pieces measured three and three-quarters feet square and seven yards long.

There is one small island where a fantastic old-growth forest survived longer than those in Hokkaidō. On Yakushima, off southernmost Kyūshū, stands Mount Miyanoura, Kyūshū's highest peak. Among the cedars were Jōmon cedars (estimated to be seven thousand years old), believed to have been the earth's oldest living things. Many others were as ancient as three millennia or more. But the majority of the woods of Yakushima have been stripped by indiscriminate logging during the post–World War II period. In the 1990s, despite a significant increase in protected areas and the avoidance of large-scale felling, continued small-scale deforestation has generated popular anger.

DEER AND SALMON

Wild animals thrived in the great woodlands of Hokkaidō. The deciduous broad-leaved forests in the lowlands, with their abundance of acorns and other nuts, were vastly more favorable to animal life than either the conifers in Siberia and high mountain areas or the broad-leaved evergreens in western Japan. Many of the plants growing under the trees also provided food.

Among herbivorous mammals, deer congregate in the largest herds. Smaller species, including the Japanese deer, live in especially dense groups. Their habitat is forests of broad-leaved deciduous trees, especially Japanese oak, and mixed forests of conifers and broad-leaved evergreens. Farther north, the rarer larger species, including red deer and moose, live amid firs. Woodland resources there do not support large populations comparable to those of the smaller deer.

Today it is difficult to imagine the great number of Hokkaidō deer that once existed. An 1858 travelogue records an experience in Hidaka: "Noticing in the distance a red patch stretching across approximately three hundred square yards, I asked the Ainu what it was. With bows and arrows in hand, they dashed toward it. The surface of the earth had seemed red, as if covered with reddish dead grass; but at that moment it suddenly stirred. It was a great herd of deer. The deer scattering in all directions probably numbered several tens of thousands."[22] This occurred on a plateau in the upper reaches of the Piu River, a tributary of the Atsubetsu, near its watershed with the Niikappu River.

Deer occupied a particularly important position among game animals. *Yuk,* the Ainu word for deer, also means "sport."[23] Large numbers were hunted, beginning in the coldest season of the year. When the accumulated snow reached their torsos and restricted their movement, it was easy to chase them with hounds called Ainu dogs. Around this time, deer hide was in excellent condition and venison was at its most flavorful.

The winter rain of mid-February was devastating for the deer. Since brown bears in hibernation gave birth around this time, the rain, called in Ainu *kimun-kamuipo hurayep,* was likened to the cubs' first bathing: "rain that washes bear cubs." When the snow, moistened by rain, iced over, the deer faced a critical situation. They could not eat the food beneath the frozen surface. Moreover, their hooves broke through the ice and sank, so that with each step their slender legs were scraped by the cracked ice. Humans, able to cross the frozen snow without sinking, could catch them easily. Venison was boiled to separate out the fat, then pre-

---

22. Matsuura Takeshirō, *Higashi-Ezo nisshi* (Eastern Hokkaidō journal) (1858).

23. According to Chiri Mashiho's *Bunrui Ainugo jiten* (Classified Ainu-Japanese dictionary) (Nihon Jōmin Bunka Kenkyūjo, 1953), *yuk* originally referred to brown bears, deer, raccoon dogs, etc., all important sources of food. It later came to refer only to the most important, deer. The Hokkaidō deer (called *Ezoshika* in Japanese) is larger than deer on the main island.

A group of Hokkaidō deer. Photo by Kurita Naojirō.

served through drying. This process was called *sakanke.* Although hares and brown bears were also hunted, deer were vital because of their quantity.

In the Meiji era, the herds of deer followed the same destiny as the great woodlands. Tens of thousands of deerskins were exported to France; large quantities of their horns and fetuses were exported to China for medicinal purposes. There were even canneries for exporting venison to the United States. The record snowfall of 1879 dealt another blow that threatened the rapid extinction of Hokkaidō deer.

If the great woodlands and the deer symbolized nature's bounty on land, salmon symbolized the bounty of Hokkaidō's

A large school of salmon swimming upstream in the Kunbetsu River at Shibetsu.

rivers. The density of salmon was once so great that, the saying went, "a pole could stand erect amid them" or "one could barely scoop river water." With the reduction of salmon fishing at sea as a result of the 1985 Japan-Soviet Fisheries Cooperation Agreement, the number of salmon returning upriver has increased; we can once again see massive numbers of them swim upstream.

Yukar verses describe salmon in the Saru River as follows:

Underwater enough salmon
to push up the water
on the river surface;
the sun scorches their backs
on the riverbed,
rocks scrape their bellies.

Youths race one another
to the waterside
throw away short-handled hooks
fight for long-handled hooks

A *tesh* (weir for damming fish), thought to date from approximately 1,000 years ago. Found at the construction site of a new dormitory on the Hokkaidō University campus (June 1982).

and dump ashore the salmon
they've caught.

People carry salmon on their backs
throw away small bags
fight for large bags
and from the river to the village
form an unbroken procession.[24]

Schools of salmon unfailingly retraced the rivers at a fixed time each year, providing sustenance and thereby securing the livelihood of the Ainu. This livelihood was far more stable than that of many other hunting and gathering peoples, such as the Evenki (northern Tungus) of Siberia or the Koin (Hottentot) of Africa. In many areas the Ainu formed small settlements rather than migrate seasonally, their houses standing side by side along a river, and only as far upstream as the salmon swam. Along the Saru River, the farthest upriver they lived was Iwachishi and its vicinity; on the Nukabira tributary, only as far as Nukibetsu and its vicinity.[25]

Salmon were so important that *chep* (fish) in Ainu means "salmon." The highest title, *kamuichep* (divine fish), was also attributed to salmon. From the Meiji era on, however, the same indiscriminate harvesting that devastated the woodlands and deer of Hokkaidō befell salmon and other fish such as capelin.[26] Japa-

24. This salmon song belongs to the subgenre called *kamui yukar* and is quoted from the version recited by Kobata Umonte of Nioi village (now Biratori city) and translated into Japanese by Kayano Shigeru in *Oki no taki* (The waterfall of embers) (Suzusawa Shoten, 1977).

25. Spawning takes place further upstream, but by that point the salmon scatter in male and female pairs, making it more difficult to catch large quantities of fish.

26. Capelin (*Mallotus villosus*) is a species of smelt: a sleek, slender fish with silvery coloring and a forked tail fin, with small scales and large eyes. See the discussion of the name *shishamo* below.

nese fishermen caught such large numbers of salmon in the sea before they reached the rivers that Ainu on the riverbanks waited to no avail. The Japanese also recklessly caught so much herring as they reached the shore for spawning that the fish were used simply as fertilizer. Yet Ainu were arrested for poaching if they caught salmon that escaped the ocean hauls and swam upstream.

Calendars we had none; it was spring when herring came
—dear to me are the *kotan* days of old.

Iboshi Hokuto[27]

THE BOUNTY
OF THE FOUR SEASONS

Hokkaidō's natural richness enabled the Ainu, who were primarily a hunting and fishing people, to satisfy their food needs in an annual cycle. Taking the Saru basin again as an example, the river would freeze from mid-December to about March 20. When it thawed, dace—*akahara* or "red belly," a large dace that grows to almost two feet—were the first fish to swim upstream to spawn, and they continued to migrate from early April until the end of May. In this area, where people had long made use of the fertile soil that accumulated on the riverbank to cultivate millet, early April was the season to till the fields in preparation for sowing. As they tilled, they were able to collect cutworms (the grubs of May beetles) for use as bait. Dace were also simple to catch with one's hands, since they laid eggs in extremely shallow waters. Dace fishing lasted until the end of the sowing season in late May.

27. *Iboshi Hokuto ikō: Kotan* (Kotan: A posthumous anthology of Iboshi Hokuto) (Sōfūkan, 1984). Iboshi Hokuto (1902–29) was an Ainu poet who composed *tanka* (31-syllable Japanese poetry, arranged in the syllabic pattern 5/7/5/7/7). *Kotan* is an Ainu word for village or hamlet.

Plants were the most important food collected from mid-April to June. The season for *pukusa* (a plant of the lily family, also called *kito*), which was gathered first and in greatest quantity, began when dace started coming upriver. Approximately ten days later, *pukusakina* (a plant of the buttercup family) was ready to be harvested. Both seasons lasted about a month. *Pukusa* was the main staple vegetable for the entire year. Large quantities were dried, to be soaked in water and eaten in soups in winter. In the Saru basin, flowering ferns were eaten, but fernbrakes were not. From mid-May, large amounts of *tulep* (another plant of the lily family) were collected. This plant was at its peak when, the Ainu would say, "the mountain azaleas bloom." Starch from *tulep* bulbs was pounded in a wooden hand-mill, then kneaded into dumplings and dried for preservation. Butterbur shoots and stalks, available from about mid-May to early July, were eaten fresh.

River trout began to migrate upstream in late April or May—at the latest in late June. Unlike salmon, trout appeared early and remained in the stagnant water of the main river. Between late August and early September, on a rainy day "around the time when *udo* berries turn black,"[28] they traveled up the narrow creeks of branch rivers to lay eggs. Trout went much farther upriver than salmon, swimming as far as the bottom of a waterfall, which they could not climb. By this time, red spots would appear on their sides, like "many embers" (*apekeshkesho* in Ainu). This is when their flavor was best. Trout could be caught all summer, but did not dry well when whole because maggots bred in them. For preservation they were split open along the belly and smoked until their skin was just barely dry; this also improved their taste. Because of their high fat content, smoked trout would sour and

---

28. *Udo* (*Aralia cordata*) grows to between three and six feet tall and bears round, blackish-purple berries in early fall. Young shoots are edible in the spring.

lose flavor by winter. So only enough were caught and smoked to last until the salmon swam upstream.

Trout could also be kept fresh for nearly a month by placing them at the bottom of a cold spring. A hole was dug where spring water bubbled out from the bottom of a river, and in it was placed a flat layer of fresh trout. Pebbles were spread over them, then another layer of fish was laid out on the pebbles. Two or three layers of trout were placed underwater like this, covered with pebbles so that cold spring water flowed over them. Venison was also preserved in this manner in the summer.

September 3 was the first day of salmon fishing. Salmon continued ascending the river until late November, "the season when a net raised from the water instantly freezes." Salmon and venison were the most important Ainu staples. Just as autumn brings the rice harvest to farmers, it guaranteed the Ainu a secure and easy harvest from the rivers of Hokkaidō. As long as indiscriminate yields did not violate nature's providence, the catch required no special labor. Toward the end of the salmon season there appeared small salmon called *inaukotchep* (fish high-ranked enough to deserve *inau,* a ceremonial whittled twig or pole, usually of willow, with shavings attached). Though small, these were not young fish; their roe and milt were grown to full ripeness. People who caught them offered *inau* to the gods and concluded their salmon fishing for the year. Success in catching this special fish was not certain; the gods bestowed it on some but not others. There were even years when none was caught. In some areas, the fish were preserved as decorations to be used at *iyomante*, the festival in which the spirit of a bear or an owl was sent back to the world of the gods.

Another important fish that swam upstream at a fixed time each year was capelin, known in Japanese as *shishamo.* According to the explanation received by Kayano Shigeru from his grandmother, the name comes from the Ainu word *susam*, combining *su* (a pot)

Fresh *shishamo* (Japanese; a species of smelt known as capelin)
drying at Mukawa town.

and *sam* (right nearby). *Susam* is a fish for which one heads to the
river after having put a pot on the fire, so easy was it to catch.[29]
Capelin did not migrate upstream over as long a period as salmon;
but for three or four days in early November, the river turned so
dark with schools of this fish that the riverbed became invisible.
A single scoop in the water could fill a hand net.

The first frost came around October 5. In mid-October, when

29. There is another version of how the *shishamo* got its name. According
to Aoki Aiko, who is introduced below in "*Kotan* and *Chise*," when she was
fifteen or sixteen (in 1928 or 1929) her paternal grandmother told her that the
name was derived from *susu* (willow) and *hamu* (leaf). Thus, *shishamo* means
"willow leaf-fish." Long ago, an elder prayed while dancing, and willow leaves
turned into fish. The willow tree continually shed its leaves into the river and
people gathered under the tree and cooked and ate the leaf-fish without re-
serve. This angered the gods, so now there is a smaller supply. Aiko knew another old woman in her village who told the same version. When she visited
the adjacent village, Yamamonbetsu-kotan, Aiko heard a seventy- or eighty-
year-old woman, Etui-huchi, tell the identical story (Nagai Hiroshi's audio
recording of Aoki Aiko's narration).

the autumn colors were at their peak, deer hunting began. A deer pipe whistle blown upwind lured bucks when does were in heat. Taking the cry as a sign of intrusion into their territory, bucks would rush furiously to attack the invader. While snow marked the onset of the serious winter hunting season, deer continued to be hunted until the thaw in early summer. Thus, the only months when deer were infrequently caught were from mid-June to early October, when the forests were covered with green and venison was gamy and unsavory. Dried meat was consumed instead, along with the abundant mountain plants and fish.

The second most plentiful catch was rabbit—specifically, wild Ezo rabbit, which was trapped in winter. The fox of the species known as "northern fox" was never hunted, because it smelled bad no matter how it was cooked; but the tastier Ezo raccoon dog was pursued, mostly in winter. It is possible that hunters of the early Jōmon period several thousand years ago shared the same taste in game. The raccoon dog, but not the fox, was among the animals unearthed from the Torihama site in Mikata in Fukui prefecture, perhaps indicating its consumption by humans.

Brown bears did not yield a sizable amount of food, but they were particularly vulnerable when they were hibernating in their dens, especially after giving birth. The stiff, icy snow was easy for both humans and dogs to run across in approaching a bear den. It was also possible at that time to "welcome" a bear cub, that is, to hunt the parent bears and capture the cub alive for the *iyomante*.

In the mountains, large quantities of acorns were gathered in the fall. If one wished, a year's supply of emergency food could be collected. Both oak and Japanese oak acorns turned blackish toward the spring, losing their astringency. They were then boiled with wood ashes to eliminate the remaining bitterness and cooked with other food in a stew. Chestnuts, too, stayed fresh until the spring if buried underground. In Kushiro in eastern

Giant butterburs. The three women have tattoos around their mouths. Photo from the 1930s by Hayashi Shunshō, head priest of Ryūunji, Muroran.

Hokkaidō, water chestnuts were also important; but in Hidaka district, which has no large marshes, they were never eaten.

Other foods gathered in the mountains during spring and summer were watercress, stone parsley, Japanese knotweed, fatsia shoots, udo, butterbur, ostrich fern, *momijigasa* (a plant of the chrysanthemum family), and *yukizasa* (a kind of smilax). In autumn, walnut, *sarunashi* (a kind of silvervine), wild peas, wild vine berries (whose leaves and vines were used in spring), and mushrooms of all kinds were collected. This list includes almost all the mountain plants utilized today.

THE CREATION
OF HEAVEN AND EARTH

This book aims to investigate the life of the *ainu* (humans) against the rich natural backdrop of Ainu Moshir (Hokkaidō, the Kuriles, and southern Sakhalin) by portraying their daily lives as concretely as possible. However, since the mythology concerning the birth of the *moshir* (homeland) deeply informed the daily lives of the Ainu, I would like to introduce these myths before proceeding.

Ainu myths about the creation of heaven and earth, and about the birth of its people and culture, differ considerably from region to region. On the mainland, too, a variety of myths must have circulated among different regions (or tribes) by the Jōmon or mid-Yayoi period, a prehistoric period (ca. 300 B.C.E. to ca. 300 C.E.) following the Jōmon and characterized by wet-rice cultivation and bronze and iron use. The so-called Japanese mythologies—the *Record of Ancient Matters* (*Kojiki*, 712 C.E.) and the *Chronicle of Japan* (*Nihon shoki* or *Nihongi,* 720), composed of mythic, legendary, and historical elements—obliterated other myths that had originated in politically and culturally independent regions. The Japanese mythologies were "political products that the eighth-century Yamato courtiers created in order to legitimize their rule."[30]

In Ainu Moshir, however, regional myths took longer to be effaced by the central Yamato power, surviving at least until early Meiji times. Many stories subsequently disappeared, but others have been recorded, however imperfectly. The creation myth introduced here is a relatively old one among recorded versions. It was left by the late-Edo explorer Matsuura Takeshirō (1818–88), who traveled through Ainu Moshir between 1845 and 1858, compiling a vast number of documents. Among them were detailed accounts of cruel Shisam conduct toward the Ainu, the misery of Ainu communities after workers were drafted for forced labor, and the failure of the Edo military government and Matsumae province to rectify the situation. Not surprisingly, Matsuura's records were not allowed to be printed intact; only excerpts were published in his lifetime.

The following creation myth appears in Matsuura's 1858 exploration record, *Yubari nisshi* (*Yubari Journal*), as a summary of a *yukar* that an eighty-three-year-old *ekashi* chanted for him all through the night by the firepit in a *kotan* called Tapkop.[31] Portions of it recall the *Record of Ancient Matters*, but we cannot readily judge whether the similarities indicate direct relationships between Ainu and Shisam myths or common ancient sources.

> Long ago, before there was such a thing as land, before there were such things as countries, a vapor appeared on the surface of the blue ocean. Like a fire flaring, like a flame sweeping up-

30. Inoue Mitsusada, *Shin'wa kara rekishi e* (From myth to history), vol. 1 of *Nihon no rekishi* (History of Japan) (Chūō Kōronsha, 1970).

31. The myth is taken from the modern Japanese translation by Maruyama Michiko, *Yubari nisshi* (Tōdosha, 1976). The original by Matsuura Takeshirō is in literary Japanese. Topkap Kotan is now Azana Maruyama in Kuriyama town in Yubari county.

ward, it eventually rose and became the sky. A long time passed, and the mud that was left behind slowly turned into an island, becoming large and solid. As more time passed, a nebulous vapor gathered and a god was born—so it is said.

During that time, in the bright, pure vapor that had risen high like a flame, another god was born and descended to earth on five-colored clouds. From these five-colored clouds, the two gods chose the blue ones and threw them toward the sea, saying, "Turn into water." And, thus, the ocean was born. They threw the yellow clouds, saying, "Cover with soil the islands on earth." Then they sprinkled the red clouds, saying, "Turn into treasures of gold and silver jewels." Finally, they commanded the white clouds, "Be plants, birds, beasts, fish, and insects." In this way those various things were created.

The two gods, the god of heaven and the god of earth, then pondered, "How should we create a god to rule this country?" An owl flew by. As they looked at it, and wondered what it was, its eyes twinkled. Amused, they did something, and gave birth to many gods.

Among the many new gods were two beautiful, shining gods, Pekerchup (the sun god) from the "she mountain" and Kunnechup (the moon god) from the "he mountain." They ascended into heaven on black clouds to illuminate the dark, misty regions of the new country. It is said that the *moshir* created when the mud solidified is today's Mount Shiribeshi.

In time, many gods were born, and each took on a different role. The god who created fire taught how to plant and raise millet of different kinds. The god who ruled the earth taught all things about plants, including how to strip tree bark to make clothes. There were also the god who ruled over water, the god who ruled over gold, the god who ruled over humans, and many others. These gods invented many useful things, including devices for catching salmon, spearing trout, and netting herring, which they passed down to their divine descendants.

Ainu revering the owl as the guardian god of their hamlet and as the deity that taught conjugal love. Drawing by Matsuura Takeshirō, "Ezo manga" (Ezo playful drawings), in *Matsuura Takeshirō kikō shū* (Travelogues by Matsuura Takeshirō), ed. Yoshida Takezō (Fuzanbō, 1977). The writing reads: "Eastern and western Ainu like to keep owls, feed them morning and night, and revere them. So I asked the reason. They answered that this bird taught their ancestors conjugal love. They said they showed their respect by offering whittled *inau* [ceremonial whittled twigs with curled shavings attached]. What is laid out underneath is a small woven mat."

Mount Shiribeshi (also known as Ezo Fuji), the site of the divine descent in Ainu lore.

Following the birth of Ainu Moshir, animals were created. Next, Ainu were made in the image of gods, and skills for living were passed down to them.

To explain how this was done, the myths introduce a character who mediates between the divine and human realms: a god, or, in some versions, "the forefather of humans," called Ainurakkur, Okikurmi, Oinakamui, and so forth. Among the many

Ainurakkur myths, the most dramatic is his birth through the marriage of Thunder (male god) and Elm (female god). The Elm deity takes the form of an elm known as *harunire* or *akadamo* in Japanese and called *chikisani* in Ainu, and always appears in relation to the creation of fire. Although details of the myth differ from region to region, Ainurakkur's mother is always Princess Elm.

According to one version of the myth, Princess Elm was a deity possessed of a beauty that was rare even in heaven. Once when the thunder god Shikannakamui was watching her in fascination, he lost his footing (in another version, he was pushed from the rear by a playful god) and fell directly on the elm tree. As a result, Ainurakkur was born.[32] Ainurakkur—the name roughly means "humanlike god"—was exactly like *ainu*, humans, in terms of appearance and sentiment. He taught the skills of living to the Ainu and protected them against demons.

Another version of the Ainurakkur legend comes from Biratori town in Hidaka in the Saru region, the region where Okikurmi made his divine descent to Ainu Moshir:[33]

Long ago there lived a god called Okikurmi, a young male god possessing both wisdom and strength. One day he heard his father and mother talking about Ainu Moshir, recently created in the world below. It was a land of beautiful mountains and limpid rivers. Pebbles in the river shimmered with the seven colors of

32. This myth appears in Chiri Mashiho, *Bunrui Ainugo jiten: shokubutsuhen* (Classified Ainu-Japanese dictionary: Plants) (Nihon Jōmin Bunka Kenkyūjo, 1953; Heibonsha, 1993); Kindaichi Kyōsuke, *Ainu no kenkyū* (Ainu studies) (Naigai Shobō, 1925); Yamamoto Tasuke, *Kaichō Furyū* (Monster bird *huri*) (Heibonsha, 1978), and elsewhere.

33. See "Ainu no shiso Okikurumi Kamui no densetsu" (Myth of Okikurmikamui, the founder of the Ainu) by Kayano Shigeru, who compiled and translated into Japanese the fragmentary tales told in the Saru region in his *Honoo no uma* (The horse of flame) (Suzusawa Shoten, 1977).

The scene of the Okikurmi legend (the Nibutani area along
the Saru River). Photo by the author.

the rainbow, and the sound of the running water suggested its
pleasant conversations with the pebbles. The twittering of nearby
birds was even more exquisite than that heard in the divine realm.
However, *ainu* who were created along with the *moshir* did not
yet know how to make a fire or bows and arrows.

Okikurmi couldn't help wishing to go to Ainu Moshir.
"Please let me go to the world down below. Let me teach the
Ainu livelihood skills," he begged his father.

Surprised, the father deity gazed at Okikurmi's face then answered, "Listen well, Okikurmi. Descending to the beautiful land
below does not at all mean only dreamlike, wondrous things. In
the past many gods have volunteered to go, but all have failed the
three endurance tests set for them. First you must endure terrible heat, then you must endure terrible cold, and last you must
never laugh no matter what happens. Some gods have died from
the heat; others have frozen to death. No one has ever proceeded

to the third test of refraining from laughter. I don't know that you will succeed either."

Although this was the first that Okikurmi had heard of such tests, he replied without fear, "I intend to endure all three hardships. Please let me take those tests."

Proudly watching Okikurmi, the father deity said, "Fine. I have always considered you a reliable son. I am sure you will be able to persevere." He consented to ask the gods to test the youth.

On the first day Okikurmi sat before the many gods. The sun's rays beating down on him were unusually hot. His scorched back was ready to peel away, and a glance at the sun nearly melted his eyes. When he placed his hands over his eyes to fend off the sun, his arms roasted and gave off the smell of broiled venison on skewers.

Okikurmi remained impassive. Watching, unseen by him, his mother covered her face when she noticed the smell of her son's burning flesh. At that moment the gods called out, "Fine. So much for today." The sun's rays grew mild.

Okikurmi tried but could not rise immediately. The flesh of his back threatened to slip down like the meat of a grilled fish, and his arms seemed thinner for what they had lost from burning. But this meant that he was that much closer to Ainu Moshir, so he mustered his youthful strength and stood up.

On the second day Okikurmi was seated in a bitterly cold place, the opposite of the previous day's environment. A cold wind began blowing, and frost formed rapidly even as he watched. At the same time, sleet covered his body and turned into solid ice. His ear lobes hurt so much that he thought they were about to tear away. Okikurmi quietly covered his ears with his hands.

The wind's intensity and the cold increased. Thinking he would indeed freeze to death at this rate, Okikurmi, while still seated, slowly leaned forward to double his upper body over his lap. The sleet pelted him,[34] turned into snow, and accumulated, so that he could no longer move at all. Still he endured in silence. Finally, the gods said, "That is all."

On the third day Okikurmi faced the final test. "This is it. I won't laugh no matter what happens," Okikurmi resolved as he sat before the gods. A larger number of deities had gathered than on the previous days. "Okikurmi, you must not laugh, no matter what happens," said the gods as they surrounded him in a circle. Two young gods jumped into the circle. The gods burst into laughter, for the two were a naked male and female.

The two young gods began an odd game. The female god walked slowly inside the ring on all fours. The male god followed her, also on all fours. Touching or smelling the female god's neck and behind with the tip of his nose, he sometimes went off to the side to lift a leg as if to pass water. The two gods were imitating dogs in heat. The gods rolled with laughter, clapping their hands and stamping their feet. Okikurmi, filled with determination, remained straight-faced.

Tickled by the tip of the male god's nose, the female god brought her hips closer to him, relaxed and seeming to anticipate his action. He went around behind her and licked her *anunukehi* (precious part). She too licked him. As they repeated this over and over, they seemed to have become real dogs; to have forgotten their divinity. The male god rose onto the female god from behind and pressed his *chinunukehi* (precious part) against her, then vigorously went on to enact a scene "like a wagtail."[35]

34. Drizzle and icy rain are far worse than snow in the coldest season. Dry snow does not wet the clothing, but drizzle and icy rain penetrate to the skin. Body heat, moreover, escapes into the wet clothing and in such conditions it is easy to freeze to death.

35. *Translator's note:* In Japanese myths, wagtails are said to have taught lovemaking.

This was now almost *uko-omoinu* (union) itself. The divine on-lookers no longer laughed; captivated by the young couple's re-alistic acting, they were utterly silent. Heedless of this response, the male god lightly touched the female god's neck, while his hands played with her breasts, her small nipples between his fingers. Far from laughing, some observers averted their eyes, blushing; and others sat still, their bodies twisted.

The wagtail gesture lasted for a while, then the male god finally removed his chest from the female god's back. The spectators were wrong if they thought this was the end, for yet another skit re-mained: that of dogs inseparably stuck together. As the male god imitated the motion of pulling the female god without separating where they were joined, she harmonized with that motion by ap-pearing to be pulled, while cooing like a puppy wanting milk. This was so hilarious that the spectators once again burst out laughing. As the naked couple tumbled and rolled without separating, the gods laughed and laughed, holding their bellies so they wouldn't burst and hitting one another on the shoulders. Finally, Okikurmi was unable to contain himself and let out a single small laugh.

"Look, Okikurmi laughed. He won't be able to go down to Ainu Moshir now," the gods jeered. Okikurmi's tears of regret fell like rapids. After enduring all the heat and cold, he felt he could not concede because of one tiny mistake. Okikurmi re-solved to run away.

That night, he stole a pinch of grain from the millet his par-ents carefully stored and hid it in a wound he opened on the calf of his leg. He trusted the dark to hide him as he attempted to set out on a journey to the world below. A dog by the door called out loudly, "Okikurmi is leaving with millet he's stolen!" An-gered, Okikurmi quickly grabbed a handful of ashes and threw them into the dog's mouth, saying, "You will never speak again!" He leaped out, and since then dogs can only bark.

Ainu Moshir, created by the gods, was a truly beautiful land,

and the Ainu who inhabited it had truly gentle hearts. Okikurmi taught them a variety of skills for living. He began with how to build a fire. Until then the Ainu had used fire taken from volcanoes or mountain fires caused by thunder and other natural phenomena, always being careful not to extinguish them. Okikurmi introduced the simple method of making a fire by scattering sparks created by rubbing stone and iron over charcoal made from shelf fungus.[36]

Again, Ainu houses until then were rock caves, knee-deep pits dug on level ground and topped with roofs, or three poles covered with bundles of thatch. Okikurmi had them construct pillars for more spacious homes that enabled them to walk upright inside.

He also introduced tools for hunting and fishing. The fishhook for catching salmon and trout, called *marep* or *marek,* is a deeply bent hook at the tip of a pole. It works as a spear when poking and as a hook when pulling a fish, thus resembling the harpoon in its double function. Bows and arrows were, of course, among the tools Okikurmi taught humans to make, including arrows with a powerful poison. An arrow covered with dried wolfsbane root that had been crushed after being moistened with saliva was potent enough to make a large bear collapse in a few minutes.

At first it sufficed just to find the day's fresh footprints, since an arrow shot at them would spontaneously follow and hit the animal. This was so convenient that humans grew lazy and began using arrows for footprints from the day before, or even two days before. The arrows, which now had to fly far to reach animals that had moved on a distance, would lose their energy, fall, and rot. Okikurmi was enraged to see this happen. He remade

36. Shelf fungus (or polypore, known in Japanese as "monkeystool") is a hard mushroom with a wooden texture. Dried shelf fungi are placed in the fire until they turn into red embers and then are buried in cool ashes. This produces charcoal that easily catches fire and lasts a long time.

A *nusa* (altar) decorated with *inau*. Photo by Nagai Hiroshi, at the Nibutani Museum of Ainu Cultural Resources.

the arrows so that they could only hit animals that humans saw before their eyes.

Before long, the pinch of Okikurmi's millet seeds from the divine land increased enough to be planted throughout all of Ainu Moshir. Okikurmi taught the Ainu how to brew millet wine and worship the gods with the wine.

He demonstrated how to make *inau*, explaining that offerings of *inau* made to the gods would please them so that they would protect humans. Willow was to be used for making *inau* because it was divine in origin. When the god who created Ainu Moshir left a chopstick staked in the ground after a meal on earth, that chopstick sprouted and turned into a willow tree.

Okikurmi, who had more or less finished teaching all the useful skills for human living, took a beautiful wife and settled on the bank of the Saru River. The place, now known as Okikurum Chashi (Okikurmi Fort), is on the left bank in Nioi in Biratori town, at the entrance of the Otasui Creek. Thanks to Okikurmi,

Ainu life became gradually richer. As he recalled the tests he had undergone in the divine land, he realized that the heat, the cold, and the mimicking of mating dogs were all necessary preparations for his life in Ainu Moshir. Thankful to the gods, therefore, he led a leisurely life.

Then one winter, a great event occurred in peaceful Ainu Moshir. There came a snowfall greater than any the oldest Ainu had ever experienced. In one night houses were buried to the roof. In two nights roofs, too, disappeared under the snow. Great herds of deer were trapped in the snow and died one by one. In spring, when the snow began to thaw, massive numbers of deer corpses were discovered, already rotten and inedible, and no live deer were seen. The Ainu, whose staple food was venison, grew weaker and weaker until no one was able to go out to hunt. In the end, only a few people survived in the village.

Pained, Okikurmi shared his food with the Ainu. In the beginning he handed out dried meat and fish. When the supply was exhausted, he heaped boiled millet into bowls with tall bases, which his wife carried to each house at night. In Shikerpe (now Nioi in Biratori town), a pair of beautiful hands holding a bowl filled with millet was nightly extended through the master window of each house. The Ainu received with heartfelt gratitude this present from the god, who was invisible save for her hands.

There was, in this village, a young man of dubious character. Because the hands extended through the window were so beautiful, he wished to hold them just once in his own hands. One night when the bowl was held out, the young man, who had been waiting for this, grabbed the beautiful hands instead of receiving the bowl. At that instant, a great explosion blew away the roof and the young man.

Angered, Okikurmi and his wife left their dwelling in Otusai and returned to the divine land. Only the winnow that Lady

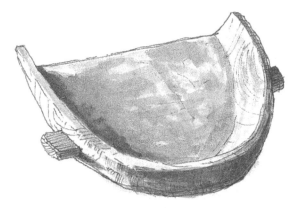

A winnow (*mui*).

Okikurmi used still remains as a rock. This rock is called Nokapira ("shaped cliff"), and a tributary of the Saru River that flows nearby is also called the Nokapira (now spelled Nukabira).

When leaving for the divine land, Okikurmi took pity and created a replacement god to watch the Ainu for him. Okikurmi fashioned a mighty god called Noyautasap, or "one who cures with sagebrush," by bundling up sagebrush into a human form. Since sagebrush was the first plant to grow in Ainu Moshir, no demon could defeat it. And while an ordinary god had only one heart, Noyautasap had five hearts of ash, made by soaking embers in clear water: one in the chest and one in each of his limbs. As a result, he was five times stronger than ordinary gods. Swords and spears for gods were also made out of sagebrush, because it was believed that demons slain with such blades could never revive.

Noyautasap, it is believed, still dwells on a hill called Apet (now Japanized as Abetsu) on the other side of the river from today's Biratori town. Thanks to this god, the god of disease is believed to bypass the Saru basin. In autumn, when Okikurmi makes his annual visit to the Saru River to collect materials for whittling

The winnow-shaped rock (the crescent rock in the center) left in Nokapira. Photo by Nagai Hiroshi.

inau, thunder roars just once in the lower reaches of the river. Whenever thunder is heard, old people tell children they have to be quiet because Okikurmikamui has come for a visit to the Ainu village.

ANCESTORS

What was Ainu life like before the changes brought about by uninvited external influences and encroachment? The chronology of these changes differs considerably from area to area. In general, the more southern the region, the earlier and faster the changes; the more northern or eastern, the slower. The closer to the coasts, the faster; the deeper in the interior, the slower.

I would like to use the Saru basin area, already mentioned a number of times, to trace this chronology as concretely as possible. Since it may be helpful to consider the lineage of an actual person, I refer to the example of Kayano Shigeru, the well-known Ainu folklorist and activist. The oldest ancestor Kayano himself directly remembers is Awa-ankur, four generations ago. However, records of the family line make it possible to trace his paternal side back seventeen generations. Since Kayano already has grandchildren, this is a family history of nineteen generations.

The earliest known generation, that of Humoshirushi, lived in Akupet in the east, or *moshirpa* (i.e., the Tokachi, Kushiro, and Kitami areas). During the lifetime of Nipetoran, the sixth generation, the family moved to the Saru area in Hidaka, west of the Hidaka mountain range. There they built a fort in Abet, across the river from present-day Biratori. This was about three hundred years ago. Kanaikar, the eleventh generation, is said to have moved to central Biratori around two hundred years ago.

If we estimate twenty-five years as an average generation, Natori Takemitsu's survey roughly dates the first-generation ancestor, Humoshirushi, to 425 years ago. A history of Biratori town

Kayano Shigeru's grandfather and grandmother, Tukkaram and
Tekatte, with their daughter Umon and granddaughter Haruno.

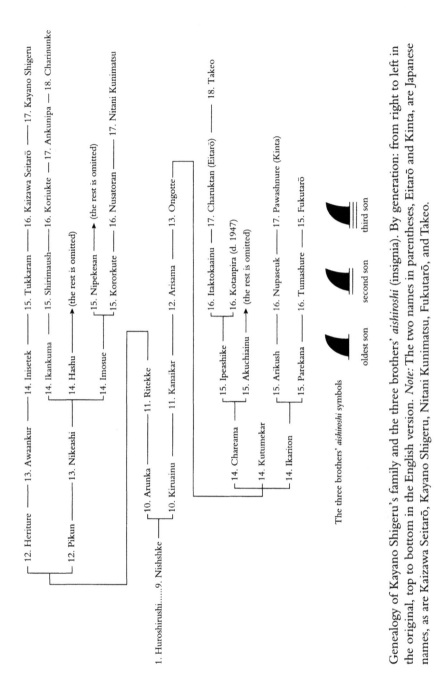

Genealogy of Kayano Shigeru's family and the three brothers' *aishiroshi* (insignia). By generation: from right to left in the original, top to bottom in the English version. *Note:* The two names in parentheses, Eitarō and Kinta, are Japanese names, as are Kaizawa Seitarō, Kayano Shigeru, Nitani Kunimatsu, Fukutarō, and Takeo.

takes the average generation as thirty years, thereby pushing back the date to over 500 years ago.[37]

This genealogy, which partly consists of what can be called mythical tradition, does not present a "scientific" chart based on modern rationalism. Different versions can, moreover, be found even within the same Biratori town. The late Nitani Kunimatsu of Nibutani village believed that Humoshirushi lived in Nikap (the present Niikappu, to the south of the Saru region), and that Wenhot, in the eighth generation, first moved to Abet, then to Koupira, and finally to Nibutani. There is also an oral tradition that directly contradicts this, claiming that the ancestors of the Saru Ainu migrated from Nanbu province (now eastern Aomori and northern Iwate prefectures) in the northeast region of the mainland.

Kayano himself heard another story from his father, Kaizawa Seitarō:[38] The family's ancestors at some point in time crossed the Hidaka mountain range westward from the Tokachi to the Hidaka district and settled near Shizunai in Hidaka. For some reason, three brothers—whether they were the original immigrants or their children is unknown—left Shizunai to live separately. On parting, they designed new symbols, different from the family insignia that had been in use since the Tokachi days.

Called *aishiroshi* and used for inscription on arrowheads, family insignias had an important meaning in Ainu hunting life. When hit by a poisoned arrow or by an unattended trap arrow, a large animal did not always die instantly; indeed, it often went

37. Natori Takemitsu, *Ainu to kōkogaku* (Ainu and archaeology) 2, contained in his *Chosakushū* (Complete works), vol. 2 (Hokkaidō Shuppan Kikaku Sentā, 1972); Kōno Hiromichi and Watanabe Shigeru, eds., *Biratorichō-shi* (Biratori town history) (Hokkaidō Shuppan Kikaku Sentā, 1974).

38. *Translator's note:* Kayano Shigeru's surname differs from his father's because as a child he adopted the name of the family into which his older sister married.

a long distance before collapsing. The insignia on the arrow in the carcass determined who caused the death.

After consultation, the three brothers, who had engaged in ocean fishing while in Hidaka, decided to model their new insignia after the dorsal fin of the killer whale. The oldest brother's insignia was to have one horizontal line underneath the shape of a fin; the second brother's two lines; and the third brother's three lines. They agreed that if their progeny encountered these symbols, they would respond to their common ancestry and help one another.

Of these three brothers, the third traced the Saru River to its upper reaches, as far as Pipaushi (one of the old names for Nibutani). Kayano Shigeru writes in *Our Land Was a Forest: An Ainu Memoir*:

> The elders of the village thought this youth somehow confidence-inspiring and decided to give him a bride so he would settle in the village. This was not all that unusual a situation and was called *menoko-epeka aeham*, "providing a wife to stop a man's feet."
>
> True to the villagers' expectations, the young man turned out to be an excellent hunter and, moreover, an unparalleled orator. One day an insignificant matter led to a dispute between Pipaushi-kotan and another village, and an *uko-charanke* was initiated. The word *uko* means "mutually," and *charanke* means "to let words fall"; the compound word *uko-charanke* thus refers to the Ainu custom of settling differences by arguing exhaustively. It also implies that the Ainu do not solve disputes by violence.
>
> *Charanke* requires the talent to argue with logic and the physical strength to sit in debate for days. Probably in recognition of his double gift in oratory and physical strength, the man with the three-lined dorsal-fin insignia was chosen as the *charanke* representative of Pipaushi-kotan.

Over a period of six days and nights, this man continued
to argue without once collapsing, and led the dispute to a
peaceful solution. The villagers were overjoyed. Although his
formal Ainu name is lost to us, the villagers from then on called
him Awa-ankur (the Seated Man) in honor of his oratorical
skills and physical endurance.

This is the extent of my knowledge of Awa-ankur, our ancestor five generations back. Awa-ankur had a son by the name
of Inisetet (To Scoop Things). His name appears in the "Saru
Journal" (1858), a diary left by Matsuura Takeshirō, who explored the Saru River during the Ansei era (1854–1860): "The
head family of eight: Inisetet (60), his wife Irapekar (51), son
Awetok (24), wife Aksake (22), younger brothers Tukkaram
(12) and Ikorohasiw (10), his younger sister Ikatoshin (7), and
another younger brother Ranhareha (5). The son and his wife
and younger brother Tukkaram were drafted for labor." This
is an excerpt from the entry on Pipaushi-kotan. The younger
brother Tukkaram, who is mentioned along with Inisetet's son
and his wife, is my grandfather.[39]

This was the story of his ancestors that Kayano heard directly
from his father. Awa-ankur's son Inisetet bears the first name to
be recorded in the birth register, and Tukkaram, his third son,
was born in 1847. When he was twelve years of age, Tukkaram
was forced by the Japanese to walk approximately 220 miles to
Atkesh (now Atsukeshi) in eastern Hokkaidō, as will be discussed
below.

Kayano still engraves the killer whale dorsal fin insignia in place
of a signature on his rulers and other small tools.

---

39. Kayano, *Our Land Was a Forest*, pp. 25–26. *Translator's note:* The spellings
of Ainu names and words have been changed to conform to the system used
in this book.

KOTAN AND CHISE

If jumping back seventeen generations places us a little over five hundred years ago, then Humoshirushi lived around the first half of the fifteenth century, or in the early to middle days of the Muromachi period of Japanese history (1336–1573). In the preceding, Kamakura period (1185–1336), a Shisam family by the name of Andō already occupied a portion of Matsumae Peninsula. Merchants were also in the area, and a commodity economy seems to have reached the Ainu in surrounding localities. Around the early Muromachi period, a band of samurai belonging to the former Andō, who had been defeated by another family called Tsugaru, fled to a corner of southern Hokkaidō. These merchants and warriors began to stir strong distrust and anger among the Ainu by further transforming the commodity economy, which already was affecting Hokkaidō, into exploitative trade. Eventually this led to the Koshamain War (1456–57), which was followed by approximately one hundred years of anti-Japanese resistance by the Ainu in southern Hokkaidō.

Although the Shisam had started to cross the sea to Ainu Moshir—an area including Hokkaidō, the Kuriles, and southern Sakhalin—before the Koshamain War, migration was limited mostly to the coastal areas in southern Hokkaidō. On coasts other than Matsumae, Hakodate, and their surrounding areas, there were not enough settlers to constitute a population. With the exception of a few mine brokers and drifters, hardly any Shisam directly entered the inland areas of Tokachi and Hidaka. In 1858, in the upper reaches of the Atsubetsu River in Hidaka, Matsuura Takeshirō wrote that "a woman was apparently surprised to see a Wajin for the first time."[40]

What was Ainu life like in this period when Ainu culture

40. Matsuura, *Higashi Ezo nisshi*.

achieved its most distinctive characteristics? Naturally, *kotan* people had heard of the Shisam, and some must even have traveled and encountered them, but it is unlikely that Shisam affected the fundamental character of the Ainu people and their culture. Even though ironware was already in use to a fair extent, this culture had retained its values from the Jōmon world. One with all the other lives of great nature, Ainu people lived with *kamui* (pantheistic spirits), leading a life of "ethnic self-determination," to use today's expression. Theirs was a spiritual life symbolized by *yukar* and other cultural forms, as well as by knowledge and skills concerning all living phenomena, including *ainu* (humans). Quite contrary to the perspective of modern Western science, which came to approach even living phenomena as "things," the knowledge and skills of the Ainu were based on viewing even "things" considered inanimate as having life.

While introducing some of their skills, I would like to try to portray daily life in Ainu Moshir several hundred years ago. First, a *kotan* was the center of a living sphere. It was normally located on a coast that offered a variety of food from the sea, or by a river with an abundant supply of salmon and where deer were also easily caught. Particularly optimal was a place like Nibutani Kotan, in the Saru River basin, with clear springs nearby; spring water was not only desirable for health reasons but also never froze, even in the coldest winter.

Since hunting, fishing, and gathering were the primary means of sustenance, with millet raised as a subsidiary crop, densely populated communities did not form easily; instead, people scattered to *iwor* (hunting areas). At its smallest, a *kotan* consisted of only one household; at its largest, a little over a dozen households. In most cases, a *kotan* was composed of kin. The late Professor Chiri Mashiho explains the idea behind the term: "A *kotan* is a *kotan* even if there is only one household, or even if families live there temporarily. Whether temporary or permanent, a place where

Nibutani Kotan. Photo by Fosco Maraini, 1933.

there is a house or houses is referred to as *kotan*. Like *moshir*, it can be used to mean 'homeland' or 'the world' in a broad sense."[41] Houses in a *kotan* stood closely enough together that neighbors could hear one another when shouting aloud, yet far enough apart that a fire would not spread from house to house. Thus they were separated by tens of feet to perhaps three hundred feet.

I have seen many traditional houses—of the Inuit in the Arctic, minority groups of northern China, native peoples of North America, inhabitants of the Karakoram Mountains in northern Pakistan, and others. What struck me when I saw them was how chilly Japanese houses were. With respect to protection against a cold living environment, Japan is, I think, the coldest place in the world—colder than North Pole regions—especially in snowy Shinshū and the northeast. In the past, Japanese in cold areas spent the winters, often at temperatures many degrees below freezing, in breezy houses with raised floors and sliding paper doors structured for southern climates. Cerebral apoplexy was a frequent occurrence.

What about the traditional Ainu *chise* (house) in Hokkaidō, where the temperature can drop to fifteen to twenty degrees Celsius below freezing? "*Chise* in the old days were warm," Aoki

41. Chiri Mashiho, *Chimei Ainugo shōjiten* (A small dictionary of Ainu place-names) (Hokkaidō Shuppan Kikaku Sentā, 1984), s.v. *kotan*.

A restored *kotan*. Outdoor pieces of Nibutani Museum of Ainu
Cultural Resources.

Aiko (1914–95) of Nibutani village in Biratori town in Hidaka
district commented repeatedly. As a child, she used to visit a *kotan*
in Yamamonbetsu, her mother's native place, where several
houses still retained the traditional construction style. The *chise*
was protected against the cold in a number of ways:

1. The roof and walls were firmly made of thatch, one foot
    thick.
2. During the winter, a dirt mound, two feet high, covered
    the walls on the outside.
3. There was no raised floor around the firepit. Woven mats
    were placed on a thick layer of thatch plants, which were
    spread directly over the dirt floor.
4. The thatch walls inclined rather sharply inward, holding up
    the loft at an angle close to that of the pitch of the roof, so
    that there was little space between the roof and the walls.
5. Windows were doubly covered by thatch curtains on the
    outside and plain mats on the inside. The slits between the
    mats were closed by twigs of *shinkep* (a kind of wild bush
    clover). Both the doorway and the inner entrance were
    curtained off with mats.

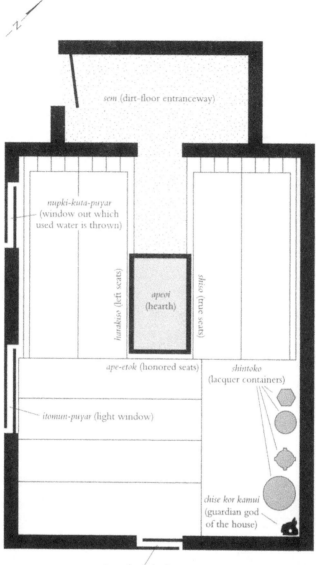

A standard floor plan of a *chise* (house). From Kayano Shigeru, ed., *Ainu no mingu* (Ainu folk utensils) (Suzusawa Shoten, 1978).

Photo of a *chise* in Shiraoi Kotan in the Meiji period. On the outside, under the eaves, thatch plants hang upside down, heads pointing to the ground, to keep the rain away. From a postcard.

The fire in the firepit was never extinguished, night or day, in houses constructed in this manner, so it was fairly warm indoors, even in the dead of winter. Food was stored in the *pu* (a raised storehouse), built separately from the warm main house, so it kept well.

Consider the following incident. Forcefully evacuated from their original hamlets, the Ainu in the Asahikawa area formed a community in the mid-Meiji period. Asahikawa town, which was responsible for overseeing their land, built approximately fifty wooden houses for the Ainu around 1907. Made with walls of boards, roofs of straight-grained wooden boards, a wooden floor for the living room, a tatami floor for the guest room, and windows of a single layer of glass, these Shisam-style houses were decidedly inferior to the traditional *chise*, which in the Asahikawa area were mostly made of bamboo grass. The *chise* were warmer in winter and cooler in summer. As a result, household by house-

A *pu* (raised storehouse).

hold, the Ainu built *chise* by the side of their new houses and conducted their daily lives in them.[42]

Favoring the "new fashion" in the Meiji era, some *chise* incorporated the wooden floor. These compromise houses also failed to stay warm, and it is said that the Ainu grew more prone to catching cold.

An older form of the *chise* seems to have been built partly underground with a teepee-shaped roof. Many examples of this construction are found in excavation sites. Among the Sakhalin Ainu, such semi-underground houses were used until the Taishō era (1912–26).

Around the time when she moved to Yamamonbetsu as a child, Aoki Aiko came upon an old semi-underground, teepee-shaped

42. The same thing happened when the South Korean military built houses for Vietnamese peasants during the Vietnam War (too hot for comfort), and when Kawasaki Steel built houses for fishermen in the Philippines in the 1970s after purchasing their land (also too hot).

house in the upper reaches of a creek, some distance from her hamlet. The center part of the thatched roof had fallen in and the moss that grew over it buried her feet to the ankles. It appeared to be at least one hundred years old. When she asked elders at home, they explained that it had been a hideout in case there was a *topattumi* ("night attack," an organized raid carried out by one village against another); they scolded her, saying children shouldn't play in such a place.

Wishing to portray the daily lives of the Ainu of several hundred years ago, I have so far given a cursory introduction to the stage on which these lives occurred, using three types of references:

oral traditions such as *uwepeker* (folktales) and *upashkuma* (factual stories or precepts), prose forms discussed further below;

the knowledge held by present-day Ainu elders, handed down to them as the traditional roots of Ainu culture;

insights gained from my visits to Inuit in the Arctic and the Moni in New Guinea, two other hunting and gathering societies.

The task, however, has proved unexpectedly challenging. Investigating even basic facts of daily life was more difficult than I had anticipated. For example, did two generations of couples—in other words, wife and mother-in-law—live under the same roof? Takakura Shin'ichirō, a professor emeritus of Hokkaidō University known for his work on Hokkaidō history and Ainu studies, writes:

> In principle, a household living under one roof consisted of one couple and underage children who were closely related to the husband. On reaching majority, these children married with the approval of the head of the household and moved into separate

houses. A woman who reached marriageable age sometimes had a separate house and waited for a husband who would be the master of the house. As the children left in this manner, only the old couple remained in their house. When the couple died, their paraphernalia were buried with them, and the house was burned for them to live in the other world. If there were dependent children or elderly persons who were not self-supporting, a brother took them in. The main branch of a family lived as *utarpake* (clan head) in an especially large house, which in troubled times could serve as a fort, with ordinary houses gathered around it. Clan meetings were held and travelers were accommodated in this house, and thus it had a public character. Instead of being burned when the family head died, it was transferred to someone who inherited the status of *utarpake*.[43]

According to this account, the wife and mother-in-law did not live under the same roof. Several Ainu researchers and Ainu elders in eastern Hokkaidō, Asahikawa, and Hidaka concur on this.

However, others disagree. Three or so *huchi* (grandames) in Biratori town in Hidaka district have suggested the contrary. "In the old days, wife and mother-in-law stayed together," they grieved. "But the world has become a tough place. Nowadays people just abandon their parents." There are, in fact, examples of *uwepeker* based on two generations living together.[44]

Records such as those of Matsuura Takeshirō can support either interpretation. A contemporary scholar observes:

As children married, starting with the oldest son, they one by one left their father's house to live in a new place. In most

43. Takakura Shin'ichirō, "Ainu," in *Ainu kenkyū* (Ainu research) (Hokkaidō University Co-op, 1966).
44. In a folk song called "The Tree-Climbing Wolf," collected in Kayano Shigeru's *Kitsune no charanke* (The fox's *charanke*) (Komine Shobō, 1974), the young couple's bedroom is in the house of an *ekashi*, who is presumably the *kotan* head.

cases, the oldest son lived next door to the father's house. The youngest child either stayed in his father's house after marriage or lived separately, like his brothers. In the latter case, only the parents lived in the old home. If the wife died first, the widower either moved into the oldest son's house or lived in a small shed built by its side, because in the old days the original house was burned for her to take to the other world. In some cases the widow did the same.[45]

An examination of various papers, reports, and oral traditions suggests that early Ainu society was based on nuclear families. What today's grandmothers think of as "the old days" when wife and mother-in-law lived together are, perhaps, the days after the Shisam influence began; they may not be aware of the truly old days that preceded.

IKOINKAR

In portraying Ainu life from centuries past, an author who seeks historical evidence must qualify every fact and action with the

45. Kubodera Itsuhiko, "Seishi kankon shūzoku gyōji" (Life, death, coming of age, marriage—customs and events), in *Ainu minzokushi* (Ainu ethnography), ed. Council on the Preservation of Ainu Culture (Daiichi Hōki, 1970). Segawa Kiyoko's *Ainu no kon'in* (Ainu marriage) (Miraisha, 1972), which documents the largest number of relevant examples, indicates that both arrangements were possible. Separate living seems to have been the older type. In a *pon oina* (small—i.e., romantic—*yukar*) told by Kannari Matsu, in *Yūkarashū* (Anthology of Yukar), vol. 1 (Sanseidō, 1959), a young female god awaits her bridegroom in a new dwelling given to her. A *kamui oina* (divine *yukar*) told by Sankirotte (in the same anthology, vol. 2 [1961]), too, introduces a young goddess's separate wing, referred to as "the beautiful little house" or "the maiden's house."

Furthermore, according to Fujimoto Hideo's analysis of an old document from the Shizunai area, two-generation households, rare in the 1810s, were fairly frequent approximately fifty years later. This accompanied the increase in adoption of Japanese personal names. Thus, while either case was possible, Takakura Shin'ichirō's description seems to present a more traditionally typical pattern.

caveat "probably," because historical evidence is difficult to find for even the most basic elements of daily life. I nevertheless hope to reconstruct daily life in an Ainu community, as accurately as possible, with the assistance of many *huchi* and *ekashi*, as well as researchers. The aim of part 2, the core of this book, is to convey the atmosphere of Ainu society long ago. To improve readability, I intend to omit the caveat "probably" and present the picture in story form. However, readers should know that part 2 is far from a product of pure imagination.

In the preceding section, I mentioned the knowledge of Ainu elders as one source for historical evidence of daily life in earlier times. This knowledge, handed down through the generations, is not limited to cosmic views and values; it also includes skills related to human life, such as birthing and healing, which are naturally vital concerns for any people.

The story I will tell of the birth of a child and the introduction of the skill of midwifery in Ainu society, for example, is based on knowledge imparted to Aoki Aiko by her ancestors and on her personal experiences. Aiko was the fifth successor to the skills of an *ikoinkar* (midwife) passed down through her maternal ancestors. Not only did she inherit practical skills in the narrow sense, but she received in the palm of her left hand, through a ritual process, a special ability called *tekeinu* (to feel in the hand). She was also an inheritor of the ability of *tusu* (divination) that belongs more broadly to shamanism, becoming one of the rare few in the late twentieth century to possess this ability.

After encountering Nagai Hiroshi, a naturalist in Sapporo city, and his wife, Etsuko, Aiko began narrating the skills and oral traditions passed down from her ancestors, following her retirement from work as *ikoinkar* in 1975. As an undergraduate, Nagai (then Ueda) Etsuko had visited Hokkaidō while preparing her thesis on Ainu food culture. After graduation, she assisted Kayano Shigeru in compiling the book *Ainu no mingu* (Ainu folk utensils).

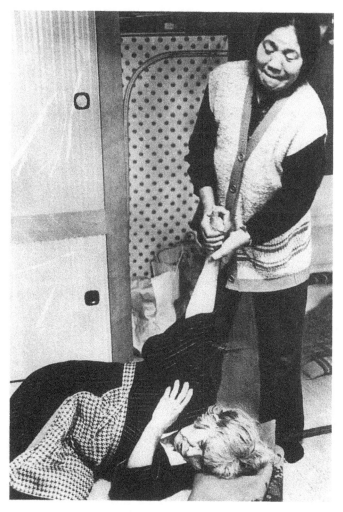

Aoki Aiko treating a patient with a dislocated shoulder. Photo by Nagai Hiroshi.

One summer day, she fell while climbing Poroshiri Peak in Hidaka and hurt her hip so badly she could hardly move. She visited Aiko, who was skilled in Ainu medicine generally.

Aiko perceived "something" in Etsuko's personality, perhaps because of her ability of *tusu* or *ue-inkar* (clairvoyance, extrasensory perception). For her part, Etsuko was surprised to see before her own eyes something that had been lost from today's world. During their first conversation, Aiko discussed, as a known fact, an event in Etsuko's past that Etsuko had not mentioned. Five years later, in 1978, in response to Aiko's wishes, Etsuko began recording what we may call the "contemporary oral tradition." The delay, which might have been an inconvenience, was instead highly fortunate: Etsuko had in the meantime married Nagai Hiroshi, an experienced documentary photographer and filmmaker. The story below of Aoki Aiko the *ikoinkar*, as well as the picture of midwifery given in part 2, draws primarily on what the Nagais learned from Aiko-huchi, supplemented by information gathered in my own meetings with her.

Seen in Nibutani as a somewhat "unusual" person, Aiko did not fail a single time in the nearly six hundred deliveries she handled; moreover, she once discovered a pregnancy at an early stage after it had been misdiagnosed at two different maternity hospitals as a tumor or a lump of flesh. "Heaven forbid, this is a perfect *ainu*!" she said. Later, she safely delivered the baby. In her own area she was renowned as a skilled midwife.

I mentioned that Aoki Aiko was the fifth-generation successor to the family art of *ikoinkar* and *tusu*. The only known birth date of her predecessors is that of the fourth generation, her mother, Ukochatek; the date of death of the third generation, her grandmother Haenure, is known, but not the date of her birth. Aiko knows about the first and second generations only through her mother and grandmother. While the Ainu had a so-

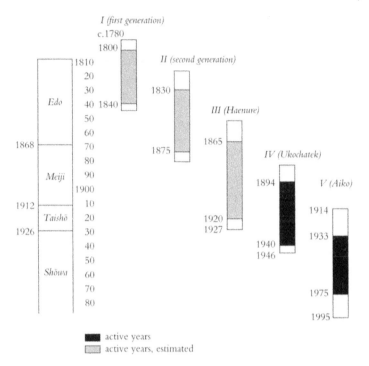

Estimated chronology of the five generations of midwives down to Aoki Aiko.

phisticated vigesimal numerical system, it was considered improper to count or ask another's age.[46]

The estimated life spans of those in the first and second generations and the periods of their activities as midwives are indicated above. While the midwife of the first generation rarely worked as *tusu*, she is said to have had powerful clairvoyance, able to see in her mind's eye what someone was doing—for exam-

46. According to Fujimura Hisakazu, Ainu people thought the god of death might decide to send them to the other world if he discovered how old they were.

ple, on a distant mountain. With this ability, Aiko imagined, the art of *tusu*, which seems to have become more intense from the third generation on, was probably unnecessary.

At the time of the first generation, life seems to have been comfortable enough. It became harder with the second generation, and beginning with the third generation the family experienced great poverty. This undoubtedly reflected the impoverishment of the hamlet as a whole, owing to Japanese exploitation and the forced labor draft that began in the late Edo period. No matter how skilled a midwife was, the hamlet and neighboring hamlets no longer had the resources to guarantee her living. Aiko's grandmother continued to devote much time to the art of delivery and *tusu*, but few households were able to make voluntary contributions, as they had done before. The fifth generation saw the time when an academic background and reading and writing knowledge of Japanese were required, and those with real strength in skills and theory of childbirth were branded as "unqualified, illegal midwives" unless they passed the new official standards.

As a child, Aiko had a strong tendency, to the extent that it bothered her mother, toward minute observation (called in Ainu *ichimchimi,* meaning "sorting out with hands"). This was an indication of her lively curiosity and inquisitiveness. When Aiko was twelve, her mother began bringing her along as an assistant whenever there was a delivery. The following is an account of one of the visits Aiko remembers from those early days.

This particular birth took place in a poor Shisam family who lived in a charcoal burner's hut deep in the mountains. There was no blanket. The pregnant woman lay on the floor under one layer of kimono. Hot water, to be used for bathing the newborn, was boiling in an iron pot over the firepit. The upper end of the hook for hanging the pot was tied to the beam with grapevine skin, called *sutukap* in Ainu. "So it's not just Ainu people; Shisam also use *sutukap*," Aiko thought.

When the baby was born with an energetic birth cry, a family member hurriedly poured the hot water from the pot into a washbowl and mixed it with cold water. Aiko's *hapo* first washed the baby's face, then its body. The family had no washcloth. Since absorbent cotton was unavailable in that area in those days, Hapo used sagebrush cotton she had brought. Good for stopping blood and killing germs, it was also used for treating the woman after she gave birth.

When all was finished, the payment from the poor family was a cup of tea. The washbowl used for cleaning the baby was once again placed over the fire to boil water, then that water was poured into a tin can used as a teapot. Instead of tea leaves, cranesbill leaves were used. "It's not just Ainu people who use cranesbill," Aiko thought. On their way home, she said to Hapo, "They didn't pay you a penny and served tea from water in the washbowl for the baby. From now on, don't drink such unclean things."

Hapo answered sternly, "If I leave the delivery house without even drinking tea, I cause *yainikoroshima* (embarrassment) to Uwarikamui (the deity of childbirth). The birth of a new life isn't a matter of bills or coins. I do it with my true love, with my heart, so I won't embarrass Uwarikamui. That's why I've been able to handle the toughest births safely."

At twelve, around the time Aiko began accompanying Hapo as an *ikoinkar* assistant, she was instructed in "the posture of giving birth by oneself" by Hapo and Huchi, who was then still in good health. Aiko does not remember if there was a special term for this way of sitting, but Huchi demonstrated *kemaha pirkano monoa* (the way of sitting with proper leg posture), then had her granddaughter try it:

Sit with the feet slightly overlapping under the hips. This is close to "sitting straight," except that the left foot is placed over the right foot in such a way that the left sole presses against the anus. Then open the knees wide and lean your back against *totta* (large woven bags). When labor begins, hold on to the *tar* (carrying rope), hung from the beam, to bear the baby. Uwarikamui should be there in front of your knees, waiting to take up the baby safely.

In this region, bending forward or prostrating oneself was considered a Shisam-style posture. According to the method Aiko inherited, an Ainu midwife always makes the woman in childbirth lie on her back, for otherwise the accomplished midwife cannot use her delivery skills.

Aiko first acted as a midwife by herself when she was nineteen. The woman was sixteen years old by Western count, and this was her first childbirth. She was somewhat petite, and her womb was "just one step away from being sufficiently developed." By then Hapo had given Aiko serious training in midwifery. For example, by letting Aiko feel the abdomen of pregnant women who came for examinations, Hapo taught her how to tell the sex of the fetus or discover an abnormality. Should two childbirths concur, Hapo believed Aiko was at a stage where she could replace her mother for one, as long as it was a normal delivery. However, Hapo had never directly shown her the *apa* (aperture) of the baby's passage. Hapo had always let Aiko observe her from the rear as she worked with the baby, and then explained the birth in detail on the way home.

That day, news of labor pains arrived almost simultaneously from Koupira, two and a half miles downstream from Nibutani, and Penakori, two and a half miles upstream. The dialogue that took place between the two went like this (in Ainu):

Hapo: You go to Penakori.
Aiko: By myself?
Hapo: You can do it by yourself, so go.

Aoki Aiko at age seventeen (1931). Two years later she became a practicing midwife.

Aiko: "You can do it by yourself, so go"—but won't it be scary?

Hapo: I've taken you to many places; you'll know what to do.

Aiko: I may know what to do, but I haven't even seen the place (*apa*).

Hapo: You can do it even if you haven't seen it, so go.
          Hapo did it that way, too. It's all right. *E=ra-*
          matkor wa e=an pe ne na arpa (You've been
          prepared to do this by heaven, now go quickly).

In the *saranip* (woven bag with one strap) that Hapo handed
to Aiko were four items: scissors for cutting the umbilical cord,
thread made of the inner skin of bittersweet for tying the umbilical cord off at the navel, sagebrush cotton, and inner skin of
wild hydrangea (*Hydrangea paniculata; rasupa* in Ainu and *nori-
utsugi* in Japanese), for use in place of soap and as an accelerant
in a difficult labor.

Hapo did not let Aiko take a washbowl, saying there would
be one in the woman's house. Though now resigned to the situation, Aiko kept thinking, "What if I embarrass Uwarikamui,
what if I'm scolded by Uwarikamui?" All that occupied her mind
and heart as she started out was the deity Uwarikamui.

At the house of the woman in labor, people naturally expected
the famed midwife Ukochatek, Aiko's mother, to come. They
must have felt uneasy when a nineteen-year-old maiden appeared
by herself. But Aiko was even more uneasy. Her heart throbbing,
she took her seat on the left side of the woman just as she had
seen Hapo do.

As instructed by Hapo, Aiko offered this prayer in Ainu to
Uwarikamui: "O, Uwarikamui, I will never set out to do this task
halfheartedly. I have brought here in my bosom the ancestral skills
and my personal deity. If, together with my deity, you protect
me, it will go well. The deity of fire is here with me, too. I would
like to be Hapo's good successor, so please help me."

As she manually examined the abdomen of the mother-to-
be, her heart-throbbing anxiety gradually disappeared, and she
grew so calm that it was strange even to herself. "If you are ready
to pray with all your heart, you can deliver the child successfully,"

Hapo had said. "Try to catch the 'heart' of the baby being born." This advice expressed a belief handed down through generations of ancestors. Since the baby was in normal position, the woman had an easy birth and the delivery did not require a large variety of skills.

At the last stage of a normal delivery like this, Aiko would use her hands carefully. At the moment the baby's head shows, the midwife lightly places the thumb of each hand on it, while avoiding the fontanel. Next, as the baby's cheeks come out from the passage, she places her forefingers on each side of the chin, where the nerves are concentrated. At the same time, she slides her fingers just slightly forward. In response, the baby pulls its chin in. This technique can also be effectively applied when, in a breech delivery, the baby's chin is stuck: doing the same thing with fingers partly inserted into the passage makes the delivery easier. By using this method, Aiko said, the baby "comes out with delight." When this is done to a newborn, "it laughs."[47]

When the head is out and it is time for the neck, the midwife feels it with the forefinger of the hand that is to catch the baby. As she touches the neckbone, she lets her finger glide forward to the base of the neck. When the chest is coming out, she palpates with the same hand the thoracic vertebrae (the most important being the third vertebra and its vicinity), from the neck down toward the hips. Her hand stops at the lumbar vertebrae, and at that point it catches the baby—in other words, the baby is now "delivered" onto her hand.

Before the delivery, the midwife stretches her left leg so as to support, with the toes, the woman's anus from underneath. When the baby's head shows, she moves her toes to the woman's coc-

47. *Translator's note:* This recalls what we know as an inborn reflex—passing a finger across the chin just below the underlip causes a baby to break into a big smile.

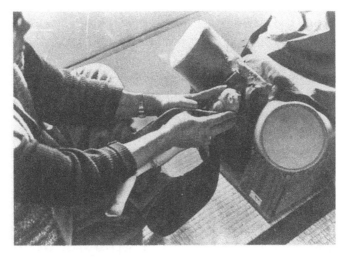

Aoki Aiko demonstrating a breech delivery with the use of a doll and a model of the female body. Photo by Nagai Hiroshi.

cyx to push it upward. This makes it easier for the pelvis to open. The baby, caught at the lumbar vertebrae by the method described above, will then land on the shin of the midwife's outstretched left leg. Occasionally the right leg is used as needed.

The function of each hand or finger is not set in advance of the entire process. The midwife chooses the fingers that are the most natural and easiest to use at a given moment. The act of feeling with a finger for each section of the backbone is called "receiving." In Aiko's words, "Giving stimulation to each part awakens the baby's nerves." Doing so helps keep the bone structure from moving out of place so that the delivery becomes smooth, ultimately making the process easier for the baby, the woman, and therefore the midwife.

Of further importance is that this technique enables quick discovery of any disorder of the bone structure or abnormality in the internal organs. Many mental and nervous illnesses that oc-

cur by early adulthood are considered to be caused, albeit remotely, by problems occurring around the backbone at the time
of delivery. If Aiko detected abnormality, she treated it immediately after cutting the umbilical cord (she was also skilled in
spinal column correction, an art of Ainu medicine). She considered incompetent midwives and obstetricians responsible for
a fair number of cases of infantile physical crippling, partial her-
nias of the groin, and dislocations of the hip joint.

Before bathing the newborn, Aiko gave thanks to the deities
for the successful delivery, then, in an act of sharing with the baby
this irreplaceable joy, put her cheek to the little body covered with
mucus and blood. With her mouth she sucked the mucus out of
the baby's mouth. She then chewed on butterbur root and fed
the juice mouth-to-mouth in order to prompt the child's first
discharges.

TUSU AND UE-INKAR

It was in October 1945, when Hapo was on her deathbed with
cancer, that Aiko, then thirty-one years old, was initiated into
the special ability of feeling in the hand. Aiko, who was married,
lived nearby and frequently went home to look after Hapo. One
day, she saw Hapo's left palm rise with undulating motions. Hapo
said to Aiko in a formal tone, "It isn't right not to pass down the
ancestral deities. Quickly, go call Sekko-achapo."

Sekko-achapo (Uncle Sekko, whose Japanese name was Kaizawa
Seitarō) was a relative and one of the few *ekashi* who could properly perform traditional rituals in Ainu. In Nibutani Kotan, only
three or so such *ekashi* then remained. Mediation between humans
and deities required a ritual performed by such a man. When
Sekko-achapo arrived, Hapo talked to him in Ainu while showing him her undulating palm: "I am now so weakened that I only
await my death. Whether with Ainu or Shisam, I have tried my

An *ekashi* (Hikawa Zenjirō) holding a *tuki* (wine cup) and, on it, a *pasui* (wine-offering chopstick). At the Shakushain festival, 1978. Photo by Nagai Hiroshi.

best as a midwife. I believe it is thanks to my guardian deities that an error has never occurred. Please give prayers so that after my death the good ancestral guardians move to my only daughter."

Sekko-achapo, known as a fluent orator, immediately left her bedside to sit by the firepit and begin praying to the fire deity. When Hapo said, "Take my hand in yours," Aiko covered it with her left palm. She felt the rising palpitation under her palm. It felt both strange and ticklish. While their palms were joined together, Hapo gravely delivered her dying will in Ainu:

I have helped both Shisam and Ainu with midwifery and mediation passed down to me from bygone ancestral ages. I haven't done this with my own power. Thanks to the guardian deities alone, there never was a failure. I have made a request to the gods that before my death, you inherit my guardians. Keep this in mind. When I am gone, do your best to help people, as I have done, no matter who calls you for help. Then, both humans and gods will protect you and you will be able to break through whatever difficulties you encounter. I leave this will, praying that both the ancestral deities and my own guardian deity move into your body. Make sure to receive them.

By the time Hapo's speech was over, the palpitation in her left hand was gone. "*Hioioi, tane isam wa* (Good, there's nothing more to say)," Hapo said. Sekko-achapo stopped his *kamuinomi* (prayer) and stepped back from the fireside to join the two women.

Hapo died in March of the next year, on a day when long icicles hung from the eaves. Her heart and breathing had stopped, and neighbors who had gathered were busily preparing for the wake. Two hours or so after her death, however, Hapo spoke out, "*Echi=nu* (Can you folks hear me)?" Those present were so taken aback that one dropped something, and another, who was removing the door, fell under it. Hapo said, "Don't be angry with me. An *ekashi* on a carriage drawn by a white horse came for me, but I remembered that I left the wine I'd prepared as a gift to take to heaven. So I've come back for it. There were three gallons. They're not here, though, are they?" Her firstborn son had lent the three gallons of wine to a neighbor. When Aiko said, "Okay, Hapo. I'll make sure that you take the wine with you," Hapo closed her eyes saying, "Sorry to surprise you. So, this is good-bye for real."

So went Aiko's story about how her mother departed to *kamui moshir* (the land of the gods).

Aiko's midwifery had evolved through a dozen years of experience before she partook in the *tekeinu* succession ritual. Hapo's technical instruction seems to have been concluded by then. Hapo's younger sister had handled a larger number of deliveries than Hapo, with skills not inferior to Hapo's. But Hapo alone had received the *tekeinu* initiation from Huchi.

A *tusu* inspiration suddenly occurred to Aiko about two months after Hapo's death, one day in May of 1946. Aiko's husband, who had contracted malaria while in military service, had been discharged following Japan's defeat in World War II. That day the couple was out in the field, planting corn. Her husband, running a high fever, began uttering nonsensical words, and, at that moment, Aiko became hazy. Though she remembers somehow reaching home, after that she lost consciousness. "I became *ruhai* (dazed)," as she put it. While she was unconscious, Aiko continuously and rapidly spoke in Ainu, her body quivering. The vibrations did not stop even after she was carried inside the house. Since no one around her fully understood her Ainu, Nitani Kunimatsu-ekashi was sent for.

The words Aiko repeated formed a message spoken by an ancestor through Aiko's voice, "This one will die if you leave her alone. Hurry and make a *kinasut-kamui* (snake deity) and let her have it." "This one" referred to Aiko. As a *tusukur*, Aiko was relaying the words of someone in the other world. Right away a *kinasut-kamui noka* (a form of the snake deity) was created, and Nitani-ekashi performed prayers. Aiko became calm, the rapid Ainu speech ended, and soon she revived.

Aiko reflected on this. While Hapo was alive, Aiko had secretly thought she would be happy to succeed to the art of midwifery, but not to that of *tusu*. The sudden visitation of the *tusu* phenomenon in this manner, she thought, meant that she was being punished for her attitude. After that, Aiko began to entertain a sense of mission about *tusu*, and thus *kinasut-kamui* became her guardian deity. As for her husband, he was eventually cured of malaria. According to Ainu medicine, cat saliva was effective for a disease accompanied by intermittent fever. Aiko repeatedly fed him food mixed, without his knowledge, with cats' leftovers.

Aiko performed *tusu* sometimes unconsciously and suddenly, but at other times by asking the fire deity to move a specific spirit to come down to her. The former phenomenon was and is quite rare, and spirits possessing her were limited to ancestors such as the first-generation midwife, or Hapo, or Aiko's own guardian deity. The latter phenomenon is similar to the so-called *itako* medium in northeast Honshū. In such instances she would speak to some appropriate spirit, such as the deceased grandmother or grandfather of the person who requested the consultation.

Going into the *tusu* state means mediating, as a kind of prophet, the words of a spirit. So the body that acts as a vehicle is also affected by the spirit. After being possessed by a heavenly spirit (for example, the first-generation midwife), the medium's physical condition improves; but after contact with a dark spirit, the medium becomes so exhausted that she may take to bed. Premonitory to the *tusu* state, vibrations occur all over the body. When the medium is for some reason reluctant to go into the *tusu* state, the vibrations are intense, whereas they tend to be modest when she feels willing. When the vibrations are over, she temporarily becomes another person. The time period of this change of consciousness is about ten seconds at minimum, and two to three minutes at most.

The gift of clairvoyance manifested itself in Aiko in 1955, when she was forty-one. Aiko was hospitalized with a tumor of the uterus at that time. After the operation, she caught the doctor saying in a low voice, "Oh, dear." When she questioned him, he confessed that he had left a piece of gauze in her body. Aiko wanted to help the conscientious doctor who had acknowledged his error, so she called to her guardian deity and stayed in a *tusu*

Aoki Aiko sending back the spirit of *Kinasut-kamui* (the snake deity, the guardian of birth). Photo by Nagai Hiroshi.

state almost all night. A long-bearded *ekashi* appeared in her vision. Slender and dressed in ceremonial Ainu clothing, he sat with his legs crossed, revealing shin hair. From around him, gentle, beautiful singing voices of other Ainu could be heard. Looking steadily at her, he gave her silent yet steady support. "I must be seeing the spiritual world," Aiko thought and thanked the *ekashi*. By the time his form disappeared, she felt at ease.

On the following day, an end of the gauze came out of the vaginal passage, so she pulled it out with her fingers. According to Aiko's explanation, each human has two types of deities: "a guardian spirit" and "a spirit that guides toward the higher." A guiding spirit instructs the person to a certain point, then is replaced by another guide leading the way toward a yet higher region. Some people continue to train and progress from height to height, as Aiko sees it, because their guiding spirit brings friends along. She interpreted the *ekashi* who appeared by her bedside that day as having been a guardian, the first of the two types.

From that time on, Aiko's clairvoyance grew stronger by the day. This power lets one see before one's eyes not only something taking place at a distance, but the future and past of someone seated before one. "To see" here means to view clearly delineated forms; it does not mean a vague, dreamlike vision or one limited within a frame, like a TV program or a movie. To borrow the words of Professor Chiri Mashiho, it is "clairvoyance that enables one to see, for example, the private parts of someone seated face to face with you."[48]

When a relative's wife was pregnant, Nagai Hiroshi asked Aiko one month or so before the birth whether the baby was a boy or a girl. Aiko, who could "see" the fetus of the woman in Sapporo, about sixty miles away, said it was a baby girl. When Nagai asked again one week before birth, Aiko said, "I see the baby

<hr/>

48. Chiri, *Bunrui Ainugo jiten: ningenhen,* s.v. *ue-inkar.*

but I'm not quite sure. Its umbilical cord is really fat and it's hiding the crucial part, so I can't see that spot. But, if it's a boy, I think I should see the *chiehe* (penis) peeking from behind it no matter how fat it is. So after all it may be a girl. Anyway, it's a plump baby with dark hair and a good complexion." When the baby was born, everything was exactly as she had predicted. I am told that it was a baby girl with an extremely fat umbilical cord.

In the preceding section, I noted Nagai Etsuko's surprise when, during their first conversation, Aiko discussed a past incident in Etsuko's life that Etsuko had never mentioned. Though she didn't know their names, Aiko said that she "saw" two young men who thought well of Etsuko. Etsuko had abandoned them, so to speak, in coming to Hokkaidō. Now Aiko "saw" another young man. Though he and Etsuko hadn't even spoken to each other, eventually she would marry him. This young man turned out to be Nagai Hiroshi.

Suffering from a heart condition, Aiko had retired in 1975 both from midwifery and *tusu*. The only delivery she handled after retirement was that of the fetus misdiagnosed as "a tumor or a lump of flesh" by two obstetricians, who were about to remove it from the uterus. The child was in elementary school in 1992.

Nagai Hiroshi estimates that Aiko treated nearly thirty thousand people with her midwifery, medicine, or consultation with the spirits by way of *tusu*.

UWEPEKER

So far we have looked at the setting of Ainu Moshir and considered the means by which to imagine the Ainu lifestyle of several hundred years ago. Drawing on the knowledge I gained from Aoki Aiko and other elders, I would like, in the next part of this book, to make use of traditional forms of Ainu oral culture to give the reader a sense of Ainu life thus imagined.

The late bard Yae Kurō (1985–1978), on whose narration the divine *yukar* about a hare in "The Day of Melting Snow" is based (p. 112). From a Sapporo TV broadcast.

It is often observed that the Ainu had no written language. But although *Homo sapiens* appeared hundreds of thousands of years ago, it is only in the last several millennia that peoples such as the ancient Egyptians began to use written language. Other groups followed much later. In this context, the difference between having and not having a written language is barely a moment of time. The Shisam, too, had no written language until the fourth or fifth century C.E.

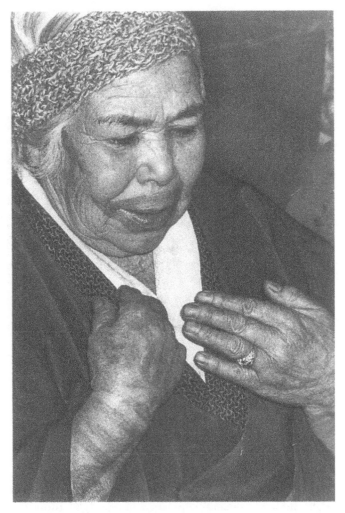

Kaizawa Turshino (1889–1982), the source of the name
"Turushno" (p. 120), at an ancestral ritual. Photo by
Nagai Hiroshi.

Moreover, most peoples have lost significant things in the process of gaining the ability to write. One of the most valuable of these was a folk culture based on memory—the world of oral transmission. Oral traditions played a far more sizable role in society and in individual lives than does written literature today. Such traditions were transmitted to a live audience in Ainu society as recently as in the past few decades. Now, however, because of the sharp decline in the number of "listeners" who understand Ainu, it is doubtful that the few elders who can take on the role of performer or reciter will be able to reproduce the world of oral transmission as a physical space that includes the audience.

The most famous of the several pillars of Ainu oral arts is called *yukar* (*sakorpe* in eastern Hokkaidō).[49] Others include proselike tales called *uwepeker* (also known as *tuitak*) and fables called *upashkuma* (or *uchashkuma*). In contrast to the performance of *yukar*, which is rhymed verse with melodies, these others have been transmitted in "spoken" form. Song and recitation also fall broadly under the category of oral arts, and poetic improvisation called *yaisama* was once an everyday cultural form. The categorization of these arts varies somewhat from researcher to researcher. On page 89 I present Haginaka Mie's chart of epic poems and prose tales as an example of the least complicated classification of the types of oral transmission, excluding songs and incantation.[50]

49. Common expressions such as "orally transmitted literature" or "oral literature" often are used pejoratively. Whether in China or in the West, the concept of "literature" implies the use of "letters," visual symbols with form. Every people had oral arts that depended upon the aural sense. Oral tradition precedes written literature, not the other way around; arts that depend on writing belong to a small minority and are recent in human history. Yet as "mainstream" peoples have emphasized written languages since "historic" times, they have privileged written "literature." My use of the term "oral arts" here is deliberate.

50. The chart is based on Haginaka Mie, *Yūkara e no shōtai* (An invitation to *yukar*) (Hokkaidō Shuppan Kikaku Center, 1980), and partially revised by Haginaka herself for inclusion here.

The late Kannari Matsu (1875–1961) is the teller of the *yukar* "Kanokanpe karitenpe," on which the story of the beautiful tattoo is based (pp. 137–41).

Kimura Kimi (1900–1988) is the teller of a legend titled "Kotan no yōtō" (The magic sword of the *kotan*), the basis for the night attack in "Days of Battle" (pp. 197–207).

Nishijima Teru (1898–1988), whose stories are the basis for the funeral scene (pp. 245–55). She had a precise memory of even extempore songs her neighbors had sung. Photo as she took a rest from work in her farm; taken by the author.

Epic Poems and Prose Tales

Verse Tales
 Divine *Yukar*
   Divine characters appearing in this type of *yukar*:
    Natural deities
      deities like fire and wind
      animal deities like the giant striped owl and mud snail
      plant deities like the wild lily and katsura
    Patriarchal deity
      the human patriarch called Oina-kamui, Kotan-
      kar-kamui, or Okikurmi
 Human *Yukar*
   Human characters appearing in this type of *yukar*:
    Male: a youth called Poiyaunpe, Poiotasutunkur, etc.
    Female: a young woman called Shinutapkaunmat,
    Iyochiunmat, etc.
Prose Tales
 Legends
   Oral transmissions related to rituals, place-names, ancestors,
   etc. (*upashkuma*)
 Old Tales
   Yukar told in prose form
   Stories of *kotan* heads and residents (*uwepeker* or *tuitak*)
 Other Stories
   Tales of Pananpe, tales of mainland Japanese, brief tales, etc.

With the exception of some didactic tales, a characteristic of *yukar* and *uwepeker* alike is that they are related, that is, performed, in the first person (or, more accurately, in "the first person of quotation").[51] In part 2 I shall use the form of the *uwepeker*, a narrated life story, to relate the exploits of a single protagonist, Harukor.

51. The narrator is not the main character of the story, but one who impersonates the main character. This "narrator's 'I,'" clearly indicated as such in the Ainu original, differs from the first person in Japanese or English.

Literally translated, *uwepeker* means "mutually pure,"[52] but the form can be considered analogous to the Japanese folktale. While the content can cover a wide range of topics, and the stories vary from fairly brief to long, almost all of them serve to instruct or reveal some kind of life wisdom. In the process of their transmission, many recitations of direct experience were transformed into *uwepeker*.

52. So says Kayano Shigeru in *Uepekere shūtaisei* (A collection of *uwepeker*) (Arudō, 1974). Chiri Mashiho defines the word as "mutually inquiring after news" (*Chiri Mashiho chosakushū* [Collected short works of Chiri Mashiho] [Heibonsha, 1973], vol. 2).

PART TWO

HARUKOR

✦

The protagonist of my story is a woman. As is true for many
other peoples, in general it was women rather than men who
truly sustained Ainu daily life, preserving and handing down traditional culture, particularly language. The setting is eastern
Hokkaidō (the region around Kushiro and Kitami) several hundred years ago. When we trace the ancestry of Ainu in the Hidaka locale, many of them have roots in the Tokachi and Kushiro
region. Humoshirush, the seventeenth-generation ancestor of
Kayano Shigeru, was of *moshirpa* (the east; see the section titled
"Ancestors"). It is believed that many forebears of Tokachi Ainu
came from even farther east. Following the conventions of myth-
making, I have avoided further specifying the area in which the
story takes place, although it is somewhere in eastern Hokkaidō.
The reader should envision a *kotan* near the mouth of a river,
perhaps in the area of Kushiro, along the Pacific coast. Relatively
close by is a lake, similar to Lake Tōro, with an abundance of
water chestnuts.

I begin with a few lines of Ainu and an English translation. I
ask you to imagine the rest, too, to have been translated from the
Ainu.

THE DAY OF THE SNOWSTORM

Acha newa hapo newa huchi tura okay=an wa, an=inwak
anakne sapo newa aki newa anokay tura ren inwak ne ruwe ne
awa, an=kor kotan rehe anak otasam kotan ay=ye, chepkaun-
pet petput orowa emakan=i=ta ekotankor wa okay=an
    Iyotta hushko an=amkir p anak, an=chikiri yoniyoni hike
tu matapa kay re sakpa kay okake ta shineanto ta upun yupke

93

A *chise* (house).

tek tonoshkeno wa an=kor hapo soy wa san wa pu orwa shirun
amam pushihi oma saranip se wa ahun siri ene an ruwe ne

I lived with my father, mother, grandmother, and
siblings, an elder sister, and a younger brother. Our
village was called Otasam, and we lived in a home
upstream from the mouth of the Chepkaunpet River.

My earliest memory is of a terrible snowstorm that
came upon us two winters and three summers after I had
started walking. Shortly after noon, my mother went
outdoors to the raised-floor storage shed and brought
back a sack brimming with millet stalks.[1]

With an "umph," Hapo lowered the woven bag from her back
to the side of the firepit. Grabbing handfuls of the millet, she
laid them on the shelf over the firepit to dry before threshing
them in the mortar. With each handful, a few millet grains sifted
down into the flames, popping and sputtering. In the dark house,
the windows shut tight against the snowstorm, Hapo's face wa-

1. The English translation is based on the Japanese translation by Fujimura
Hisakazu.

A *saranip* (bag woven of
the inner skin of tree bark).

vered in the red glow of the fire. The
bursting of the grains almost seemed to
soften the mighty roar of the storm.
Sapo (big sister), four years or so
older than I, was sitting by Huchi as she
spun thread. Sapo came over to help
Hapo. Barely tall enough to reach the
shelf, however, she kept spilling the
grain, and the popping sound grew
louder. "I'm fine, you just stay over
there," Hapo told her. The sound of
the millet was so enticing that I scam-
pered over to the firepit, but Huchi
told me, "You're going to get dust in
your eyes, Opere (little one)."[2] The
millet grains became black dots as they
fell onto the embers; then, once they
popped, they turned into bright spots
that vanished.

Acha (father)[3] was silently carving with his knife, but the object was so small that I couldn't tell what he was making. I wanted
so much to take a closer look, but since he'd scolded me harshly
the other day, I had avoided moving close to him while he was
carving. I knew that sometimes when a child fell into the fire,

2. "Opere" literally means "little crack." See Chiri Mashiho, *Bunrui Ainugo jiten: ningenhen* (Classified Ainu dictionary: Humanity) (Nihon Jōmin Bunka
Kenkyūjo, 1945; Heibonsha, 1993), s.v.

3. *Michi* in Biratori, Shiraoi, and other areas. Dialectal differences of this
type are not followed very strictly here.

A *parapasui* (spoon for women).

an adult with a knife in his hand reached out to catch the child and accidentally cut the child with it.

From the edge of the firepit, I asked, "What are you carving, Acha?" He replied only, "An arrowhead." After a period of silence, however, he finally looked up and said, "Once I finish this, I'm going to make you a new spoon, all right?" Acha's eyes were hidden by the shadow of his eyebrows, but I could feel his gently smiling gaze.

Perhaps the rumble of the blizzard shaking our *chise* increased a notch, for my sleeping Akihi (younger brother) woke up crying in his cradle. Huchi picked him up and sang a lullaby in a low voice.

> "*Oho-rurururururururu mokor totto ran ran*
> (Your sleepy-time milk came down, came down)
> *oho-rurururururururu mokor shinta ran ran*
> (Your sleepy-time cradle came down, came down)
> *oho-rurururururururu*"

Akihi was born when the salmon were swimming upstream, but I have no recollection of that time. Maybe it happened while I was asleep, but more likely I was simply too young to remember. Although he could sit up on his own, he couldn't crawl yet.

From the kitchen, where she was filling a pot with various ingredients, Hapo spoke, partly to Sapo, partly to herself, "We're low on dried salmon, so we'd better get some from the raised storehouse once the storm lets up." She moved the pot to the

A *shinta* (cradle).

fire, and I realized that tonight we would again have *chep ohau* (fish and vegetable soup).

We rarely had *kam ohau* (meat and vegetable soup) these days. I liked both, but if it was fresh, I preferred fish, especially salmon; if it was dried, I preferred meat. Today, we had eaten plenty of smelt for our snack, so I wasn't very hungry.

Akihi had fallen asleep again in Huchi's arms, so she placed him back in the cradle, rocking it briefly before returning to her thread

A *kanit* (spindle stick). It is left standing by the fireside and used for winding twisted thread in the shape of a figure eight.

spinning. Sapo, sitting by her and collecting scraps of thread in a bag, pleaded with her for a story. I was watching from the edge of the firepit, ready to join them if she were to tell one. Huchi turned to me and said, "You come over, too, Opere. I'm going to tell you children a story." Before she finished speaking, I had jumped up and unthinkingly stepped over the corner of the firepit.

No sooner did an "Oh, no!" flash through my mind than Acha reprimanded me. I was constantly scolded for stepping over the firepit, but I always forgot in moments of excitement. Sapo never made this mistake, but she did sometimes get a scolding for running near it. It made the ashes swirl about, and it was dangerous near the fire and the cooking pots.

Huchi asked, "So, shall I tell you about Pananpe and Penanpe?"[4] "Oh, yes," replied Sapo, "but a different version than the last one you told us." Without resting her hands from twining, Huchi said, "Well, let's see. How about when Pananpe and Penanpe traveled to a distant land in a scallop-shell boat?" Huchi,

---

4. Pananpe-Penanpe is a genre of Ainu oral arts that has relatively young children as its audience. Different episodes are told in various regions.

with her seemingly endless supply of stories, was like a *"kamui* of storytelling,"* able to relate one tale after another.

"There were two brothers named Pananpe and Penanpe," she began. Sapo and I listened attentively without making a sound; we were certain of being transfixed by the wonderful story that was about to start. The roar of the blizzard showed no signs of waning.

"I, the younger brother, Pananpe, lived downstream, while my older brother, Penanpe, lived upstream." So saying, Huchi looked at each of us with an impish expression. She was purposely heightening our impatience with the familiar introduction. "And then what?" we responded in unison.

"One fine day, when the waves were calm, I was walking along the beach and found a tree standing between one dune by the mountains and another dune by the beach. A bird was perched on its branches, singing like this:

"Konkani kokinkin
shirokani kokinkin[5]
kokishakisha
kokiriri-i-i-i. . . .

"That's how the tune went."

Huchi's imitation of the bird was so delightful that even as we nodded "Mmm hmm," we burst into laughter. I could see by the light of the firepit that Acha was holding back a smile.

"I was fascinated by this rare bird and managed to catch it. I discovered that if I caressed it gently from its head down its back;

5. *Konkani* is gold and *shirokani* silver. The rest has no particular meaning. This episode is based on Fujimura Hisakazu's Japanese translation of a version told by the late Shitaku Yae of Shiranuka in Kushiro. Although some Pananpe-Penanpe stories are told in the third person, Fujimura believes that the first-person narration represents the older form.

and then lightly tugged its tail feathers, it warbled just as beautifully as before:

> *"Konkani kokinkin*
> *shirokani kokinkin*
> *kokishakisha*
> *kokiriri-i-i-i. . . . "*

Huchi repeated the bird's call, and her singing was so convincing and entertaining we once more erupted into laughter.

"I put this bird in my bosom and went down to the beach. And what should I find at the shoreline but an unbelievably large scallop. When I commanded it, '*Hakketek makke* (Open, scallop)!' the huge scallop slowly c-r-e-a-k-e-d its mouth open.

"Full of wonderment, I stepped inside, this time saying, '*Hakketek chupke* (Close, scallop)!' to which the scallop c-r-e-a-k-e-d its mouth shut. I started singing a song beginning with '*Hakketek te-e-shke teshke* (O scallop, swim on, swim on).'

> *"Hakketek te-e-shke teshke*
> To the town of Repun Kotan[6]
> *hakketek te-e-shke teshke*
> that's where I'm going so
> *hakketek te-e-shke teshke*
> keep up the hard work
> *hakketek te-e-shke teshke*
> and carry me there
> *hakketek te-e-shke teshke . . .*

"In rhythm with my song, the scallop swam smoothly across the vast sea."

Huchi paused. Brought back to the present, we again said, "Mmm hmm." Her turns of phrase in the song were so evoca-

---

6. *Repun Kotan* means "*kotan* far out in the sea," here Tsugaru (the northernmost area of the mainland). Some traditions name the place as Matomai (Mat-

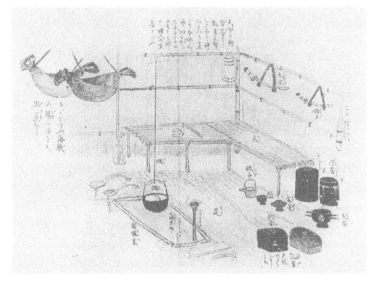

A corner of the interior of a *chise*, drawn 200 years ago, from
Murakami Shimanoin, *Ezotō kikan* (Curious sights on Ezo Island),
in the possession of the National Museum of Tokyo. This drawing,
which seems to bring all pieces of furniture to one corner, may
not be accurate in terms of their relative position.

The writing on top reads: "A large arrow holder is left dedicated
to the gods, with offering of *inau*, for a few years. It resembles the
family shrine found in many mainland homes. Called *nichineikorokamui*, it is said to be a treasured vessel for women." The writing on
the left reads: "These are hung with oil from a marine animal called
todo (Steller's sea lion)."

tive of the scallop swimming rhythmically through the sea that I
felt as if I, too, were headed toward that distant land. When her
voice came to a stop, I awoke, as if from a dream, to the world
of the *chise* where our firepit burned and the blizzard roared out-

sumae province at the southern tip of Hokkaidō); but in hypothesizing a provin-
cial governor over five hundred years ago, I have in mind the Andō clan seated
in Tosaminato at the mouth of the Iwaki River in fourteenth-century Tsugaru.

side. Looping her newly spun thread on the spindle, Huchi continued her story.

"Finally, we arrived at the banks of Repun Kotan. I told the scallop, '*Hakketek makke!*' and it c-r-e-a-k-e-d its mouth open. I jumped down onto the shore and intoned, '*Hakketek chupke!*' whereupon the scallop c-r-e-a-k-e-d its shell closed.

"I went into to the town of Repun Kotan and found it jam-packed with *chise*. It was the biggest *kotan* I'd ever seen. Large numbers of Shisam ladies, gentlemen with birds on their heads,[7] and children milled about a lively shopping area lined with stores carrying exotic products.

"Wandering through to the center of the town, I came upon a crossroads. I brought out the bird from my lapel, caressed it from the top of its head down its back, and gently tweaked its wings.

"Konkani kokinkin
shirokani kokinkin
kokishakisha
kokiriri . . .

"The bird started its fine warbling, causing the people around us to gather closely in surprise. I let them listen several times to the bird's unique song and was soon surrounded by ring after ring of onlookers.

"Somehow hearing about this, a messenger arrived from the castle in Repun Kotan and invited me up to it. And my, how big

7. "Shisam gentlemen with birds on their heads" refers to samurai with top-knots. There is a similar Ainu description of mainlander samurai as "appearing to have crows on their heads" (see Kayano Shigeru, *Our Land Was a Forest: An Ainu Memoir,* trans. Kyoko Selden and Lili Selden [Boulder, Colo.: Westview, 1994], p. 27). *Translator's note:* Although the shaven forehead with *chonmage* (or *Honda-mage*) is associated only with the Edo period, *motodori* (topknots) had long been worn, though usually under black samurai hats called *eboshi* (crow hats) that were used until late Muromachi.

that castle was! On entering, I was guided along an incredibly winding passage that led to a Great Hall. The lord sat at the front, flanked by his ministers and his consorts.

"'I hear that you have an unusual bird with a gorgeous singing voice,' he said. 'I greatly desire to hear it warble.'

"Bringing out the bird from my lapel, I caressed it from the top of its head down its back, then lightly tugged on its wings.

"Konkani kokinkin
shirokani kokinkin
kokishakisha
kokiriri-i-i. . . . "

Huchi's birdcall was so amusing that we laughed just as gaily each time she repeated it. Acha got up and went out into the unrelenting blizzard to check on the shutters around the *chise*.

"The lord exclaimed with joy, 'What a truly wonderful warble!' He wanted to hear the bird's call again and again. His ministers and ladies also clapped their hands in delight. I was asked to make another appearance the next day so that they could listen to the bird. From then on, I made at least one visit a day to the Great Hall for the entertainment of the lord and his vassals. Each time I was treated as an important guest and fed handsomely.

"Soon, however, I wished to return to my homeland. When I made my farewells to the lord, he answered, 'So the time has come. Thank you for staying so long,' and presented me with treasures. His ministers and ladies also gave me mementos of various kinds, and a parade of well-wishers carried all these treasures and gifts to the seashore to send me off.

"I told the waiting giant scallop, '*Hakketek makke!*' and it c-r-e-a-k-e-d its mouth open. Placing all of the gifts from everyone inside, I entered its mouth and said, '*Hakketek chupke!*' whereupon the scallop c-r-e-a-k-e-d its shell closed. So let's go back now—

"Hakketek te-e-shke teshke
   Back to my *kotan*
   hakketek te-e-shke teshke
   because I want to return
   hakketek te-e-shke teshke
   keep up the hard work
   hakketek te-e-shke teshke
   and carry me there
   hakketek te-e-shke teshke . . .

"When I started my song, Hakketek set off *teshke* (swimming with one shell up like a sail), smoothly crossing over the sea to the shore of my *kotan*.

"I said, '*Hakketek makke!*' and it c-r-e-a-k-e-d its mouth open. I went home and immediately called for my wife, and we spent the next few days moving the mountain of gifts. Both our *chise* and our storehouse were filled up. Bringing the bird out of my bosom, I thanked it profusely and let it go.

"Hearing of this story, elder brother Penanpe showed up."

Huchi took a breath here, so we again said, "Mmm hmm," and looked at her with pleading expressions to urge her on. Just then, Hapo called out, "Okay, dinner's ready. Come over and give me a hand."

Hapo probably had been listening to Huchi's tale while she was cooking, and thus timed her interruption for the moment when Huchi paused. Telling us, "Come on, time to help, give Hapo a hand," Huchi made us stand up. Sapo begged her, "Please tell us the rest later, okay?" She turned to me and, imitating Hapo and Huchi, said, "Okay, time to help, give Hapo a hand." Pushing me from behind, she moved over by Hapo. I felt as frustrated as if I'd woken up during the best part of a dream, and, besides, was annoyed by Sapo ordering me about like Hapo. So I yelled, "*Hakketek makke!*" in hopes of flinging away my irritation.

Acha came back in. Brushing off the snow as he stood in the dirt floor entrance, he observed, "Looks like a bigger blizzard than we've seen in a long time." The sun would have been shining if the weather were fine, but the light coming in from the entrance when he opened the door was almost like that of nighttime.

Hapo broke up pieces of kelp between her fingers and stirred them into the fish and vegetable soup, then lowered the pot before pouring the stew into each bowl, starting with Huchi's. Sapo always carried the bowls over, while I knelt next to Hapo and handed the bowls to her, one by one. Huchi sat properly before the bowl of soup placed on the edge of the firepit, hemming up a robe, and now and then brushing her hair out of the way.

As Acha sat down in front of his carving table, he told Huchi and Hapo in an unusually cheerful voice, "I just saw a snow owl outside; it was perched on the sacred fence. Well, a white owl in the midst of a blizzard when heaven and earth are all pure white—I went right up close before I even noticed! It turned to me and looked me over with its golden eyes before flying off. Something good's bound to happen this year."

I'd never seen a white owl, but I knew what owls looked like because one of the families nearby kept one with great care. Acha's story felt as special as Huchi's earlier one about the bird. I looked at him with a mixture of curiosity and dread, whereupon Huchi whispered to Sapo and me, "Don't tell anyone about this."[8]

When everyone had been served, Acha faced the firepit and, as usual, said, "*Iyairaikere* (We thank you)," as he performed *onkami* (ritual greeting) to the fire god.[9] Huchi, Hapo, Sapo, and I fol-

8. It was customary not to tell others of sightings of precious objects, as good luck might escape. Snow owls travel south in the winter from the North Pole area. They are occasionally seen in the vicinity of Sapporo. The sacred fence, *nusa san* in Ainu, is an outdoor altar formed of a fence of *inau*.

9. The fire god is female, called Ape-uchi-huchi in eastern Hokkaidō.

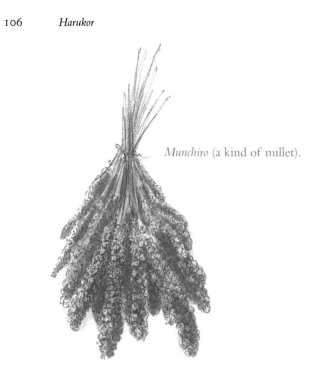

Munchiro (a kind of millet).

lowed with "*Hunna* (We partake)," raising our bowls and chopsticks with both hands.

The soup contained meat and dried vegetables that, other than the wild lily bulb, were unfamiliar to me. Finding a favorite, Sapo excitedly announced, "Oh, *raha* (liver)!" Hapo scolded her, saying, "Eat quietly without making noise." She also told me, "Don't chew so noisily." I always forgot this indiscretion of mine. Huchi continued, "Chewing like that is rude *shitaipe* (chomping like a dog)." Huchi definitely was silent when she ate; you didn't even notice that she was chewing unless you watched her. Even Acha commented, "It's also called *wenkuripe* (poor manners). *Wenkuripe* is *konotohewehewe* (gobbling away)." I was so em-

A *kemonuitosayep* (spindle with a needle container).

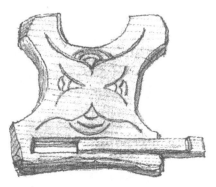

barrassed I made myself small, wishing I could hide myself in my own wrinkles.[10]

After the soup, I drank up my millet gruel.[11] Careful to avoid being scolded, I used my index finger to clean out the inside of my bowl, then said my "*Hunna* (I've partaken)."

Sapo and I were putting away everyone's dishes when Hapo, nursing the now-awake Akihi, told us, "The cold may get very bad late tonight if the blizzard stops, so make sure you bring in extra firewood from the entranceway."

When we'd finished with the firewood, Huchi called to us from her thread spinning, "If it's fair tomorrow, we'll have to go out early and stamp the snow down for pathways, so hurry along to bed. I'll come tell you the rest of the story. Sapo, when you prepare the beds, add an extra layer of fur to each. Opere, you go potty."

Going to the bathroom at night was actually less bothersome when the weather was bad. I only had to go to the tree-bark

10. "To hide in one's own wrinkles," *yainikoroshima,* is an Ainu expression for embarrassment.

11. The most common meal consisted of *ohau,* which was the staple food, and soupy gruel as a side dish.

A mat being woven on an *iteseni* (mat-weaving table).

chamber pot in the entranceway. Usually, we had to go outside closer to the hills, and it always felt like evil spirits would come out; sometimes you could even hear the wolves howling in the distance.[12] All the dogs in the neighborhood would bark, too, and it was quite frightening. Huchi and Acha always said, "Wolves are our friends." But I just couldn't bring myself to like the sound of their howling.

Sapo and I, wanting to hear the rest of the story as soon as we could, snuggled among our fur blankets and clamored at Huchi, "Come over here quick, we want to hear the story." Brushing away the bits of thread in her lap, Huchi good-naturedly replied, "All right, all right," and standing up unsteadily, came to us and lay down. Sandwiched between Sapo and Huchi, I waited patiently for Huchi to start her tale. Pulling a deerskin over herself, Huchi leaned on her elbow and faced us as she started.

12. These would have been the large Ezo wolves, related to the continental wolf. They became extinct in the late 1880s. Since these wolves assaulted grazing animals, they were killed with strychnine nitrate under the guidance of an American named Edwen Dun (1848–1931). Some say that the animals responsible for the attacks were wild dogs, and that wolves died of distemper carried by dogs from Honshū. In the Ainu tradition, wolves help rather than harm humans. In fact, there hardly seem to have been any incidents of humans being attacked by wolves.

"Let's see, we were where Elder Brother Penanpe came over because of the rumors he'd heard, weren't we?" "Yes," we replied in unison.

"'Well, well, Elder Brother Penanpe, please come in,' I told him. 'We'll serve you a feast, and while you eat you can listen to everything I experienced.' But this is what Penanpe said in reply, 'You think I don't know what you've been through? All you did was jump in ahead of what I wanted to do.' He left in a huff, even going so far as to urinate in the doorway."

I giggled, while Sapo said loudly, "What a horrid elder brother!"

"Now, here's the story of me, Penanpe. After I left my brother's house, the weather was fine, and the waves were calm, so I went walking along the shore, where I noticed a tree standing between the sand dune by the mountains and the sand dune by the shore. A bird had alighted on its branches, and it was calling like this. . . . "

Huchi paused, so we chimed in with the call that we had by now memorized.

"Konkani kokinkin
shirokani kokinkin
kokishakisha
kokiriri—"

"That's right," Huchi praised us before continuing. "My, you've learned it so well. . . .

"I thought, 'Ah hah! This must be the bird,' and caught it and stuffed it in my bosom. I went down to the beach and found a gigantic scallop lying at the edge of the waves. And what did I say?"

We immediately shouted, "*Hakketek makke!*"

"It's bedtime," Huchi warned us, "so you shouldn't be making such a racket." She continued, "Everything went smoothly, just like when Pananpe did it, and the scallop c-r-e-a-k-e-d its shell closed. So we set out on our travels.

"*Hakketek te-e-shke teshke*
 To the town of Repun Kotan
 hakketek te-e-shke teshke
 because I want to go
 hakketek te-e-shke teshke
 keep up the hard work
 hakketek te-e-shke teshke
 and carry me there
 hakketek te-e-shke teshke"

This time, we sang along with Huchi. The fire in the hearth crackled and sparks flew up toward the ceiling, hitting against the dried fish and fading away.

"The scallop glided powerfully through the sea and finally arrived at Repun Kotan. I again told the scallop, '*Hakketek makke!*' and it c-r-e-a-k-e-d its mouth open. I got out and shut it, saying, '*Hakketek chupke!*'

"Exactly as I'd heard, the town of Repun Kotan was crammed with houses. Just as the rumors had it, there were stores carrying exotic products, the Shisam ladies, and Shisam gentlemen with birds on their heads. When I came upon a crossroads, I brought the bird out from my bosom, just as Younger Brother Pananpe had, to make it warble. But before I could even caress the bird or tweak its tail feathers, I was completely surrounded by people. They must have noticed me even before I got to the crossroads, because they had already formed a line behind me."

Huchi spoke as if all of this had happened to her rather than to Penanpe. "Then, as I got all ready to induce it to cry, a messenger arrived from the castle. 'Welcome, please follow me,' he said, leading me there. I don't even know how we got there, that's how confusing the way was, and then he led me into the Great Hall. Just as Pananpe had said, the lord was sitting in front with his ministers and ladies crowding around him on both sides. 'How wonderful of you to come again,' the lord said. 'I was so pleased last time when you allowed us to hear such beautiful warbling from your bird, but I was just thinking how lonely it had gotten after you left us. I hope you will treat us to even more splendid calls this time.'

"I enthusiastically brought the bird out from my bosom. If the lord was this excited, I was going to really get the bird singing and earn myself a whole lot of treasures. And so I just gave those tail feathers a mighty pull. Well, the bird was so surprised, it pooped.

"And, do you know, it kept pooping and pooping, until the huge hall was full of poop and that mountain of poop just stank and sent everyone into an uproar. . . . "

We'd started giggling when the bird started to poop, but by now we were laughing so hysterically that our tummies hurt. Huchi always put on a straight face at times like this, so it was even funnier.

"At first, the lord and his ministers just sat there in astonishment, but they soon became quite angry about the mountain of poop and yelled threats at me. The warriors drew their swords, while others began to chase me with spears at the ready. I don't know how I fled the huge castle or ran through the town, but though I was cut and slashed and poked and pierced during my desperate escape, I finally returned to the shore where the scallop waited. I barely managed to rasp out, '*Hakketek makke!*' and the scallop c-r-e-a-k-e-d its shell open. I practically crawled into it, and quickly said, '*Hakketek chupke!*' whereupon the scallop c-r-e-a-k-e-d its shell closed. Now we just had to get out of there.—

"Hakketek te-e-shke teshke
To my *kotan*
hakketek te-e-shke teshke
because I want to return
hakketek te-e-shke teshke
keep up the hard work
hakketek te-e-shke teshke
and carry me there
hakketek te-e-shke teshke . . .

"Somehow I was able to get through the song and get back to the shore of my village. Now, '*Hakketek. . . .*'"

Huchi paused, so we responded, "*Makke!*" She said, "But no, that's not what happened," and continued, "I was so frantic by then that I accidentally said, '*Hakketek renren* (Sink, sink).' The scallop blew bubbles as it sank and sank, and so I met my death. . . . The end."

"Ahh," we said. "Okay, now you've got to go to sleep," declared Huchi as she stood up and headed toward her thread-spinning stick by the fireside. "I can't believe neither one of you fell asleep before the end." Listening to the low murmurs of Huchi and Hapo talking and the sound of the blizzard, seemingly quieter now that I was drowsy, I sank into a deep sleep.

THE DAY
OF THE MELTING SNOW

My memories of events after that blizzard day increase in number and clarity. I think that the fact that I don't know when I got my ears pierced means that it must have happened earlier, perhaps when I was just starting to walk.[13]

---

13. In the old days, both men and women Ainu had pierced ears. Depending on the region, ears were pierced in infancy or at six or seven years of age.

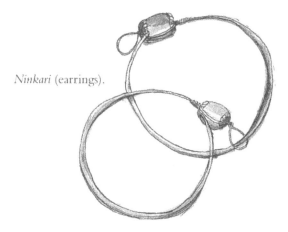

Ninkari (earrings).

One of the most unforgettable memories from my girlhood occurred at the time of the melting snows. During one year when I began to be told constantly, "You're not a baby anymore," or "You're a big sister now," I was given my name. Akihi had grown up enough to run around outside and play with his friends from the neighborhood.

That night, Akihi fell asleep early as usual, and even Sapo went to bed before I did. I was up later because Huchi was telling me a *kamui yukar* about the hare.[14] Sapo had heard this story before, and although she usually would have wanted to listen anyway, Hapo had kept her busy helping with other things. Thinking back, I'm sure that must have been part of a strategy to get Sapo asleep first so I'd be alone.

"*Horka tush tush*
  horka tush tush . . . "

14. *Kamui yukar*, which introduce animal or plant deities (see chart above, p. 89), are shorter than human *yukar* and are characterized by the use of refrains and set melodies. The following *yukar* of the hare is based on a recording by the late Yae Kurō, an eastern Hokkaidō bard (translated into Japanese by Haginaka Mie).

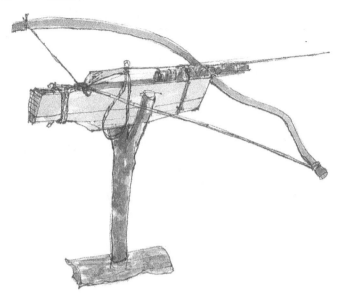

A *kuwari* (trap arrow), a poison arrow for shooting bear.
A smaller kind was used for fox and raccoon dog.

Huchi started singing the refrain. She kept rhythm with a slight movement of her hands as she spun thread.

> "*Horka tush tush kim ta okay=an* (I'm in the mountains)
> *horka tush tush isepo an newa* (I'm a hare)
> *horka tush tush kim ta okay=an ike* (this hare in the mountains)
> *horka tush tush ainu opitta* (all the people)
> *horka tush tush an=ronnu kuni* (try to kill me)
> *horka tush tush kani ku kani ai . . .* (with metal bows and arrows)."

A large hare with magical powers who boasted that no arrow could touch him was finally pierced by a sagebrush arrow. He failed in his attempt to escape, and was cut into bits that were then strewn about.[15] Ever since then, the mountains and fields have been filled with much smaller rabbits, which are easily caught and eaten by *ainu*, and even by birds of prey.

I was now the only child awake, and Huchi left the fireside and went out to the storehouse where Hapo was working. It was a moonlit, windy night. Acha, who had been mending his rabbit traps, called me in a formal manner. Sure that he was going to scold me for something, I tried to review my possible transgressions during the day as I approached him tensely.

"I want you to sit down with your best manners and keep quiet," Acha told me, and started bowing to the hearth fire. It was a relief to know at least that he wasn't going to reprimand me, but my anxiety about all this solemnity remained. I watched over Acha as he calmly bowed with his arms spread. The wind seemed to blow more fiercely as the night deepened.

Completing his ceremonial bows, Acha started to speak to the fire deity:

"Dear fire god, thanks to your grace, our Opere has grown healthily into a girl old enough to learn embroidery patterns. As she is now of an age where we must name her, I have discussed the matter with my wife, and we would like to name her Harukor, but I wish to consult with you.[16] You know many other gods, so please ask them as well, and grant me your answer in my dreams tonight. If things are fine, we would like to proceed with 'Harukor.' If this is not acceptable, we will most certainly reconsider the matter. Thank you."

---

15. Most animals, plants, and utensils that appear in *kamui yukar* are associated with the spiritual world, and hence hold differing degrees of supernatural power.

16. The name Harukor means "having food" and carries a wish for a secure livelihood with enough to eat.

Listening to Acha, my tension dissolved into a burst of happiness. I, too, as an *ainu*, was about to receive a real name. I wasn't going to be just Opere anymore. I tried hard to keep control over my excitement, which reminded me of the birds flitting about in the melting snow. When Acha finished another bow, he spoke to me, "Well then, Opere, let's get you to bed. Your name isn't settled yet, understand? So don't tell anyone for the time being."

When I went out to the bathroom, the wind was strong but the night air wasn't fiercely cold yet, and the snow that had melted at midday was still slushy. Hapo, who had been talking next to the storehouse with Huchi, noticed me in the moonlight and said, "Tomorrow morning after you haul water, I want you and Sapo to go gather firewood." Because of the strong wind, many dead branches would fall to the ground that night.

The call of a turtledove drifted into my morning slumber, then Hapo's voice. "I was just thinking how unusually warm it is," she said, "and here we already have a turtledove crying." The strong wind seemed to have subsided. I immediately recalled the events of the night before, but I kept silent. I didn't know if Acha had had his dream or not, for he was nowhere to be seen. He had probably gone out to check on the rabbit traps.

On our way to get water after breakfast, Sapo and I encountered another turtledove crying in an oak tree. Sapo started singing in imitation:[17]

"*Kusuwep toy ta* (the turtledove tills the fields)
huchi wakka ta (grandma goes to get water)
katkemat suke (mistress cooks a meal)
pontono ipe (young master eats his meal) . . . "

17. "The Song of the Rufuos Turtledove," handed down in the Saru region.

Sapo was singing exactly what she had learned from Huchi and Hapo; but to me, always scolded for being slow with the water, the "*huchi wakka ta*" part sounded like "*hokure wakka ta* (hurry up with the water)." And I was sure that the actual cry of the turtledove was much closer to these words.

Once we got the water home, we immediately set out for the mountains in back to get firewood. It was another warm day, and the melting snow made the climb difficult. Here and there, a patch of earth was visible, and butterbur shoots were budding. At the entrance to the woods, there was another bare patch where the melted snow had formed a pool of water. An assembly of birds was pecking at the ground and drinking water. There were perhaps five different kinds, totaling forty birds in all, merrily chirping away.

"What's that bird called?" I asked Sapo.

"That tiny one with a long tail is a long-tailed tit, and the ones with the black heads are chickadees. The one with the red bosom, you don't see all that often."

What a racket they were making, and how cheerful! Sapo went on into the woods, but I was so taken by the birds that I squatted in a patch of snow a little distance away and listened to their chatter. Watching more closely, I realized that the birds were equally intent on both *isoitak* (chatting) and poking at something in the ground. An *ainu* who talked so much during a meal would be considered rude, but it seemed like such fun that I wanted to join in, and I tried even harder to understand what they were saying. There were only two of the red-breasted birds Sapo had said were rare. They must be an *acha* and a *hapo*. I idly named them "birds of the red neck ornament." From the manner of the birds' *isoitak*, it seemed that these two had returned from a distant *repun moshir* (foreign land) or a distant *kotan* and were sharing their adventures with the other birds.

A *rekutunpe* (neck ornament).

"Birds of the red neck ornament, I wonder if you know the *re-pun kotan* Huchi's told me about. . . . " So saying, I entered into the *isoitak,* putting a voice to my thoughts.

"Opere!" Sapo's voice from the woods brought me to my senses and I stood up. I became aware that my rear was wet from the snow. It was cold, but I was more concerned about Sapo calling me "Opere." "I'm not Opere any more, I've got a name now," I wanted to retort. But I had to hold back, since Acha had warned me not to tell anyone.[18] I wondered whether or not Harukor had been approved as my name.

"What *are* you doing? Hurry up and help me with this!" Not knowing a thing about the previous night, Sapo berated me. I realized that I'd never heard her real name. I thought about asking her very quietly since no one was here but us, but decided against it. Lots of tree *kamui* would overhear, and there might even be some evil spirits lurking unseen.

The strong winds had broken off a lot of branches, and without having to walk over a large area, we were able to gather almost more than we could carry. We bundled the small branches and tied them up, then we each chose a heavy branch to drag behind us. The birds had finished their *isoitak,* and not a single one

18. Ainu people called one another by nicknames and endearing names. Revealing one's real name made one vulnerable to evil gods and persons. It was impolite to ask others their name.

A portrayal of *attush* weaving, painted about two hundred years ago. From Murakami Shimanoin's *Ezotō kikan*, in the possession of the National Museum of Tokyo. The original caption reads: "*Attushkar* illustrated: *Attush* is the name of tree-bark cloth and is woven from inner skin of *nikap*. *Kar* is also a term for production. I think *atu* means to collect; *tush* is a dialectal word for tissue. I suspect that *attush* means gathering thread both along and across. Again, ropes are generally called *tush*."

remained. Two cranes flew above our heads toward the Chepkaunpet River. Their white and black wings, spread out full, were beautiful. It was even warmer than the day before, and we could hear melting snow making puddles here and there.

When we got back down to the *chise*, Hapo was weaving an *attush* on the bare ground next to the storehouse.[19] She was preg-

19. *Attush* is correctly *atrush* in Ainu, from *at* (tissue from the inner skin of

nant with the baby that came after Akihi, so she looked large. The baby was due when the azaleas bloomed.

Apparently waiting for us to return, Hapo told Sapo to pound the millet that had been drying on the drying rack above the fire. Her words to me were, "Put away the firewood and then come back, I have a task for you." I was hoping that Acha would have returned to tell me about his dream, but he wasn't there.

When I went back to Hapo, she told me in a low voice, without pausing at her *attush* weaving, "Acha said this morning that your name is set on Harukor. He said that everything was fine in his dream."

I replied, "Ahh," and repeated softly, "Harukor, Harukor." "It's a good name," Hapo observed, then warned me, "Don't tell anyone, okay?" I agreed that it was a wonderful name, and was filled with the same happiness that I felt last night. I suddenly remembered and asked, "What's Sapo's name?"

"It's Turushno (Covered with Grime).[20] Hers is a good name, too. When your Sapo was an infant, she was sickly and often had a fever. She almost died two or three times. Ekashi, who set off for Kamui Moshir (the realm of the gods) a little while before you were born, said that the gods of illness were too fond of her, so he named her 'Covered with Grime' to make them dislike her. Turushno's been much healthier since, thanks to her name, I guess."

I could hear Sapo near the entranceway pounding the millet with a pestle. The sun was high in the sky, and the air was as wind-

---

tree bark) and *rush* (fur). The skin is soaked in water, for example of a pond, to soften; thread is taken, then woven into cloth. *Ohyō* is the main source of *attush*, but *harunire* (also called *akadamo*) and *shinanoki* are also used.

20. I borrowed the name of a *huchi* who lived in Nibutani in Hidaka district. Kaizawa Turushno died in February 1982 at ninety-three. She was known as an oral artist with rich knowledge of *uwepekere* and other forms of Ainu culture.

less as if it had never been blowing the night before; the warmth was reminiscent of the time of the young shoots. I asked about Acha's and Hapo's names also.

"Your Acha's name is Isonash (Great Hunter). He was named in the hope that he'd become a good hunter and that's the way he turned out—you're very lucky that you can eat deer all the time. I'm Resunotek (Skilled at Child-Rearing), and it is true that I'm quite good, but our very first baby—a boy, born before Sapo—died at about a month. He was healthy enough to surprise even the *ikoinkar* (midwife), and so cute! Huchi and I both cried for days on end. And your Acha, well, he'd been looking forward to going hunting with his son, even before he was born, so—yes, we knew before he was born that he'd be a boy. The *ikoinkar* can tell the difference. Anyway, this really made me sad—for a while I couldn't sleep at all, and I often watched Acha get up at midnight and bow to the fire god. That's why we buried that baby near the door to the entranceway.[21] Sapo was our next baby."

As she talked, Hapo got teary-eyed and her nose stuffed up, so she stopped her *attush* weaving and blew her nose into her hand. "You know, we named Sapo 'Turushno' because, even before her sickliness as an infant, we'd already lost our first baby. We were afraid that a god of sickness would take Sapo away, too."

A sudden barking from the dogs stopped our conversation. When I looked in the direction where two of them were leaping about—Acha had taken the other with him—I could see the forms of two children coming upstream toward us. From their outlines and the way they walked, I was sure it was my cousin Hotene and her younger brother.

"It's Hotene!" I yelled and, scolding the dogs, dashed over to

---

21. A wish for rebirth led to a belief that a dead infant should not be given a formal funeral. If buried where the family stepped back and forth, its rebirth would be hastened.

A woman's greeting. "A woman makes
a gesture like embracing another in both
arms, then passes her right index finger
three times under her nose." From an
edition of Murakami Shimanoin's *Ezotō
kikan,* transcribed by Hirasawa Heizan,
now in the Northern Resource Room
in the Hokkaidō University Library.

welcome them. Hotene was a year older than I, but she was my
closest girlfriend. Her brother Resak was about the same age as
Akihi, and they, too, were good friends. Akihi noticed their arrival and came running out of the *chise.*

Hotene, with the dogs barking at her, held some kind of package high above her head. When I'd caught up to the dogs and
quieted them down, she handed me the package, saying, "It's a

gift for Huchi." She suddenly knelt to give me an adult woman's formal greeting. We never did anything so polite to each other, so thinking that she was teasing me, I responded with an ultra-dutiful salute. Bursting into laughter, she said, "My mother told me, when you get to Ipokash's house, you do a proper bow, all right? So I decided that before I greeted your parents, I'd practice on you, Ipokash."

Ipokash (Not Fit to Be Seen) was my nickname. Hotene (Wet Bottom) and Resak (No-Name) were also pet names. Seeing Akihi, Resak immediately suggested they go ring throwing, and they ran off toward the storehouse. The dogs joyfully bounded after them.

Hapo stopped her *attush* weaving and welcomed Hotene at the entrance to the *chise*. Hotene again knelt for her formal greeting, then called to Resak over at the storehouse, "Don't start playing until after you've bowed." She sounded like a mother scolding her child.

Huchi, who was weaving a bag by the firepit, greeted my cousins with great delight. Hotene again did her full bow and made sure Resak greeted Huchi as well. Huchi, even more satisfied, straightened her back as she said, "My, my, you've really become a big girl." Their gift to her was fatty venison.

For Hotene, an even greater pleasure than playing with me, when she came to our house, was listening to Huchi's *uwepeker* and *kamui yukar*. Huchi knew that quite well, so she pulled out a snack left over from the day before, divided it among all of us, and sitting before her unfinished bag, asked, "Let's see, shall I tell you a story today?"[22]

---

22. A snack, *ratashkep* in Ainu, was a mixture of special foods that were not part of daily meals, especially those attractive to children: for example, Amur cork nuts with Chinese millet flour and wild peas, or chestnuts and preserved salmon roe.

"Yay!" Hotene answered, chewing on her snack, "Tell us, tell us!" Resak and Akihi, however, wanted to throw rings, and went back outside.

"Well, then, I'll tell you about something important to girls." Crinkling up her eyes and narrowing them until they were hardly visible, Huchi beamed a gentle smile to each of us in turn.

When Huchi started out, "I'm a bear god," Hotene edged closer to Huchi and murmured, "Mmm hmm," as if she'd already been drawn in. It seemed as if Huchi were putting special care into telling today's story, so I, too, felt a lump of expectation forming in my throat.

"And a pretty highly ranked bear god, too. I was the protective deity of the highest mountain in the Yupet River basin. . . . "

Just as she started her tale, Acha came back. Hotene repeated her proper bow yet again. Having caught six hares, he was in fine spirits. "Why don't you take a hare home with you," he told Hotene, giving me a special smile to signal his happiness over my name. But Hotene wanted to hear the rest of the story, so she reseated herself next to Huchi, barely aware of the hares.

"Even the highest-ranked gods must visit the land of the *ainu* every few years, and go back with gifts of *inau* (ceremonial whittled twigs). They don't visit just any *ainu*, of course, but they pick one who's skilled at making *inau* and is good-natured.

"I'd heard before that an upright *ainu* lived along the upper reaches of the Ishikari River, and seeking to be invited to that place, I lumbered down the mountain one day. I'd seen that very *ainu* hunting near the mountain where I served as guardian deity.

"I wandered out purposely to be seen by him, whereupon he swiftly hid behind a tree and put an arrow to his bow as he waited for me. Pretending not to notice, I passed by him. The twang of the bowstring sounded, and the god of the arrow pierced me.

Sending the bear to the spiritual world. Murakami Shimanoin, *Ezotō kikan*, in the possession of the National Museum of Tokyo.

As I heard the bowstring sound two or three times more, I lost consciousness."

Huchi turned her bag inside out to check on her weaving before continuing. "When I came to after a while, my head and body were separated, with just my soul resting atop my head, right between my ears. The *ainu*, realizing from my huge size that I must be the mountain deity of the Yupet River, had decided to halt his plans for an abbreviated bear send-off at a hunting lodge nearby and instead to welcome me to his *kotan* so that he could send me back to the realm of the gods in full ritual splendor from his home. He was therefore carrying on his back an *oshkur-marapto* (bear's head with the entire fur still attached) down to the *kotan*.

"When he got home, close to dusk, the *ainu* placed me on the ritual altar outside, entered his house, and informed the deity of his firepit that a bear deity was paying a visit. The fire deity, dressed

A *kaparimip* (unlined appliquéd robe).

in six layers of robes held together with a sash, and six more layers left free to flap about, came outside, leaning on a staff made of twisted iron. With an *onkami* he told me, 'O, deity of high rank, thank you for gracing our *kotan* with your presence. Please enjoy a leisurely stay with us.' He then returned to the house.

"I was invited into the house, through the sacred window, by members of the *kotan*, then ensconced in the seat of honor near the window, opposite the lower end of the hearth near the dirt floor. One by one, the assembling villagers addressed me with respectful words of welcome. Wine and dumplings were being prepared, and soon a feast such as had never been seen in the land of the gods was laid out. I joined all the *ainu* in drinking wine and eating dumplings, and enjoyed myself enormously. Soon, songs and dances were performed before me as well. I noticed a youth, on the short side, who was an absolutely magnificent dancer. His movements were lithe, and he seemed to float in the air as he moved left and right, forward and back; he sometimes even threw in a flip or two in the air. My eyes were glued to him the whole time he danced.

"After a while, a gifted teller of *yukar* arrived and began his oration. But whenever a bear is sent back to the realm of the gods, *yukar* are left unfinished at the most exciting part. This is so the bear deity, wishing to hear the next part, will want to be hunted down for another visit to the *kotan*. And so, around daybreak, the *yukar* came to a pause at a crucial point, and I came back to the land of the gods laden with gifts on my back.

"For some reason, though, the image of that fantastic young dancer kept flitting before my eyes."

Here, Huchi left the plot of her tale to explain something. "If the bear deity wants to hear the rest of the *yukar* or see the fine young dancer again, he has to visit the *kotan* again. That's why bear gods are hunted by *ainu*, and why the bear gods take pleasure in showing up so they'll be hunted. And that's why we put so much effort into giving them a proper send-off."

Responding to our "Mmm hmm," Huchi went on.

"So, I was shot by an arrow exactly the same way the next time. When I got to the *kotan* in the form of a bear's head with the body fur still attached, I was again welcomed as a guest at the same home. As I expected, the songs and dances started, and the same slight youth again danced for me. I was so absorbed in his dancing that, forgetting that I was a god, I began to dance with him. Thinking that he wasn't just anybody, that he must be some kind of deity, I explored his identity with my supernatural sight, but I couldn't see anything. I'd about be able to perceive something when a haze would blur my vision. The continuation of the *yukar* related by the great storyteller was indeed wonderful, but I was so taken with the dancer that I barely listened.

"I again received many gifts and was sent back to the land of the gods, but still remained in the dark about the youth. I went down to Ainu Moshir repeatedly in order to be shot by an arrow and invited to the *kotan* so that I could find out about him and see more of his mesmerizing dances.

"I wonder how many trips I made. One day after dancing with him until we were both exhausted, I drifted off to sleep. Out of the corner of my eye, I suddenly noticed that among the many pots hanging from the right wall as you entered the large house, the littlest of the thin-rimmed small pots had shifted the slightest bit. I looked around immediately, and noticed that the youth was nowhere to be seen. I finally had it! He was the deity of the little pot. I wanted to go over to the pot and express my gratitude, but I withheld my desire and waited for the deity to wake up.

"After a while, the youth again made his appearance, so I darted a glance at the pot and found, as expected, that it was missing. I smiled at the youth and started talking to him. 'I've come to this house over and over again so that I could see more of your dancing and also find out who you are. I've finally figured it out and can now go back to the land of the gods without any regrets. Before I return, I'd like to ask you why you're such an amazing dancer, and why you're so generous as to entertain the gods.'

"The young god of the little pot answered shyly, 'I've lived in this same house for a long, long time. The mistress of the place loves cleanliness, and even if she uses me for a stew, she always washes me immediately afterward. I'm always feeling cleansed and lighthearted, so whenever I have a spare moment, I feel like dancing and thus have developed some skills at it. Besides, whenever we have a bear sending, it's the bigger pots that get to provide service, and I'm left with nothing to do. So I dance for the gods, in part also to thank the mistress for taking good care of me. I've danced for quite a few gods over the years, but not a single one has been able to discover my identity. You, being of high rank, though, have finally figured it out.'"

Huchi here waved her hand in a gesture of disagreement.

"'Oh, my goodness, no. This is not something you can discern in one or two tries. I came here many, many times just to find out. I've been hunted so many times, making this house that much more prosperous, which means that you, the *kamui* of the little pot, have made your thanks quite well known.'

"And so, bearing even more gifts than the last time, I thanked the *kamui* of the little pot and returned to the realm of the gods."

Huchi stopped to catch her breath, so we murmured, "Mmm." Hotene asked, "Is that the end?" From outside came the sounds of Akihi and Resak playing with their hoops.

"No, there's more. I must let the good-hearted master of the house know about this," Huchi said. "After returning to the land of the gods, I sent a dream to the *ainu* and let him know in detail about the little pot. In response, this good *ainu* made yet another offering of *inau* to me and also thanked the deity of the little pot with lots of ritual wine and *inau*. . . .

"And so that's why I was hunted so frequently and visited the land of the *ainu* so often. And now, a word to the *ainu* of today: 'Treat every one of your tools and implements well, washing what should be washed and cleaning what should be cleaned, for you will surely be repaid by the deities of those tools.' Those are the words of that high-placed bear deity."[23]

Bringing her face close to us as if to confirm that we really

23. "*Tuitak* of the Small Pot." I borrowed this story from "The Small Pot at Leisure," told by Hikawa Tsuru of Osachinai, Saru region, and recorded in Kayano Shigeru, *Hitotsubu no sacchiporo* (One salmon egg) (Heibonsha, 1979).

A pot and a lid. A large pot is called *su*, a small pot *poysu*, and a lid *suputa*.

understood, Huchi smiled with her eyes as she looked from one to the other of us. I felt like the pots could see right into my heart and glanced at the pot cooking a deer-bone broth over the firepit and a little pot left hanging after being washed. I reminded myself that I'd never been particularly neglectful of any tools and that I had no fear of being scolded by the gods of the pots.

"Let's draw embroidery patterns and see who comes up with a better one," Hotene suggested. She was really good at it, so I was nearly always outdone. But I'd recently become quite enthusiastic about learning from Huchi and felt that maybe I wouldn't lose so easily. "Okay, sure," I said happily. Huchi also encouraged us with a "Yes, why don't you give it a try? I'll judge whose is better."

Hotene immediately smoothed the ashes in the firepit and drew two equal squares. We had to fit patterns traditional to our region in those boxes, and the trick was to make interesting trimming at the edges and links between patterns. And what pattern were we going to use for this competition? "How about . . . ," Hotene started, when Acha, who had been tending to the hares, sharply interrupted with, "Silence!" His face tense, he seemed to be listening intently. I, too, could hear a low rumble from far off, a sound I couldn't place as either thunder or rumbling from the mountains. Huchi stopped her knitting with equal solemnity.

"Isn't that a flood?" Huchi asked. Simultaneously, we heard women's high-pitched screams from Akpet Kotan, up the river.

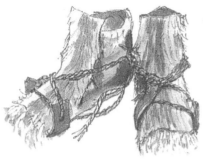

Yukker (deerskin shoes).

"It's a *peutanke* (emergency call)!"[24] Hapo exclaimed.

Acha grabbed Huchi's hand. "We've got to get away. We'll run for the hills."

"It's a flood," Huchi told us as she stood up. "Go get the boys from outside."

The *peutanke* was relayed by the high, thin, but piercing "wohh-y wohh-y" screams from women. Their voices, as if calling us from the recesses of hell, roused an eerie, hair-raising dread. From outside, Hapo responded upriver with the same "wohh-y" scream, then immediately sent two or three *peutanke* shouts downriver with a penetrating voice completely different from her normal one. From other houses in the neighborhood and *kotan* below ours, there was a wave of responses to her cries as well as attempts to send the *peutanke* alarm farther downstream. These calls overlapped with their echoes. Caught amid the rumbling and roaring of the earth and the hills, I was overcome with the terrifying thought that the world was coming to an end. But I was too frightened even to cry.

I left everything as it was, considering even the time it took to put on my shoes as too precious to waste. Yet, for once strangely conscious of a very small spider making its tangled way through

24. Also *peutank:* a female call that carries far, warning of an emergency. In principle, men do not use this warning voice.

the fur on the toes of my shoes, I scooped it up in my hand as I ran with Hotene toward the hills. I mused that it must have come out because of the unusual warmth and felt that I should save this spider *kamui* from the flood.

People came running out of their homes in the *kotan* and swarmed toward the mountain. Since Hapo was heavy with child, Sapo helped her along. Acha led Huchi by the hand, and they all began the ascent, not too far behind the others. Huchi, in a surprisingly calm voice, though of course out of breath from running, observed, "Okay . . . we should . . . be fine here . . . for most . . . floods. . . . We . . . needn't worry."

The flood came toward us with ferocious speed. "Look, Ipokash!" Hotene yelled, and I turned back toward the Chepkaunpet River just in time to see what looked like a mixture of white ice and black water leap out from behind a hill in Akpet Kotan and gush down in a torrent, filling up the whole river. Everyone who was still running also looked back, frozen silently in place. The floodwaters, seething with chunks of ice and stones, slammed into the rocks in the riverbed with dull thuds and tremors, then crashed along below our Otasam Kotan. The rushing waters instantly buried the riverbanks, but even the homes in the *kotan* closest to the river were placed far enough and high enough away from the rising waters. It seemed that the water level peaked when the crest of the flood disappeared downstream, for the water began to withdraw immediately.

"What a terrible *chiurikin* (flash flood) that was," said Acha.[25] Members of the *kotan*, relieved that nothing disastrous had occurred, chatted with each other.

---

25. When the snow alongside a river thaws while the river and earth are still frozen, the water from the melting snow starts to run rapidly. Once it has become dammed up, for example by solid ice, it may suddenly overflow. The type of flooding caused by such dammed water is called *chiurikin* in Ainu.

"This type of flood is pretty common at the start of spring, but this one was really big," Huchi said to Acha. "The last time we had one this size was the year you found yourself a bride, I guess."

"You're right, " Acha answered. "That time a house in Akpet Kotan was swept downstream. . . . I was just thinking earlier that it's unusually warm today."

"Okay, let's go home and thank the fire god for everyone's safety," he told us and skied down the hill over the loosened snow, standing straight up. Akihi and Resak tried to imitate him, but couldn't slide as well and ended up on their rears. Hotene and I had a race, sliding on our rear ends, but Sapo was too embarrassed by such things to join us anymore.

Sitting by the fireside, Acha faced the hearth fire and delivered a particularly respectful *onkami*, then addressed the deity, "I thank you profoundly for your response to our daily observances that has allowed us to survive this disaster without incident. We will continue to pray diligently in the future, and would appreciate it if you, the deity of fire, would ask the deities of water and the mountains also to protect us. . . . "

Thinking that Hotene's family downriver would be worried, Acha decided to walk her and her brother home. Akihi tagged along, while Sapo and I helped Hapo prepare the evening meal.

MOON'S DEW

One autumn, seven winters and seven summers after the day of the flood, the *kotan* was full of happy faces because the salmon harvest was particularly abundant.[26] However, perhaps moved by the sun that set earlier day by day and the scattering of the

26. In keeping track of time, the Ainu divided each year into *mutapa* (winter year) and *sakupa* (summer year).

brightly colored leaves, I found myself sinking daily into darker and more melancholy thoughts. I knew exactly why, but I suppose the brevity of autumn days made me feel that much more unsettled.

My anxiety lay in my fear that I might never become a full *ponmenoko* (maiden). Sapo had already wed last year, marrying into the neighboring Akpet Kotan, and was soon due to give birth. Even Akihi had recently come of an age where he covered his *chiehe* (penis). And, to reveal my secret, I had passed my fifteenth birth month without my first *chuppe* (moon's dew).[27] My cousin Hotene, one year older than I, and all the *ponmenoko* close to my age in nearby *kotan* already had their *chuppe*. Yet even my breasts remained forever the same as Akihi's.

Hapo had first told me about *chuppe* when our next-door neighbors rebuilt their *chise* and the members of the *kotan* gathered for a *chisenomi* (house-warming celebration). That was three winters and summers ago. Having lost the son after Akihi to sickness, Hapo had aged terribly from heartache, but her next and sixth baby looked exactly like the one before, as if he were its reincarnation. The fire deity must have been truly moved by Acha's earnest prayers. The day of the *chisenomi* next door was soon after the rebirth of my tiny second brother.

Hapo had regained her cheery smile and was nursing the baby when I came home after dancing at the dedicatory *rimse* (circle

27. One never revealed one's age or asked others their ages. *Chuppe* means menstrual flow, *chup* (moon) and the suffix *-pe*, which indicates various modes of water in combination with such words as *kina* (grass), *noki* (eaves), *shirokani* (silver), *kinape* (dew on grass), *nokipe* (raindrops), and *shirokanipe* (silver drops). Different terms for menstruation are used from region to region; other examples include "moon illness" and "woman's illness." This section of Harukor's story is based on the experience of a *huchi* who was in her eighties in 1982.

A *chisenomi* (house-warming celebration). The photo was taken
on June 5, 1992, at the Kussharo Resource Museum Hall.

dance) held after the *chisenomi*. The rest of the family hadn't returned from the banquet. Calling me over, Hapo told me matter-
of-factly about *chuppe*. "It's something every girl has on the way
to becoming an adult. There's nothing to worry about. If you
don't have it, that's when it's a worry."

I think Hapo told me early because of Sapo. The summer of
the year of the flood, several girls in the neighborhood had gone
to play in the river. Because it was hot, we had jumped into the
shallows and were horsing around with the water up to our hips,
but when Sapo sat down on the bank, the rock under her not
only got wet from the water but also turned red. Thinking she
was sick, we both turned pale, and she ran home. Later, she told
me, "I'm okay now. It was nothing." Thinking that it was just a
mild illness, I hadn't given the matter further thought, but now
I knew it had been the start of her *chuppe*.

Perhaps there was another reason Hapo told me about *chuppe*

A *yarnima* (container made of tree bark).

on that particular day. One rainy day soon after that, Sapo and I were both given tattoos by a woman from a *kotan* downriver.[28]

Whenever I saw older girls with their pretty tattoos, I hoped that I'd get one soon, but I'd also heard that it was extremely painful, and so my anticipation was mixed with an equal amount of fear. When the Tattoo Woman came by, I felt a strong desire to run away, but Sapo was overjoyed.

Around that time Sapo spent every spare moment pouring water into a wooden container so as to let it mirror her face, playing with her hair or fiddling with her earrings. Sometimes, she even went to the storehouse without our parents' knowledge, and wiping around her lips the black soot from the bottom of a pot in imitation of a tattoo, she would ask me, "Am I pretty?" Gazing at the reflection of her face in the container from all different angles, she would sing a *yukar* melody praising the beauty of tattooed maidens. I was sick of having to put up with her tilting her head and looking sideways at the water's reflection; but I too wanted to be pretty and sometimes examined my reflection when I went to draw water.

28. Ainu women wore tattoos around the mouth and on the hands and arms. Tattooing occurred at seven or eight at the earliest and by fourteen or fifteen at the latest. It was repeated about three times and was completed before marriage.

We were given no forewarning the day that the tattooist came. Acha and Akihi were away on an overnight fishing trip upriver to catch trout. Despite the gloom from many days of rain, our aunt from down the river had come with her daughter Hotene for the first time in a while. Resak, who usually came as well, wasn't with them. I'd assumed that it was because he was getting big like Akihi and was therefore too involved in activities such as archery to bore himself going about with women.

With hindsight, there were all sorts of signs. Usually, around noon, Hotene and Sapo and I were served a light snack, but today we were presented with a meat and vegetable soup that was as generous as any evening meal, and furthermore we were urged by our aunt and Hapo to eat plenty. It was all so strange that, puzzled, Hotene and I asked what was going on. But they said, "Come on, just enjoy it," and laughed.

After we had stuffed ourselves, Huchi told us the old tale about the Monster Bird Huri.[29] When we tried to jump-rope beneath the raised storehouse, however, Hapo told us, "Don't go out today." Suspiciously, I asked, "Why?" but Sapo seemed to know what was going on. When Hapo tried to reply, there was a cough at the entrance.[30] "Anyone home?" a woman asked as she entered, removing her rain gear of butterbur leaves.[31]

My aunt and Hapo went toward the entrance, answering, "Yes,

29. *Translator's note:* "The *huri* is a huge mythical bird mentioned in legends and epics; we might possibly call it a griffin" (Donald Philippi, introduction to a "Song of a Huri Bird," in *Songs of Gods, Songs of Humans: The Epic Tradition of the Ainu*, trans. Philippi [Princeton: Princeton University Press, 1979], p. 165).

30. Visitors warned of their arrival at a house with a cough outside and waited for someone to come out, but here the tattooist simply goes in because she not only is a close acquaintance but is expected.

31. Butterbur in Hokkaidō is large. Sometimes it grows taller than adults, and the stem can even reach the eaves. Eight or nine leaves are enough to cover the head, shoulder, and torso of an adult.

we're here." "How wonderful of you to come in this rain!" they said, as they took her hands in theirs to rejoice that they were all fine, their voices revealing that they were nearly in tears. The woman also greeted Huchi formally.

After they chatted for a while, the woman got out a small, empty pot. She put it over a small flame in a corner of the hearth, placing something like bark inside it as she hummed an *upopo* (festival song) melody. In another empty pot she borrowed from Hapo, she heated up some white birch bark until there was a heavy black cloud of oily smoke, and the pot became sticky with a thick layer of soot. I finally realized that I was looking at tattoo ink.

"Isn't that for tattoos?" I whispered in Sapo's ear. She nodded with an infuriating expression that said, "Of course, what took you so long?" She'd admired those tattoos so much, I was sure she'd be ecstatic, but in the shadow of her eyelashes, I could read her fear and nervousness.

"Okay, now, we're going to make you all pretty. Shall we start with the oldest?" The Tattoo Aunt had turned the pot upside down, so the soot was now on top. Still smiling, Hapo told Sapo to lie down in front of the Tattoo Woman. When Sapo obediently lay down with her face up, as she was told, Hapo held down her head lightly with one hand. As the Tattoo Aunt drew a sooty rim around Sapo's lips, she sang the words from the *yukar* that Sapo used to sing every once in a while:[32]

> "Even without it
> she's so beautiful
> the tattoo around her lips
> how brilliant it is
> it can only be wondered at."

---

32. Beautiful tattoo is a recurring theme in *yukar*, as in "*Kanokanpe karitenpe*" told by the late Kannari Matsu (translated into Japanese by Kayano Shigeru).

The Tattoo Woman pulled out a small knife from her bosom, then said, "It's going to hurt just a little, but it'll turn you into a truly fine maiden, okay?"[33] She inserted the point of her blade into the sooty rim. Hapo simultaneously clamped her knees on both sides of Sapo's head, which she was pressing with her hand. She peered into Sapo's eyes and said, "Stay still, she'll mess up if you move. She's the best tattooist there is. It's not going to hurt too badly, so don't worry." As the blade pierced through, Sapo's body jolted, but she didn't make a sound.

"Good girl," the tattooist spoke. "You're so strong—you'll be sure to win a fine groom." Whenever the blood started to flow, she wiped it off with sagebrush cotton she'd soaked in the juice in her pot. Aunt and Huchi helped to make sure Sapo didn't move by holding down her arms and legs. Moving her knifepoint skillfully as she added soot to her fingertip and rubbed it into the wound, the tattooist told the three of us a story.[34]

"I'm a frog *kamui* who lived in a certain *kotan*. And a female frog, at that. One day, a lightning deity and a wolf deity came to a nearby *kotan* to find a bride. This is because that *kotan* had two maidens reputed to be peerless at handicrafts. The two deities came one by one to see. As promised, the first maiden was marvelous at embroidery, the second one peerless at weaving mats. They had nice figures and handsome faces; furthermore, they were of impeccable lineage in the *kotan*, and had been educated accordingly. So the gods were quite satisfied.

"Sadly, they both failed on one point. And that was that they were *tekehontomta charohontomta* (arms half-done, lips half-done); that is, the tattoos around their lips and on their arms were only

33. Leaving only the tip of the blade visible, the knife was covered with cloth. Tattooing was done not by poking with a needle but by cutting and rubbing.

34. "The Frog Deity" is a summary from a story from Shiranuka in eastern Hokkaidō (translated into Japanese by Fujimura Hisakazu).

half complete. The lightning and wolf gods were quite disap-
pointed and went away, saying, 'There's just no way they'd be fit
as brides.'

"Soon, the gods came to my *kotan* as well. I'm pretty good at
handiwork, but more important, my tattoos were fully completed
and the best done in the *kotan*. The lightning deity was genuinely
happy with me and welcomed me as his bride, and another maiden
with a similarly fine tattoo was wedded to the wolf deity."

Sapo clenched her hands into fists, but remained silent. The
tattooist continued her tale of the frog deity. "If you have to quit
midway, just because it hurts a bit, you won't be able to with-
stand childbirth once you've become a bride. And if you go to
Kamui Moshir without a tattoo, they'll tattoo you with a bamboo knife, and that, I tell you, will *really* be painful."

Hotene and I watched wordlessly. Sapo looked like she was in
pain, but she wasn't making a sound, so maybe it wasn't all that
bad. My earlier anxiety was lessening somewhat. The Tattoo Aunt
swiftly continued her hand motions as she said, "I'm almost
done," or "You're going to be so pretty," or "Lovely, lovely." Then
she raised her voice and announced, "All done," as she pressed
the tattoo with the boiled juice from her pot. Sapo slowly sat up
with a glazed look, as if she'd woken from a long sleep. You
couldn't tell if it was soot or blood around her lips, and they
seemed slightly swollen, so you couldn't really say she was
"lovely" yet. Remaining expressionless, she continued to be mute.

"The wound's going to swell up and hurt tonight, so why don't
you go to bed?" said Hapo. "You won't be able to eat dinner anyway." I finally understood why they'd fed us so much earlier.
Hotene was next. Although she wasn't as excited as Sapo, Hotene
was much more interested in getting tattooed than I was, but she
cried quite a bit from the pain. Held down by my aunt and Hapo,
she eventually quieted down. My anxiety had increased when
Hotene started crying, but her total silence was even more dis-

quieting, and I later found out that she had fainted. When it was my turn, I endured the first shock of pain without a cry, but heard the tattooist's comment, "She's a brave one, like her Sapo," fading gradually away as I lost consciousness.

I felt something burning, as if embers had been placed around my lips. Wanting nothing but to shut everything out, I staggered over to my bedding, my face frozen, as if I'd forgotten how to laugh, cry, or be angry. Hapo lent a hand to support me.

The pain worsened during the night, and by morning, I could see the swelling of my own lips. We were feverish and the pain had kept us from getting much sleep, so we stayed in bed the whole day. Food was the farthest thing from our minds. When we got thirsty, Hapo dipped cotton grass in water and placed it against our lips for us to suck on.

And so three winters and summers passed after our first tattoos, which were followed by two more sets of tattoos around our lips and arms. After her first *chuppe*, Sapo had been taught even more strictly to perfect her cooking, thread spinning, and *attush*-weaving skills. The year after our final tattoos, she got married and left home. Even though I hadn't had my *chuppe*, I was held to more exacting standards, too. Especially with embroidery and mat-weaving patterns, the entire family had praised and flattered me no matter how poorly I did. But now, however well I did, they would point out flaws or say, "This part's no good."

I took the increased expectations for granted, but the growing weight of my anxiety prevented me from raising my voice in joyful laughter like other girls my age, even when the *kotan* was getting in a festive mood for its Autumn of Abundant Harvest.

Before dawn one day, when the salmon was at its final peak and the fall colors were fading as early trees began to lose their leaves, I went to the fishing hut along the banks of the Chepkaunpet River to carry out my usual role, during fishing season, of carrying and putting away the salmon. A weir was set up across a branch stream by the fishing hut, and Acha and Akihi spent each night catching salmon by torchlight. As it got lighter, Hapo and I would move the salmon to the fishing hut, cut them open, smoke them over a bonfire, and hang them to dry.

The eastern sky had just started to whiten, and it was still dark as we trudged along our way. When we crossed a bridge at a pond on the way, I picked up a pebble and threw it into the water, praying under my breath, "O Water Deity, please give me your protection." Because it was earlier than usual, perhaps still night-time, the water god might be asleep and possibly forget to watch over me. I woke the deity with the pebble the same way I did whenever I crossed a bridge at night. As the pebble plopped into the pond, a waterbird took flight with a loud flap of its wings. It was too dark to see clearly, but it was about the size of a wild goose.

As I approached the weir, I heard a dull thud, then Acha shouted, "*Osh* (It's a female)!" Watching Akihi bustling about in response, I smiled. That dull sound was Acha pounding the head of a salmon, which he had just lifted out of the river, with his fish-hitting stick.[35] He had probably murmured to the fish, as he beat it, "*Inau kor* (Take with you this *inau*)." He had then an-nounced "*Osh*" to prepare Akihi for his role. With *cha* (males) he wouldn't have yelled so loudly. With *osh*, just before spawn-ing, the egg sac would have slid out, so Akihi had to quickly in-sert a small willow branch into the passage.

Just as I was about to call out to Akihi, I felt a strange sensa-tion in my lower abdomen. Come on, I can't possibly have wet myself, I thought. Then in the next instant, the realization—could

35. The fish-hitting stick (*isapakikni*) was made from a fresh willow branch. It had the function of *inau* as well. A salmon hit with this stick willingly went back to the world of the spirits, with the *inau* as a gift, eventually to return again to the human world. In other words, every strike of this stick performs the "salmon sending" in a simplified manner.

it be?—that it might be *chuppe* flooded my mind. My heart began to beat rapidly, and I rustled through the growth of reeds
along the riverbank, conscious of Akihi and Acha's wondering
gazes. I raised my underrobe.[36] I was right.

"*Chuppe!*" I softly exclaimed. The faint crimson pattern on
my inner thigh in the dim light before daybreak became im-
printed as one of those lifelong memories. I was filled with the
joyful thought that I had finally become a young woman. Wiping myself off at the edge of the reed thicket with sagebrush
leaves, already withering from the frost, I quickly made my way
home. I ignored everything, including Acha's "What's the matter?" echoing behind me.

Hapo, at the doorway with my younger Akihi, ready to take
him along to the fishing hut for the day's work, welcomed my
news wholeheartedly. She showed me how to attach cotton grass
and cattail cotton to a *mattepa* (belt for menstrual pads) she had
stored away for me. Huchi also noticed, and although I was now
taller than she, caressed my hair and face as she told me, "That's
wonderful Opere! Oops, I guess you're not Opere anymore,
you're a woman, a little woman." For some reason, my tears
welled up and flowed without end; as they say in the *uwepeker*
and *yukar*, "like a swift river."

"If you study the shape of the moon tonight, you'll pretty
much be able to predict your next *chuppe*," Hapo said. Then telling
me to follow her, she led the way to the storehouse area.

We had three storehouses. Hapo took me to the one for stor-
ing wild plants and climbed up the ladder. Once we were inside,
she firmly closed the unpatterned mat curtain at the entrance and
pulled out from her bosom what looked like a pile of string. The

---

36. In the old days, the woman's underrobe called *mour* was made of softened deer leather. It was cylindrical and was slipped on through an opening for
the head.

An *ishma*, also called
raunkut (woman's
underbelt).

autumn light of the increasingly tardy sunrise was at last streaming though the thin cracks in the eaves of the storehouse, gleam-
ing against the neatly woven rope of bleached, white thread.

"This is something I wove with love for just such a day," Hapo
said, her expression more solemn than I'd ever seen it. Affected
by her intensity, I also became self-conscious, and gently touched
the graceful, delicately woven rope.

"See, take a good look. It's called an *ishma* (underbelt). I'll teach
you one day how to make this, but women always wear one when
they've reached adulthood. I'll tie it on for you, so raise your underrobe."

As she tied the *ishma* around my hips in set form, she explained
further, "I'm tying this according to the instructions handed down
from generation to generation by our matriarchal line. Your Huchi
here is Acha's mother, so she ties her *ishma* differently from our
line. This is something very, very important that you must take
to heart—never, ever remove your *ishma*, or show it to outsiders.
Even among family members, a husband is the only exception
apart from the women in your matriarchal line. Don't you show
this to anyone other than your future husband, much less let anyone touch it."

Women of our line tied the *ishma* so that the rope went twice
in front and six times in back. When she finished tying it, Hapo
emphasized once again, "You have to understand, your *chuppe* is

a sign that the gods have recognized you as a full-grown woman. They've signaled that it's time to give you your *ishma*. So I'm going to treat you as a full-grown woman from now on. I've raised you so far as a child, but now we have to prepare you to be a woman who can stand on her own without embarrassment. You're nearly as skilled as Sapo at embroidery and cooking, but your manners at mealtime and your behavior when we have guests still show that you're a child. Remember, your shame is Hapo's shame, Hapo's shame is Huchi's shame, and Huchi's shame is a shame to our ancestors."

When we opened the mat curtain and left the storehouse, the sun was gloriously playing on all the hills with their falling leaves, and the frost on the ground was beginning to melt and dampen the earth. The mundane scene took on a new significance for me.

Hapo told me, "Don't lend a hand with the fish until your *chuppe* ends. Don't even go to the fishing hut, or you will displease the salmon and the catch will be bad. Stay at home and help Huchi with the housework." She went to the fishing hut, holding Little Akihi by the hand.

From then on, Hapo became even stricter in teaching and disciplining me.

IYOMANTE DAYS

Two winters after the day of my *chuppe*, close to the day of the longest night of the year, our *kotan* was full of anticipation as we awaited the first full-scale *iyomante* festival in a while.[37] The festival of the giant striped owl was going to be held in our Otasam Kotan. The giant striped owl was called *kotan kor kamui* (the

37. *Iyomante*, "god sending," is a term employed for the two largest ceremonies, bear *iyomante* and the giant striped owl *iyomante*, in which the spirit of the animal is sent back to the spiritual world. The owl *iyomante*, which was even

A *shitopera* (wooden spatula for making dumplings).

guardian deity of a village), and its festival was much more important and solemn than that of the brown bear, which was called *kimun kamui* (mountain deity).

The main roles onstage for *iyomante* are performed by the men, but the backstage preparation demands more from the women. Beginning weeks in advance there is the pounding of millet for making wine. Then wild lily-root dumplings and other snacks must be made in vast quantities. The women of the village are also called on to exert themselves to the utmost to prepare feasts and lodging for guests. When it comes to an owl *iyomante*, there are sure to be visitors from faraway Kutcharo Kotan and Kusur Kotan (now known as Kushiro). Sometimes, our invitation is accepted by young men all the way from the depths of the Tokachi Plain.

While the preparations were exhausting, no other event gave the women, especially those of marriageable age, as much fun or excitement. However busy our hands, our mouths were free, so we talked endlessly, often about eligible young men. Even if they were from quite far away, men who were popular with the women would come up in discussion, their hunting and oratorical skills assessed in detail.

---

more important than the bear *iyomante*, has rarely been observed since the Meiji era, and no detailed record of it remains. The giant striped owl, whose habitat ranges from Hokkaidō to Sakhalin, the Kuriles, and Siberia, is the most ferocious of all owls in Japan, even preying on dogs and cats. Its numbers rapidly declined with the decrease of deciduous forests.

This winter had just seen the second abundant salmon harvest in a row, and for several years there hadn't been any major misfortunes such as contagious diseases or natural disasters, so the *kotan* was bursting with gaiety as the *iyomante* approached. When the day finally arrived, the young women would secretly compete for the talked-of youths who appeared. During the long night they would find themselves captivated by the heroic dramas related by master orators of *yukar*. I often went with my friends to *kotan* that were holding *iyomante*, so even though our *kotan* only had one every two or three years, I'd been to an *iyomante* nearly every year.

Not only was I directly involved in this *iyomante*, if only in the backstage preparations, which were more serious because it was for the grand *kotan kor kamui*, but in addition I had high personal expectations and anxieties. First, my fiancé would doubtless appear; and second, another young man, a suitor who was even more passionate about me than my intended, was also certain to be there.

It was at the beginning of the previous winter, a few days after a blizzard cleared and not long after the day of my *chuppe*, that my parents told me I had been promised to a youth from Akpet Kotan up the river, known by the nickname "Petennouk." He had spent the night at our place on his way back from a *kotan* along the seashore when the blizzard got dangerous. After he left, Hapo informed me that he was my fiancé. His family was among those from Akpet Kotan with whom we were quite social, so I had met him many times. I didn't dislike him, but I had not foreseen this in the least.

Since then, Petennouk had appeared more frequently at our *kotan*. Around the end of the summer, another young man from a *kotan* even farther upriver suddenly began to deepen his acquaintance with my family—specifically, with me and Acha.

Twelve or thirteen days before the *iyomante*, festival wine was

A *sakekar-ontaro* (vat for wine brewing, used in eastern Hokkaidō).

brewed at the *porochise* of the *kotan korkur* (village head),[38] and the heart-pounding countdown to the *iyomante* began. Gathering in the *porochise* after breakfast, we pounded the millet for wine on a straw mat outdoors, for the weather was fair even if the air was sharp and biting. The snow had piled up only as high as our ankles. For each of five mortars, there were three pestles for threshing millet. People took turns being one of the fifteen pounders. The rest of us, the thirty or so wives and maidens who assembled from our *kotan* and others, worked at screening the threshed millet in sieves or carrying it inside. Around the hearth were men waiting to cook the millet in buckets for brewing wine.[39]

The rhythmic *"Hessa-ho-hoi, hessa-ho-hoi"* of the women

38. Called *porochise* (fine, large house), the *kotan* head's house functioned both as a family residence and as a meeting hall.

39. In Hidaka and other areas, wine is brewed almost entirely by women. In eastern Hokkaidō, according to Fujimura Hisakazu, brewing for important rituals like *iyomante* was men's work, while women handled the threshing and sorting of the grain. Some disagree.

pounding with their pestles echoed through the bitterly cold *kotan* sky. Sometimes we could hear the children playing at pole-jumping and hooting in anticipation of the festival. While pounding the millet for the ritual wine, our topics of discussion were relatively discreet. Once we had relaxed and moved on to preparing food for guests or distributing woven mats at a separate *chise*, we progressed every now and then, as was customary, to a comparison of men's attributes.

"I met Ipokash's fiancé, Petennouk, about five days ago." The first reference to me came from someone nicknamed Umakashte, one of the most direct young women in our *kotan*. Umakashte lived only four houses away and was a year or two older than I. In contrast to her demure face, she had a strong will. Because she was so blunt in her speech, the young man whose parents had arranged with hers for their marriage had come to dislike her and had broken off the engagement. But I was fond of her straightforward personality. Because my untalkative nature made us a good pair of opposites, we were known throughout the *kotan* as inseparable. Just because we were best friends, though, didn't mean that Umakashte would hold back about my fiancé in front of everybody.

"When I went to see some relatives in Akpet Kotan, he was visiting, too. He's a pretty pathetic hunter, but his carvings are amazing. He was teaching a young relative how to carve *pasui* (ceremonial chopstick used for offering wine). There aren't too many people who can match his skill."

Once the conversation shifted to Petennouk, a *katkemat* (married woman) from next door seized the opportunity to touch on a topic I wasn't particularly eager to discuss. "But you know, I get the feeling that Ipokash likes Unayanke better than Petennouk. Unayanke seems to stop by her house pretty frequently on his way back from fishing trips out on the sea. If you ask me, his motive for coming out this way is Ipokash, not the fish. He's a fantastic hunter, so Ipokash's Acha seems to like him really well, and I'd say that her fiancé's got quite a rival on his hands!" Unayanke was from a *kotan* fairly far up the Chepkaunpet River. Not all the young women in Otasam Kotan had heard of him, but he gained instant notoriety. What was more, things were exactly as the *katkemat* from next door said, and my heart *was* leaning toward Unayanke. My face reddened, as if flames had crept up on it. I'd never felt so strongly like "hiding inside my wrinkles."[40] But everyone's curiosity was only further aroused.

Women who had married out to neighboring *kotan* had come in with their daughters to assist in the *iyomante* preparation, creating an opportunity to hear what kinds of reputations Petennouk and Unayanke had in their own *kotan*. Sometimes I put on an air of indifference, while at other times I tried to change the topic of conversation; but in truth, I was listening with every fiber of my being and secretly hoped that the talk about them would continue.

Unayanke's Chichap Kotan was far away, so only two women from it had come to help. The one working in our group was a married woman named Umoshmatek, a distant relative of his. Presumably not only for that reason, she described Unayanke as a rare find, a likable young man with the three most essential qualities.[41] Especially in his hunting skills—he favored archery—he was said to be head and shoulders above the youth of any *kotan* along this branch of the river.

"But you can't forget Petennouk's carving. I think it wouldn't be a lie to say that he's far superior to any young man in the whole region, not just a branch of the river." This was from another

40. The face reddening "as if flames crept up" and wanting to "hide inside my wrinkles" are metaphors for shame that recur in *uwekeper* (*tuitak* in eastern Hokkaidō).

41. The three qualities are *shiretok* (good appearance), *rametok* (courage), and *pawetok* (eloquence). These were especially essential to *kotan* heads.

married woman, Etonrachichi (Runny Nose), from Petennouk's Akpet Kotan, who must have felt that she couldn't remain silent when the honor of her *kotan* was at stake.

The gossip about the two continued as we prepared food. Umakashte glared at me, saying, "So, Ipokash, what are you going to do with two such extraordinary young men chasing after you? Perhaps I'm just jealous, but being too desirable must certainly be annoying."

As she had pointed out, this dilemma couldn't be ignored. I would eventually have to decide my own feelings. With this much gossip, it would not take long for Unayanke's name to reach Petennouk's ears. I wondered how much Petennouk actually liked me. He had given me a *menoko makiri* (small knife for women) with an elaborately carved design. In return, I had embroidered *tekunpe* (hand covers) for him; but for some reason, I didn't sense the same passion I felt from Unayanke. Acha seemed to be unhappy with Petennouk's shortcomings in hunting skills, but what I found more unsettling was that he always seemed lost in thought and not all that interested in me.

In the evening I discovered to my surprise that Unayanke had arrived early for the *iyomante* as the representative of Chichap Kotan.[42] This meant that at least in his *kotan*, he was perceived to have a bright future.

Soon after I returned home from completing the day's work, Hapo came back from the *porochise*. She looked at me meaningfully, handing me a small package as she said, "Unayanke asked me to give this to you." I tensed as I accepted it, my gaze darting back and forth between my mother's face and the gift. I moved over to the hearth fire to open it. Inside was a *mukkuri* (mouth zither). I felt inexplicable joy, but at the same time was

---

42. The head of a *kotan* who was invited to *iyomante* often sent a capable youth as his proxy to help with the preparations.

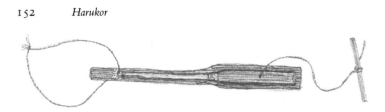

A *mukkuri* (mouth zither), an instrument found throughout countries bordering the Pacific Ocean from New Guinea to the African continent. The player holds the right end and pulls the thread on the left to vibrate the valve at the center, while using the upper chest as a sound box. The pitch and tone color are controlled by moving the tongue.

annoyed with Unayanke. He must have noticed me wearing the knife from Petennouk. Plotting some careful strategy, he had begun by sending me this *mukkuri*. He probably realized that he couldn't measure up to Petennouk in carving and wanted to avoid a head-on challenge. Instead, his plan was to see if he could get me to play the *mukkuri* and eventually respond favorably to him. When I tried it out, I realized that he must have picked it out of dozens that he'd made, for I had never produced a more magnificent sound.

As the day of the festival approached, more and more helping hands came from other *kotan*. In addition to being responsible for the preparations, women were given the task of seeing to the needs of guests. Unayanke seemed to be racing about as one of the messengers between the *ekashi* from other villages who had assigned roles, so he rarely had a chance to be near us. On one rare occasion, he was part of a group of young men who had gone up the mountain to obtain a cork tree for a sacred ritual. Several of the women had also gone up for firewood.[43] He was clearly aware of the women's group from his position by a clump of trees.

43. Amur cork, or *kihada* in Japanese, was used as a tree of the highest grade for *iyomante* of the highest god, the giant striped owl. It was believed to turn into gold in the world of the spirits.

At that moment, something happened that caught me completely off guard. From within our group, Umakashte began singing a *yaisama* (improvisational song).

"*Yaisamane-e-na*
   yaisamane-e-na[44]
   What shall I say?
   What shall I do?
   My heart
   is so full of sorrow. . . . "

The content of her song was so vague that it wasn't possible to determine for whom the song was meant, but she clearly intended it for one of the youths by the trees. This in itself was not unusual. But I was startled by the realization that Umakashte was singing for Unayanke. Something in the way she sang made me feel that she was keeping me, her closest friend, at arm's length.

Could it really be? Struck by a feeling I'd never had before, I seethed with envy and competitive spirit at my best friend's aggressiveness. I found myself unconsciously pulling hard on the ropes as we tied firewood in bundles. Hardly aware of the light snow that was melting on my wrists, I forgot to brush it off.

Not much happened in the rush of the next few days, not until the day before the *iyomante* and the prefestival rituals began. All the important *ekashi*, invited from neighboring and distant areas, were dressed in their most formal attire. Led by the festival chief, Shiratekka-ekashi from Akpet Kotan, who was famed for his erudition,[45] a complex set of rites was performed by the

---

44. "*Yaisamane-e-na*" is a refrain used at the beginning of *yaisama*.

45. The *iyomante* host requested that an eminent *ekashi* of another *kotan* serve as festival chief. Under this elder's leadership, the roles of other *kotan* elders were determined according to established ritual practices.

A *heper-set* (cage), used for raising a bear cub or owl in preparation for an *iyomante* (spirit-sending festival).

men, starting with ceremonial bows to the fire god at the village head's *porochise*, then moving on to the striped giant owl in its cage.[46] By this time, the shortened day of winter had come to a close. The women, even as they took care of the guests and the feasting, surrounded the cage and sang *upopo* and danced *rimse* for the guardian bird, whose journey to the realm of the deities awaited it the next day.

As it got darker, the bonfire burned ever more brightly, and with the addition of wine, the frenzy of the prefestival multiplied. Huchi and young men joined the circle dance. The giant striped owl was such a proud bird that if fed by someone it dis-

46. The cage was called a *heper-set* (see photo above).

A rare contemporary surviving painting of an owl *iyomante*. From *Ainu fūzoku emaki* (Picture scroll of Ainu customs and manners) by Nishikawa Hokuyō, a late Tokugawa painter, in the possession of Hakodate City Library.

liked, it would ignore the food; but tonight, its full attention was drawn to the uproar. It was so used to the *kotan korkur* family that had raised it since it was a fledgling that when let out of the cage, it would fly out to the river and feed on fish, then return. More-wash, the ten-year-old daughter of the family, was crying bitterly, saddened by the impending separation.

I left the circle dance for a while to take a turn at hosting, then returned to the dance. Umoshmatek whispered to me, "You know what, Umakashte gave Unayanke a pair of hand covers."

So, after all. . . . My face tensed as I realized that my flash of insight had been confirmed, but even Umoshmatek probably missed the change in my expression on this night when the bonfires roared away and everyone's face was washed in vermilion. The best unmarried embroiderers in Otasam Kotan used to be Sapo, myself, and Umakashte. Now that Sapo was married, it was commonly held that Umakashte and I were an equal match. As close friends, we had been good rivals at embroidery, but for us to be competing at something like this must be the trick of some evil spirits.

Wondering if I should consult a *tusukur*, I found my attention to the dancing and singing waning.[47] While some girls were even weeping from the emotional impact of the event, my own fervor gradually diminished. I didn't even notice that Petennouk had arrived from the next village until Etunrachich, dancing behind me in the circle, told me. His appearance had little effect on me, however. I was at a loss about to how to respond to Umakashte's challenge. Unable to reveal my torment to Huchi and Hapo, I quietly left the party still at the peak of excitement and returned home, hoping at least that an ancestor would appear in my dreams to offer advice.[48]

Huchi had come home shortly before me, leading my younger Akihi by the hand. "You don't seem yourself, Opere," she worried. Even though I was taller than she, she reverted to treating me like her Little One. "Are you all right?" Without answering, I hastily entered my own room.[49] None of the relatives staying with us were back yet. Unable to fall asleep, I chewed on the cat-

47. A *tusukur* is one who conducts *tusu*, a shaman. See pp. 75–79.

48. Dream interpretation, called *yaichinita kokanu* (or *wentarap kokanu* in Hidaka), was often used as an important guide to action.

49. In the old days, it was customary to prepare a separate area called *tunpe* for a daughter who came of age. Depending on the region, a part of the house was sectioned off with straw mats, a separate compartment was extended under the eaves, or a separate cottage was constructed (though some scholars question

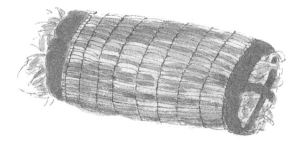

An *eniupe* (pillow).

tail straw sticking out of the end of my pillow and let the tears flow.

Snowflakes flickered here and there the morning of the day of the *iyomante*, but the wind was not strong, so the weather was fairly good. No ancestors visited my dreams, but strangely enough, one appeared in Hapo's dream. As she changed into her finest, she casually mentioned to me, "You seem to be concerned about something, but last night one of our ancestors left me a message for you, to follow your heart." Repeating to myself that I should "follow my heart," I felt the tension in my chest gradually ease.

It was time for the giant striped owl to be released from its cage and transferred to the center of the cross made of the logs of the cork tree. The festival was approaching a peak. In seeming deference to the owl's prestigious position as the guardian deity of the *kotan*, the light flurries dwindled to nothing and patches of blue sky became visible. The women formed a ring around the cage, entertaining and consoling the *kamui* with send-off songs and dances. The *ekashi*, who had completed preparations for the festival stage, came toward us with great dignity, lead-

---

the last possibility). In this story, the separate space is a compartment within the main house, made for the heroine's older sister and handed down to her.

A *kotan kor kamui* (giant striped owl) from a contemporary
owl *iyomante*, December 1989, at the Ainu Ethnic Resources
Museum in Kasshuraro Kotan.

ing the rest of the men.[50] They joined us in the ring, shaking
takusa (bundles of purifying plants) up and down. Unayanke and
Petennouk, in formal dress, were both present.

As the women in the circle accelerated the pace of their clapping and singing, the owl was welcomed out of the cage, according
to ancient custom, by the *ekashi*, and attached with string to the
center of the sacred Amur cork. Ten young men selected for their
strength greeted it somberly with *onkami*, then lifted up the tree.

50. The style of the owl *iyomante* differed widely from region to region.
In eastern Hokkaidō, the Kushiro area had especially rigid rules. "Only high-
ranking elders who knew the old ritual procedures could participate. Women,
children, and rankless people could not even approach the site of the ceremony,"
says *Kotan seibutsuki* (Animals in *kotan*) by Sarashina Genzō and Sarashina Kō
(Hōsei Daigaku Shuppankyoku, 1977/1992). In the Harukor story, the rules
are not as rigid, but women do not directly participate in the ritual.

Moving in time to the even more intense pitch of the festival song, they raised and lowered the sacred tree as they wound their way from the festival ground to the ceremonial altar. The sight of the full-grown owl flapping its wings open and closed, as the cross moved up and down amid the fervent singing, cheering, and clapping by the children and infants of our *kotan* and the several hundred visitors from faraway *kotan*, seemed majestically befitting a send-off to the land of the gods. And there, among the young men chosen to carry the sacred tree, was Unayanke.

Under the solemn direction of Shiratekka-ekashi, the "Ceremonial Arrow Rite" was performed with five decorated arrows. This ceremony of the separation of the soul and its physical body, skinning and dismembering, took place as the *kotan* was gradually covered in the evening darkness. While the venerable rituals were carried out solemnly by the men in front of the ceremonial stage, the ring of women surrounded them at a distance. The women created the atmosphere by responding to the different rites—first with lighthearted *rimse,* then somber song, and so on under the guidance of Toitoi-huchi. She was the older sister of Etunrachich, a married woman from the neighboring village, and was well known for her great knowledge.

Because I had been appointed to help with the preparations for the grand banquet being held that night, I left the dance for a while and busily moved about between the *porochise* and various *chise* around it. At one point, I passed by Petennouk but could only nod slightly to him, as I was carrying a pot in both arms.

As I bustled about, preoccupied with my tasks, the men's rites progressed so that the main events were now in the *porochise*. The giant striped owl's sacred form (its head and the skin of its torso) was placed on the altar prepared at the honorable seat, on the far end of the firepit. Its soul was still seated between the ears of the form and would join us for the banquet, after which it would enjoy a *yukar* master's performance of a full-length tale. The men seemed relieved, having finished the first half of their rituals without incident, but we still had long hours of work ahead of us. The soup made of the guardian bird's body, which was the gift it bore when it arrived in this world, was served to all the evening's participants.

For many women, it was the *yukar*, rather than the banquet before it, that was the highlight of an *iyomante*. This was especially true today, for the celebrated Apniainu-ekashi, admired as the greatest storyteller among the eastern Ainu, had been invited all the way from Shipetcha Kotan. This was a once-in-a-lifetime opportunity, and many of the girls from *kotan* along the Chepkaunpet River had gathered for this reason above all. According to rumor, one of Apniainu-ekashi's *yukar* was a massive tale that could not be finished in four nights, and girls who sat through it found themselves moved to unrelenting tears for the six days and six nights following it.

"I hope Apniainu-ekashi will tell a story like that tonight!" I told my cousin Hotene, as we distributed bowls of soup. She enthusiastically replied, "Yes, we've got to serve him very properly and please him so he'll do that!" Hotene was to be married soon. Her breasts were probably fuller than anyone's in the *kotan* around us, and I wondered if they didn't get in the way of carrying things. Mine had grown some after my *chuppe*, but they were still fairly small.

When all the most important personages, starting with the *ekashi* invited as honored guests, had been seated at their designated spots, the grand feast to celebrate the guardian deity's departure began with the dignified chanting of the festival chief, Shitekka-ekashi.[51] This was followed by prayers to a number of

51. Elders with more important roles were seated at the far end of the firepit, close to the sacred window. The right side of the firepit, looked at from the

A *tuki* (wine cup).

deities by each *ekashi* sitting around the hearth. As we offered wine to the gods, I became aware of a restlessness in my heart. When I searched it to see what was making me so anxious, I had to recognize that it was how Unayanke was affecting my relationship with Umakashte.

After the *ekashi* and the already-married men, who were seated around the firepit, had offered ceremonial wine to the gods and each had a sip, they passed the wine cups to their wives and related widows who were seated behind them. Accepting the wine cups, the women bowed formally and drank. Whenever there was an elderly woman without male relatives, some considerate man would call out her name and give her his cup.

Once the older generation of *ekashi* and married people had finished, the younger men took over their seats and repeated the process. They were supposed to hand their cups to girls close to them, and this was where complications arose. Since they could call out not only to family and relatives but also to a sweetheart or betrothed, subtle emotions were sometimes in play. Petennouk would naturally call for me, his fiancée. I didn't think that Un-

---

entrance, was occupied by guests. On the left sat people of the host *kotan*. In the old days, *porochise* often had two firepits, and women sat around the firepit closer to the entrance.

ayanke was bold enough to call for me in front of Petennouk, but maybe he would name Umakashte. My pulse quickened at the thought, but the ritual forged ahead, indifferent to my feelings. When "Harukor!"—my real name—was called out, it was Petennouk after all.[52] As I approached him, conscious of numerous pairs of curious eyes, I heard Unayanke's voice call out Umakashte's true name, "Keutoranke!" I felt as if I had been struck by lightning. Many other people seemed surprised as well, and their gazes shifted from me to her. However much I tried to control the shaking in my hands as I accepted the wine cup from Petennouk, I couldn't stop a slight trembling. Wondering whether or not Petennouk knew, I briefly raised my eyes to glance at him as I offered the wine cup and saw that he was watching me with a smile like an *ekashi* who understands all, yet also with a remnant of shyness. He was always as difficult for me to read as some kind of *kamui*. I was so intent that it took me a moment to realize that the wine for this *iyomante* was especially good.

The banquet was in full swing, and after the feasting came an array of performances to please the guardian spirit. I went out at one point to bring something to Huchi, who was already at home, and to tell her that the *yukar* would soon start. When I returned to the *porochise*, making my way from the entranceway to the banquet hall, Unayanke was at the entry decorated with *inaukike* (curled shavings from whittled branches). He must have been waiting for me, for he whispered, "Sorry about earlier, Harukor." His expression was blurred by the backlighting, but his sincere words, at the same time exasperating, instantly softened my heart, much like the sun during the season of melting snow.

Once in the banquet hall, I set to work putting away dishes in preparation for the *yukar*.

---

52. Real names were used at sacred rituals.

Apniainu-ekashi, the great master of *yukar*, had a long, beautifully trimmed beard with some white hairs in it and a broad
chest, from which emanated his powerful voice. He was adorned
in ritual attire that lent him an air of godliness, as if he had appeared from Kamui Moshir. He was quite young for an *ekashi*,
perhaps not yet sixty years old, but his fame had made his name
known, even in our *kotan*, for over ten years. I recalled hearing
his name from Hapo at an early age. For most of us girls along
the Chepkaunpet River, though, this was the first time we had
seen him in person.

Tonight's masterful *yukar* was of course an *ainu* epic meant for
adults.[53] Several *huchi* in another *chise* were presenting the children with *uwepeker* and *yukar* about animal deities. My Huchi was
a fine *uwepeker* performer but had a strong desire to hear Apniainu's *yukar*, and so she had come back to the large *porochise*.

The people in the hall, crowded around the two hearths with
the storyteller at the center, quieted down for the long heroic
epic that was to begin. Lamps had been lit in two areas, and as
the noise from the previous entertainment dissipated, there was
only the occasional crackling of the bonfire to disturb the silence.
There was no wind at all, and the clear night air was bitterly cold
and still. It was only once in a while that we heard, from the direction of the Chepkaunpet River, the sound of cracking ice.

"O Venerable Kotan Kor Kamui and Deity of Fire," so started
Apniainu-ekashi in his dignified voice, intoning a chant to the
gods. "It is a great honor for an insignificant person such as myself to perform the *yukar* for this grand *iyomante*. I shall draw upon
my every humble resource to present a respectable performance.
I beg that even if portions of my tale are related in a displeasing
manner, you will magnanimously overlook such inadequacies and
someday grace us again with a visit to Ainu Moshir."

---

53. See p. 89 for the classification of *yukar*.

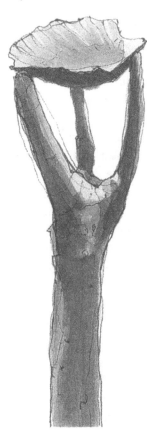

A *ratchako* (lamp stand). Grease from fish, bird, or animal is placed on a scallop shell set on a three-forked branch, and a wick soaked in grease is lit.

The master's sonorous voice, perfect to mediate between Kamui Moshir and Ainu Moshir, made me feel alert. While reciting the sacred chant, he began to keep a quiet beat with his *repni* (time beater), and the *ekashi* around the fire began, barely audibly, to match his beat with their *repni*.[54] The rest of us held our breath in anticipation, our hearts already leaving Ainu Moshir, sucked into the realm of *yukar*. When the beats of the narrator and the men by the firepit began to merge, Apniainu started his recitation:[55]

"For what reason
  is it that I live alone
  in such a house as this?

54. A stick about a foot long is used to beat the rhythm on the wood by the firepit. The beat provides an important accompaniment for the narrator.

55. The beautiful rhythm and melody of rhymed Ainu verse cannot be conveyed here, but let me note that the performer and listeners together create an art of singing, narration, acting, and poetry.

Repni (time beaters), approximately one foot long. They could be made of remainders of wood; for example, willow left after making *inau*.

In this large house
the altar overflows
with golden vessels
and silver bowls,
with golden treasure chests
and silver treasure chests.
Above them
lies the sword of a brave soul,
its tassels swaying in the wind,
and by it is the sleeping chamber
where I grew up.
Where, alone, I grew up. . . . "

The *yukar* he had started to perform was one of those featuring the hero Ponyanpe. The masterful Apniainu had a resonant voice, but he continued for a while in a low, subdued style, which nevertheless carried to every nook and cranny of the *porochise*. Even Hotene and I, sitting in a dark corner so far away that the light from the lamp stand couldn't reach us, could hear every word clearly. This quality alone told us that this *yukar* performer was in a different class from others we had heard before, but the emotion contained in his phrases seemed to evoke *itak-kamui* (the spirit of words). Our hearts were captured, and our bodies numb as if a spell had been cast on us. Even though he had just started, Hotene was already pressing her eyelids.

"It truly is a mystery but
  when I felt hunger
  bowls of food lined up
  of their own accord by the fire.
  And when I had enough
  I played with the ashes.
  When I laughed aloud,
  playing with the ashes,
  the blizzard *kamui*
  and the wind *kamui*
  were amused by my gestures.
  When I felt sleepy,
  six furs piled up of their own accord
  in the sleeping chamber
  for a peaceful dream. . . . "

This *yukar* about Ponyanpe was one I had never heard in our *kotan*.[56] Apniainu had completely assumed Ponyanpe's character, and his narration remained at a steady, low pitch. Its richly expressive portrayal brought alive the young Ponyanpe's life of solitude. We had no idea who was looking after the young boy's

56. There are a few major characters in "human *yukar*," but Ponyanpe (originally Ponyaunpe or Poiyaunpe) is a representative hero. There are many completely different narratives about the same hero. The version introduced here is based on the narration of Yae Kurō of eastern Hokkaidō, translated into Japanese by Fujimura Hisakazu. I also used details from the version of Kannari Matsu (see glossary), translated by Kayano Shigeru.

needs, but Ponyanpe grew up freely before our eyes by the hand of some invisible being.

As he grew old enough to play with bows and arrows, the master's pitch rose slightly, and the *repni* accompaniment responded to this change by increasing in vigor. These subtle changes had to match the master's shifts without disturbing the overall effect, and so the *repni*-beaters tonight were all chosen for their finely honed sensitivity to *yukar*. Many of the onlookers were also keeping time by lightly tapping their knees with their hands.

When Ponyanpe had gained familiarity with archery games and released an arrow into a swarm of dancing mosquitoes, he found that if he aimed high, he could impale seven or eight at once against a pillar, and if he aimed low, that he could pierce an equal number, sending them into a windowsill. Each time, he laughed merrily to himself. As he gradually deepened his mastery of the art of archery, he grew sturdier.

One day, he noticed something odd behind the treasure boxes on the altar at the honored seat. It was shaped like a seated human being. It had never been there before. When he approached and examined it, it was empty inside, for it was a set of armor. And what a marvelous set it was.

"With gilt-woven robe
and armor woven of thin thread,
armor woven of tender thread.
Black cord,
white cord,
and red cord
form a design.
On the collar and the hem
was a finishing touch of
broad, flat metalwork,
with a carved pattern
of two swirls,
of three swirls. . . . "

Long and short treasure swords.

Apniainu's eloquent speech gradually began to reverberate more and more.

Above the altar hung Ponyanpe's precious sword.

"On the long, curved sword
  bestowed by the gods
  were entwined
  the dragon god
  and his mate.
  The male dragon god,
  his powerful horns
  on the sword-guard,
  his face brought near
  the female dragon god. . . . "

Ponyanpe, protected with his armor and treasure sword, departed from the home of his birth, led by the will of the gods.

In depicting Ponyanpe's departure, Apniainu's style changed abruptly from that of the steady rhythm of epic poetry to the tumultuous tone suggestive of a swift river. The *repni* beat also peaked, and excited "Ho," "Ei," and "Hou" calls were inserted. The audience's breathing also became charged, and young women forgot themselves as they began projecting their husband's or sweetheart's faces and forms on Ponyanpe's.

Having left his birthplace, the hero stood atop a hill to look back. Surrounded by a long fence, the large house floated, golden in the morning mist. But birds had built their nests on the fence and rats had claimed the base of the house. Everything was in disrepair. Although Ponyanpe had been raised by the invisible being, the house had been left in ruins for years. . . .

During the moments when the hero was filled with emotion as he looked back at his house, the narrator's style returned to the lyrical mode. As Ponyanpe's state of mind was being depicted, a *huchi* near me made a hesitant movement. Hotene also noticed and whispered, "Hey, Ipokash, isn't it about time to 'go close by?'"[57] Just as I responded, "Yeah, I want to go too. Why don't you say something?" someone five or six people away said, "Excuse me . . . ." It was Umakashte. "I'd like to go sit close by. May we have a break?"

The master paused, put down his *repni*, and quietly announced, "Well, then, everybody, let's take a break." Once again I felt left behind by Umakashte, but wondered if this was nothing more than her usual assertiveness. About a third of the listeners stood up and filed out toward the entranceway. I went out with Hotene. The late moon must have been trying to rise from the eastern hills, for the stars in that direction were starting to diminish. Among the men who went outside were several who walked in leisurely and dignified fashion up to the entranceway; but the mo-

---

57. "Going close by" or "sitting close by" was a euphemism for passing water. "Close by" was appropriate because it took a short time; for bowel movement, "far" instead of "close by" was used.

A *sapanpe* (ceremonial crown).

ment they stepped out, they would suddenly dart out into the darkness, find an appropriate corner by the festival ground, and relieve themselves.

Once everyone had returned to the hall and their voices had died down, one of the *ekashi* wielding a *repni* invited the storyteller, "Well then, Ekashi. Shall we begin?" Adjusting the ceremonial crown on his head, the famous storyteller resumed his tale.

Having left his home, propelled by divine will, Ponyanpe was visited early in his travels with a dream about his fiancée. The maiden was an unparalleled beauty blessed with all the virtues of a woman, but she lived with her six evil older brothers. From kotan *far and near, self-confident men came to seek her hand, drawn by her beauty as well as her womanly virtue, good upbringing, and skill at craftwork.*

The home where this beautiful woman and her brothers resided was on a high hill by a volcano crater, and there was a clearing before the house. The youths who came all the way to court this young woman had to wrestle with the woman herself in that open space, while her evil brothers watched. This woman, however, possessed incredible strength,

*and she tossed aside one courageous youth after another. On one side of
the clearing was a cliff that faced the mouth of the volcano. Near it was
a pile of the skeletons of all these young men.*

*"This maiden is none other than your intended bride"; thus Ponyanpe
was informed by his divine guide. As Ponyanpe made his way toward
the mountaintop where this powerful beauty lived, he encountered a
maiden sitting alone on the path. She asked to accompany him to his
destination.*

Apniainu's resonant voice took on the tone of an internal
monologue as the hero considered the request:

"How, now, for what reason
   would this stranger ask
   to join me on my travels?
Her countenance,
   her garb,
   her gestures
are all unusually graceful
   and hint at fine breeding.
Yet this is where spirits walk
   deep in the mountains.
Is this some malign spirit
   wishing to tempt me
   and thus disguised
   as a lithe maiden?"

*Ponyanpe declined the young woman's request and, steadfastly ignoring
her, continued walking. But she insisted on following him, and when
dusk fell and he gathered fir branches and leaves to build a temporary
hut for the night, she busily set to work preparing a meal for him. The
chastely mannered maiden offered her services only and did not try to
sleep in the same hut. Because the soup could have been poisoned,
Ponyanpe first only sipped at the broth. There was no trace of poison,*

A *hupcha kucha* (hunting hut of fir branches).

and it was far tastier than anything he had ever had. Half in disbelief, he accepted serving after serving.

When he awoke at dawn, the maiden continued to serve him in the same chaste fashion, now preparing breakfast. As far as Ponyanpe could tell, she did not seem to be some kind of supernatural creature. But determined not to reveal any vulnerabilities or weaknesses, he set off without saying a word to her. In silence, she followed him. In this way, they crossed six valleys and six mountaintops, and several days later arrived at the mountain peak along the volcano.[58]

58. Six, which is more than the number of the fingers on one hand, is often used in Ainu to symbolize a large number.

Apniainu's style changed again, to the quality of tumultuous rapids, and sharp exclamations joined the high beating of *repni*.

"The awesome roar of the volcanic fire
   the scorched walls of the cliff.
   Scattered about the depths of hell
   are the bleached bones of young men,
   the bleached bones of brave men,
   the bleached bones of broken dreams.
   Beyond that strange sight
   and the red-brown sulfuric smoke
   look upon
   the six scoundrels
   of all evil deeds
   baring their hideous faces
   now pouring wine."

Ponyanpe stepped into the area around the wrestling ring where the brothers were having a drinking bout and proclaimed, "I, Ponyanpe, have come to court your sister, a maiden of great virtue, as my future bride." Delighted to claim yet another victim, the brothers told him, "Please make yourself comfortable. We'd like to see you wrestle a bit with our sister. If you win, we'll gladly offer you her hand."

Laying eyes on their younger sister, Ponyanpe was overwhelmed by her beauty and elegance, and utterly convinced that this must be the woman he had come seeking, the one the gods had told him was his intended.

Apniainu-ekashi described at length the details of her beauty and fine bearing, then returned to the monologue style.

"How, now, is it
   that such a regal maiden
   should mingle with men of such ilk
   and with her magical powers

come to have murdered
untainted youths,
courageous youths,
big-dreaming youths?"

As Ponyanpe prepared to wrestle with the beauty of supernatural might, the maiden who had followed him said, "Please let me take her on." About to step into the earthen ring, he replied, "You have nothing to do with this. Why are you so . . . " But the maiden's resolve was firm. "No, please. You must allow me to go first. I have no regrets if I die in the process. It is surely not unuseful for you to find out from my match just how strong this woman's power actually is. I beg of you. . . . "

The six ruffians, who had been watching with amusement as they drank their wine, were quite pleased by this turn of events. "Well, this should be fun. Let's get the women going at each other first."

"I had thought her but a maiden,
    that mysterious one,
    yet when she faced off
    with the mighty beauty,
    she revealed her own magical strength
    as they grappled and broke away
    neither side claiming victory or defeat. . . . "

As the master narrated each move of the match, the audience responded audibly, but because it was difficult to determine which side to take, the murmuring that arose among the sighs sounded hesitant.

Battling back and forth across the clearing, the maidens eventually stepped over the rim at the edge of the volcano, and, still entangled, fell down the cliff toward the depths where the magma boiled. But both women possessed divine powers, and they floated in midair as they grappled, neither one winning. They began the fight over, and again they rolled down the cliff and found themselves afloat. They repeated this process over and over.

As this strange event unfolded, Ponyanpe tried to see all that his clair-
voyance allowed him to see. Opening one eye as wide as the full moon,
and narrowing the other to a needlepoint to focus his gaze, he glared at
the villains. What he saw was this. The six evil brothers, exploiting their
sister's sweet nature and peerless beauty, were plotting to subjugate and
rule the moshir *throughout the region. Their strategy was to cast a pow-*
erful spell on their younger sister and have her wrestle with and kill each
of the praiseworthy brave youths who came from various kotan *to seek*
her hand. They could then invade the weakened structure of kotan. *Re-*
alizing that the root of evil lay in these six brothers, Ponyanpe imme-
diately drew his treasure sword.

"This matchless treasure sword of mine,
  sent as a gift from the realm of the gods,
  its white blade
  now leaves its scabbard
  and releases a flash of lightning
  and roaring thunder. . . . "

Apniainu's sonorous recitation ascended to its peak, urged
along by the increasingly vigorous pounding of *repni*. As he was
transformed into the wrathful Ponyanpe, his fierce mien reddened
by the light of the fire, his long beard shaking, and his thick eyebrows moving up and down, Apniainu's presence grew until he
overwhelmed the area around the firepit.

The six scoundrels drew their swords and a battle ensued.

At this point the energy and noise from the crowded listeners
began to drown out the beat of *repni*; scattered men's voices
throughout the hall were raised in *okokse* (shouts of support). Once
into the great battle, the narration switched into a free-flowing
style, much like a rapids of words. Between the cheering for
Ponyanpe, "Ohohohoho—i, Hohohohoho—!" the pounding on
floors and knees, and the beating of *repni*, the hall itself became
a battlefield. Young women identifying their husbands and sweet-

hearts with Ponyanpe were dragged into the storm of excitement, even forgetting to brush aside their welling tears, and raising their voices in unformed words.

Thinking they'd just slash and dispose of this urchin as part of their drinking entertainment, the six villains had underestimated Ponyanpe. In the course of the battle they realized that he was not just anyone.

"Panicking,
the evildoers
now covered their noses,
now covered their mouths,[59] saying
'Things being thus,
we must plead with our guardian deity
for a helping hand.'
See
the evil spirits materialize—
around one side of each sword
a red viper entwines,
around the other side
a blue viper entwines.
Red flames from the mouth of the red viper,
blue flames from the mouth of the blue viper,
six red flames,
six blue flames,
six blade points
leap this way and that above me. . . . "

Ponyanpe leaped upon his six enemies as if the backs of their swords provided bridges for his own attack. Both sides, along with their protective deities, spent the fullest extent of their secret powers and magical

59. Gestures of surprise. Covering the mouth and nostrils kept the soul from escaping through one of these openings.

spells. The enemy side unleashed a tornado as the vipers spit out poisonous foam, while Ponyanpe used his magical powers to create doubles and triples of himself.

The fearsome battle continued, and although it was six against one, the enemy side had only their evil spirits. Ponyanpe was protected both by the armor bestowed on him by the land of the gods and by his mysterious but mighty protective deity. Realizing that they could not win, the six fled from the clearing along the mountain ridge. Ponyanpe, who had become a demon of vengeance for the hundreds of youths killed by the wrongdoers, denied them passage. Cornering them against the cliffs, he cut off the heads of these six, already abandoned by their protective deities, in one motion of his treasure sword.

"These most villainous
  six souls,
  six evil spirits;
  in the black clouds that spring forth,
  the heavenly skies
  are shrouded in the darkness of midnight.
  See, amid that darkness,
  leaving behind what regrets I don't know,
  the six glowing lights
  sway to the west,
  sway to the east,
  until a bolt of thunder
  chases them as they, lurching,
  fade toward the western sky[60]
  blood-red at sunset. . . . "

A sense of relief filled the hall with Ponyanpe's victory, but there was still the matter of the battle between the women. It

---

60. At death, the spirit of a good person flies to the east, and that of a bad person flies to the west.

was a long time since our last break, and some of the elders must have wanted to "go close by." It would be an embarrassment if a young woman from the *kotan* didn't take discreet action. Being shy, I usually let others take care of things, but I must have been reacting to Umakashte, for I spoke up with confidence I never knew I had. Feeling that Umakashte would read through me, I was annoyed at myself. Yet the happiness I felt when Unayanke smiled at me, from his seat in the direction of the firepit by the seat of honor, more than made up for my irritation.

Wanting to hear the next part of the *yukar* and enjoy Apniainu-ekashi's mastery, people returned to their seats more quickly than the last time.

Having vanquished the six villains, Ponyanpe dashed over to the site of the battle between the two women. But he was too late, for a split second before his arrival, he heard a scream of death agony. It was the voice of the chaste one, who had followed Ponyanpe and seen to his needs, as she dropped into the volcano. Her strength finally exhausted, she was thrown aside by the mysterious, magical, beautiful younger sister of the sinister brothers. Just as Ponyanpe arrived, the virgin's soul left her body and flew in a straight line with a bolt of thunder toward the eastern sky. His gaze, full of deep emotion, followed her . . .

"O unknown sweet maiden,
   your poor soul,
   your eastward-heading soul,
   forgive me
   for my eyes that saw not
   your lofty identity,
   for my blindness. . . . "

The audience was overcome with grief as Apniainu, impassioned, chanted Ponyanpe's soliloquy. Young women were in tears, and some *huchi* protested, "That's too cruel!" "How dreadful!" "You must save her, Ekashi!" But the master's recitation suddenly quickened.

That mighty beauty, the mystery maiden, returned to the ring with a stunned expression. Because her evil brothers had been destroyed, the powerful spell on her had been broken, and she now reassumed her kind and virtuous character. Unaware of what had taken place, she had no inkling of what she herself had done. How sad was this maiden's circumstance. Deceived by the very brothers who shared her blood, then to have them murdered and to be left all alone. Ponyanpe held her tightly, whereupon the divinely fair maiden shed tear after tear and related her story. Clasping her bracelet, the maiden sang a yaisama *of her shock and grief.*

"'*Yaisamane-e-na*
yaisamane-e-na
O spirits of my remote ancestors,
O protective deities,
O gods of fire and water.
For whose sake
do you exist?
For these evil deeds,
evil deeds,
evil deeds,
evil deeds,
evil deeds,
evil deeds
I committed unknowingly,
are you abandoning me?
The only power left me
is to fall to the netherworld
and disappear into the western skies.'

This poor maiden,
a godlike maiden,
desiring to plunge
to the depths of the fiery opening
from my breast,
ran out. . . . "

"Stop!" "No!" "Save her!" "Woooy!" . . . The hall was filled
with pathetic voices. I joined in before I knew it. By then neither the sound of *repni* nor the great storyteller's recitation was
audible. I began to worry that a *huchi* or two might faint. Even
men were brushing away tears or wiping their noses. At that moment, the *ekashi*'s voice, once drowned by the noise, reverber-
ated through the audience with added vigor.

"'Wait!'
Grabbing her sleeve,
I drew her back to my bosom.
'My betrothed,
worthy beyond words,
no need is there for haste.
You and I, by the gods
are brought together as man and wife,
so dare not take this lightly.
To repent for the evil deeds unknowingly done
the two of us together
will send the souls
of the dead youths,
of the dead brave men,
of the bleached bones of broken dreams,
to the land of the gods
and labor to ensure
the prosperity
of the *kotan* left behind. . . . '"

Weeping pure tears once more in response to Ponyanpe's suggestion,
the maiden returned with him to the estate of his birthplace to wed him
and create a new home.

As we sat enthralled by the world of *yukar*, light from outdoors began to seep in between the cracks of the closed windows of the *porochise*. Though this was the season of the longest
nights, the great storyteller's *yukar* had not begun until well after nightfall, and it was now morning. When the tale reached a
point of rest, Shiratekka-ekashi announced in an authoritative
voice, "Well, then, let's stop here for now. Please look forward
to tonight's continuation."

And so ended the most important day of the *iyomante*. Exhausted by the long preparations preceding the festival, the intensity of the day, and much drinking and feasting, people
seemed to feel sleepy the moment the long-awaited *yukar* ended.
They quickly scattered to their respective *chise*. Many villagers
from elsewhere were staying in the *porochise*. It would be another
five or six days before the guardian bird's soul departed for the
realm of the gods, and the grand *iyomante* was to last the entire
time.[61] While the men would be involved in several rituals until
the final god-sending rites, none of them was as crucial as those
of the first day. Instead, the central attractions became chatting
and socializing with rare visitors from other *kotan*, and the nightly
recitation of *yukar*.

The vast amount of grain wine brought by people from other
villages was consumed so that its end would coincide with the
final day of the grand festival. For young men and women coming of age, these several days constituted a second festival criss-
crossed by feelings of anticipation and insecurity. Youths and

61. In recent times, in most regions the soul-sending ritual seems to con-
clude the *iyomante* at midnight or dawn of the second night, but in the old days
iyomante are said to have lasted for five or six days.

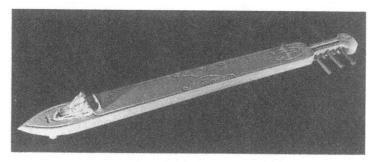

A *ka*, also called *tonkori* (five-stringed zither).

maidens from other villages, known to us only through gossip, made their appearance. Some of them were equally curious about particular young women and men from our *kotan*, and all this contributed to competition, jealousy, public give-and-take through courting songs, incidents of romantic encounters even in the cruelly cold outdoors, and various athletic and artistic competitions in the form of archery contests or performances on *mukkuri* and the five-stringed zither.[62]

In the thick of this chaos stood Unayanke, Umakashte, and myself. Whether and to what extent my fiancé Petennouk was taking part was unclear, however. He seemed to be participating and responding, but always at a distance and with an air of indifference. If I hadn't known his family background, I would surely have suspected that he must be some kind of *kamui*.

Apniainu's continuation of his *yukar* on the second evening again started fairly late. As on the first night, he opened with the solemn chanting of prayers to the giant striped owl on the festival altar.

Having returned to Ponyanpe's castle, the two strove to fulfill their

62. The five-stringed zither was particularly favored by Ainu in Sakhalin and Sōya.

A *tukipasui* (ceremonial chopstick, used for offering wine to the gods).

mountaintop vow for the regeneration of the kotan. *Ponyanpe's bride, who possessed all the feminine virtues, soon restored the dilapidated house and made it as comfortable as a brand-new one. One day, the chaste maiden who had aided Ponyanpe, the mysterious one who had died in the battle on the mountaintop, appeared in his dream.*

"'Hear my words, Ponyanpe.
I am the daughter of the Eagle King.
By order of my father, the King,
it was my duty to aid
your every noble task,
never showing myself
yet in your presence always,
from your tenderest days,
with the cooking,
sewing,
and skills of battle. . . . '"

And so it was in the form of the strange maiden of chastity whom he encountered during his travels that she had finally revealed herself. Why should the Eagle King have sent his princess to Ainu Moshir? Before his birth, Ponyanpe's parents had wholeheartedly revered the Eagle Kamui and observed proper rituals. Whenever they brewed wine, they had invariably made an offering to him, and in the course of many rituals, always honored the spirit of the Eagle King. So when Ponyanpe's parents departed this world soon after his birth, the Eagle King decided to reward them by providing his daughter as a surrogate parent.

When Ponyanpe went out to quell the six brothers, the Eagle King himself intended to serve as a second. But because of responsibilities in the spirit world and his advanced age, it was, in the end, his daughter who accompanied Ponyanpe to repay her father's debt and who risked her life to protect him. It was thanks to her true identity as the Eagle Princess that she could rise up out of the volcanic fires so often during the battle.

Apniainu, about to narrate the climax, resembled a heroic warrior quietly reminiscing about days of battle. He spoke in a voice that sounded as if it came from the realm of the gods. To the barely audible accompaniment of *repni*, which also seemed to sound from the land of the gods, he related the words of the spirit of the Eagle Princess in a simple, unembellished style. The audience, silenced by the solemn closing, was enveloped in a different, more profound emotion than the earlier straightforward excitement and tears.

"'Thus it is, Ponyanpe,
   a couple wedded by divine will,
   you must not neglect
   my Father King's noble heart
   and, as your mother did,
   must offer *kamuinomi*
   with every thought,
   with every occasion.
   My Father King and I
   shall protect
   as your guardian deities
   your children and your children's children.'"

When Ponyanpe tried to respond, the Eagle Princess faded like rising smoke. Waking, Ponyanpe told his wife all that had transpired. He sponsored a grand festival to thank the spirits of the Eagle King and the princess and invited many visitors from kotan *in the area,*

Two kinds of *inau*. Right: *shiroma-inau*.
Left: *chiehorkaikap-inau*.

*thinking to atone for his wife's past as well. The wine for the event
amounted to six casks at the seat of honor and six casks at the lower
seats. A row of beautiful* inau *were newly laid out at the altar his father had built. The scale of the festival was grander than any ever witnessed in the region.*

*Eventually they had children, then grandchildren, and the couple be-
gan to age, never forgetting the Eagle Princess's words.*

"'As our mothers did,
   we shall offer *kamuinomi*
   with every thought
   with every occasion
   and for generations
   pass this down.'
With this wish, I have recited this tale.'"

The master returned to the low, tranquil voice of last night's opening as he finished his oration. Looking around the crowded hall of subdued listeners still affected by lingering reverberations, he spoke solemnly, "*Tanpe pakno* (That will be all)."

The *porochise* overflowed with sighs and half-words of emotion. It was as if we had been struck by thunder, but we were brought back to the moment by the lively voice of a young woman saying, "Thank you very much, Ekashi."

People began to exchange murmurs of admiration: "I've never heard such a magnificent *yukar*." "That Ekashi must be a *kamui* of *yukar*."

Some young women, still in the grip of emotion, remained in tears, unable to speak a word, their voices caught in their throats. I was one of those, and so I was a moment behind everybody else in realizing that the woman who had thanked the *ekashi* at the firepit, and who then handed him the wine cup, was Umakashte. However strong-willed she might be, it was unclear whether this was an impetuous act on her part, or she had been designated by the owl god. In either case, it was a great honor for a *kotan* maiden. My enchantment was diminished by a storm of jealousy.

The master, accepting the wine that Umakashte gracefully served him from a wine pourer, placed the *pasui* on the wine cup. Raising it in obeisance, he touched his left and right shoulders and head with the wine-soaked *pasui* and in a quiet voice expressed his gratitude to his guardian deities before drinking.

"Thank you for the success of this *yukar*, which I offered to the owl god and which many people enjoyed. Please help yourself to this sacred offering of wine."

The great Apniainu's *yukar*, "Gratitude of the Eagle King," ended thus in the middle of the second night. The third day was a short *kamui yukar* that ended in a single night, performed by Otasam Kotan's most skilled Huisak-huchi.[63] She was my Huchi's younger sister. On the fourth night the master Apniainu once again narrated a long tale, this time for three days. It actually required four days to complete, but the tale was cut short by the closing day of the festival so that the owl god would desire to hear the rest and come back to visit Ainu Moshir.

However, an incident of such great personal significance for me took place during that time that even this performance of the age by a superlative artist, spoken of for years afterward, left only a vague impression. Of course, this incident involved the relationships among Unayanke, Umakashte, and myself, as well as Petennouk.

I panicked as a result of Umakashte's almost aggressive courtship of Unayanke. In this situation, I absolutely had to stand up to her challenge. I decided to embroider onto a pair of *tekunpe* an even finer pattern than Umakashte's. I chose a swirling design that was charged with life: "the two divine clouds, the three divine clouds, rising into the skies," often mentioned in *yukar*. I resolved that my handiwork should be so skilled that the pattern would appear ready to move in swirls at any moment.

During the grand festival, the *kotan* was quiet in the mornings

---

63. The *kamui yukar* was traditionally recited by a woman. In eastern Hokkaidō, it was called *oina* or, because of its female association, *matyukar* (women's *yukar*). See the *yukar* classification on p. 89.

Tekunpe (covers for the back of the hand) to shield
those journeying through mountain and forest against
brambles and cold.

as people caught up on their sleep after staying up all night. By
afternoon, the atmosphere began to change, and outdoors—even
when there were light flurries—there was spirited fun with such
games among the youths as "breast squeezing" or displays of martial feats.[64] Besides my cooking and other duties as a maiden of
the *kotan*, however, I thought only of the embroidery that I hoped
to have ready for Unayanke by the time he left after the *iyomante*.
At the same time, I tried to respond to his gift of the *mukkuri*
by performing wherever he might hear me. This was no time to
be shy if I was to fight against Umakashte's assertiveness. I was
confident that my skill at the *mukkuri* was superior to hers. I sang
an *iyohaichish* (improvised song of longing) in the hopes that at
least my feelings, if not the meaning of the words, would be conveyed to him.

64. "Breast squeezing" was a game of catching a young woman at an un-
guarded moment, slipping in a hand to grasp her breast, and running away.

But one night, as I made my way late to the *yukar* hall, something nearly made my heart stop. From below the storehouse of a *chise* near the *porochise* came the anguished love song of a woman. It was Umakashte.

"*Yaisamane-e-na*
yaisamane-e-na.
A bird I wish to be, a bird.
If a bird I were, I could fly
among the tall trees,
brushing them with my wings,
among the low trees,
caressing the treetops with my wings,
and go to the *kotan* of my beloved.
And as I soared above Akpet Kotan,
two pure tears,
three pure tears
I'd shed from the sky,
and gazing at the sky, my loved one
would wonder,
'How is it that in such fine weather
it should rain?'
Ah, would that I could touch him
if only with the tips of my wings."

My shock came from the name of the *kotan* in the song: Akpet. This *chise* was where Petennouk was staying with his relatives, and Umakashte's song was so heartfelt a love song that even I, her rival, was moved to tears.

"Umakashte!" I called out before I knew it, flooded with a passion I couldn't recognize as bewilderment, anger, or grief. It was a clear, windless, biting cold night with so many stars that it was difficult to distinguish between the stars I knew and those I didn't. Realizing that I'd overheard her, Umakashte abruptly stopped singing. For three or four breaths, she stayed perfectly still in the darkness. We were about twenty steps away from each other.

Suddenly, she screamed, "Ipokash!" and crying aloud, came running toward me. Nearly knocking me over—I was rooted to the spot in shock—as she hugged me, she spoke in muffled fragments, "Forgive me, I'm sorry I was so mean."

I found myself crying just as hard. After we cried for a while, not even noticing the cold, we went to Umakashte's house, which was always empty at this hour. The adults were earnestly listening to the *yukar*, while the children were engrossed in stories or indoor games. Using a poker to pull and push the embers in the hearth, Umakashte returned to being my best friend and talked away.[65] Because she couldn't yet sort out her feelings, she was uncharacteristically halting. Still, we felt that we understood thoughts we could not explain in words, and our friendship seemed to deepen.

I realized much later that, while Umakashte had fallen in love with Unayanke, she knew that she was too late. She had thus tried to draw the interest of my actual fiancé, Petennouk, in order to goad me and lead my heart back to him. In truth, she was also attracted to Petennouk's unworldly philosophical nature. Although I was not provoked as she had hoped, it occurred to me that Petennouk and Umakashte might in fact be a perfect couple. Seemingly exact opposites, they were complementary in character. I cannot deny that a little part of me wanted to let her have Petennouk as a gesture of friendship.

This was the next to last night of the *iyomante* that was to become the most important memory of my girlhood, and it was the largest event in the *kotan* in decades.

Deep into the night on the final day, Apniainu cut short his

---

65. A conventional expression in *yukar* and other forms of oral tradition for hesitantly confiding a suppressed feeling.

Kamuinomi prayer to the fire divinity, performed while offering wine to a special *inau* by the late Nitani Zennosuke-ekashi. Photo by Nagai Hiroshi.

monumental *yukar*. It was time to send the owl's spirit to the land of the gods. The person who was to take the role of the *kotan kor kamui* and greet the *kotan* in farewell was Shinriki-achapo, considered the best dancer along the river branch. He was about fifty years old and, like Hotene, was from the next *kotan*, Shumkari, located at the river's mouth in the lower reaches. Holding a wine cup, Shinriki-achapo offered *kamuinomi* to the fire god; then holding a feather from the owl, he extended words of thanks to the people in the hall.

"Already having passed two summers and a winter since I came to this *kotan*, I have grown into a fine adult and, now in my second winter, am returning to the land of the gods. While I am overjoyed to return to that land where my ancestors await me, it is indeed saddening to part with all of you in the *kotan* who have taken such great care of me. I am torn equally by the desire to stay longer and the wish to return, and I truly will miss you, but it is the will of the gods that I return. How fortunate I am to be sent off with such a glorious *iyomante*. When I return once again to Ainu Moshir, I hope that it is to this *kotan* that I come. . . . "

As he gave his address, Shinriki-achapo gradually became one with the *kotan*'s guardian deity. Or rather, its spirit must have possessed him, for even his voice quality took on the character of the owl. When he named the people who had cared for him, starting with the *kotan korkur*, his face was wet with tears, inducing others in the hall to weep as well.

The farewell *tapkar* (stomping dance) that he serenely began to dance afterward was genuinely absorbing—as it should have been, since that was his real gift—and the people in the *porochise*, by now further cramped with the addition of all the children, could only watch entranced when he assumed the owl deity's very being, silently gliding above the *kotan* in his dance. The moves of the dance gradually shifted to gestures of parting. He approached the window by the seat of honor that was to be his exit, returned again and again as if hesitating to leave, and then, circling above the *kotan*, dropped two, then three tears. He thus moved back and forth six times between the window and the firepit, dancing his sorrow at parting. The sacred essence of Shinriki-achapo's seemingly divine gift of dance lay in his ability to express simultaneously his grief at leaving and his joy at returning to the realm of the gods. The movement of his wings and his face, tears streaming and nose running, skillfully presented the contrasting emotions, inviting yet more tears from the audience and making the *porochise* the site of the final place of lament for the *iyomante*.

When Shinriki-achapo danced his final steps and moved to the window, a second dancer waiting outside continued on, until he arrived at the festival altar outside. All the *ekashi* went outdoors to sit before the altar, and the austere, closing prayers began. The flames of the bonfire burned ever higher. The festival song of the women surrounded them from afar. The *kotan korkur* who had raised the owl since it was a fledgling stepped forward and sat, then gave a particularly worshipful *onkami* before chanting a prayer to celebrate the moment of its departure and to wish for safe passage. The sky, which had been cloudy since afternoon, looked as if it could start snowing at any time, and the light and sound of the bonfire in the darkness, so deep that sky and earth could not be distinguished, created an even more somber mood.

The final ritual of the owl's departure involved releasing a ceremonial arrow into the dark heavens. To ward off evil spirits, the arrow was sent far beyond the festival altar, which was decorated lavishly with *inau*, and was sucked into the endless black space as if it might truly reach the land of the gods.

The next day, our visitors from other *kotan* began to head home in groups. Especially those who had been invited from great distances were unsure when we'd meet again, and those who were elderly wept as if reliving last night's dance of parting. Among the young men and women, however, were many who had taken full advantage of this wonderful opportunity to implement various schemes for developing "relationships" significant or casual, and this could be read in their expressions and gestures as they made their farewells. Some maidens, far from seeing development, must have felt entirely neglected. Forlorn figures stood at the entrances of their houses, looking sadly after those leaving. Because Apniainu's Shipetcha Kotan was far, far away, the many gifts bestowed upon him by the *kotan korkur* were borne by a young man from the *kotan* who also served as his travel companion.

The pair of *tekunpe* I made for Unayanke was quite impres-

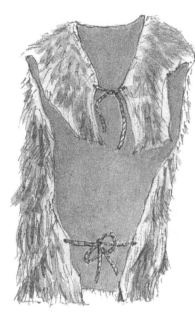

A *yukur* (sleeveless deerskin jacket).

sive, if I may say so myself. I presented them to him through Hapo. He had come to make his farewell greetings to Acha in his deerskin jacket, having changed from his formal attire to his ordinary garb. Admiring my fine embroidery by the firepit, he said, "It really looks like divine clouds about to rise." Apparently, he and Acha had promised to go together on their next fishing out to sea.

After seeing Unayanke off, Hapo whispered to me, "We'd better formally break off your engagement with Petennouk. . . . Isn't that right, Ipokash?"

DAYS OF BATTLE

About twenty days after the *iyomante*, we held a ceremony to annul my relationship with Petennouk. Our representative was Hotene's father, Acha's younger sister's husband. For the third-person intermediary, we asked our *kotan korkur*.[66] The representative for the other side was Akpet Kotan's *kotan korkur*, Petennouk's uncle.

There were relatively few problems, and we only had to offer three pieces as compensation for the annulment.[67] Umakashte had won Petennouk's heart and they had quickly become very close. As I had thought, her outgoing personality perfectly complemented his introspection. She found one excuse after another to visit Akpet Kotan, often helping Petennouk's mother with her work, and was therefore liked by his parents as well. Although she had previously been rejected by the fiancé chosen by her parents, she was highly skilled at embroidery and singing and also was quite beautiful. Three or four youths in the *kotan* had already tried to court her, with little success. She revealed only to me, her best friend, that she had allowed just one of them to visit at night by letting him in from the window of her separate quarters. Only one youth from the *kotan* had taken an interest in me, perhaps because of the delay in my first *chuppe*. But because of Hapo's strictness and because I lacked Umakashte's spirit, I had never opened my window.

We had an unusual amount of snow that year, and by the end of the "month when days get longer," or the first month of the lunar calendar, it was above knee level.[68] About that time a formal proposal of engagement came from Unayanke through three matchmakers. The matchmaker on our side was Hotene's father. Theirs was the husband of Umoshmatek, the younger sister of

66. Formalizing or canceling an engagement normally required three people: the man's representative, the woman's representative, and a third-person intermediary who was considered impartial.

67. Each part of an object was counted. For example, a sword was regarded as five pieces, counting the sheath, sword guard, blade, hilt, and sword stand.

68. In eastern Hokkaidō, snowfall generally peaks later than in the north and in the Japan Sea coast in the west. Big snowfalls often occur near spring.

Unayanke's maternal *huchi* and one of the women who had attended the *iyomante*. The intermediary for both sides was the *kotan korkur* of Unayanke's Chichap Kotan. The village head, firm in his belief that Unayanke was the river branch's best hunter and warrior, apparently had volunteered for the post.

This ceremony was followed by the comings and goings of our families between Unayanke's home and mine. I also visited Chichap Kotan with Hapo. Normally, the walk to the *kotan*, at the uppermost reaches of Chepkaunpet River, took a day in winter and a little over half a day in summer. Unayanke had two younger sisters and a little brother, who was the youngest child. One of the most reassuring things about this *kotan* was that Monashir, the best midwife along the river branch, lived there. Aunt Monashir had raised all eight of the children she bore without losing a single one. She clearly was a skilled midwife with knowledge of medicine. Moreover, she had great faculties of clairvoyance. Thanks to her, the mortality rate for children in this *kotan* was low. Hapo was especially pleased about this.

Winter had passed its peak and spring could be felt in the rays of the noontime sun. One night when the mountains had become easier to climb on *chinru* (snow sandals),[69] our Otasam Kotan dropped its guard because of the deep snow and almost faced a great calamity.

The possessor of the strongest *ue-inkar* abilities in Otasam Kotan was Horpecha-huchi, who lived with her grandson in her retirement hut at the top of the *kotan*. This retirement hut was actually within the *kotan*, not so far from the rest of us. It was about fifty steps above her son's home, and she had in her care the oldest grandson, who was about ten.

Horpecha-huchi's clairvoyance was not as powerful as Aunt

---

69. *Chinru* are ring-shaped sandals for walking on crusted snow without slipping.

Chinru (sandals for walking on crusted snow).

Monashir's, but she was the only *tusukur* in the *kotan*. Though she had retired in her old age, there had been a time when numbers of people from other *kotan*, as well as ours, sought her advice. It was this Horpecha-huchi who rescued our *kotan* from a danger that threatened our very existence.

That night the sky was clear and windless, the *kotan* brightly lit by the late half moon. I was woken late at night by Acha's sharp, quiet call to our family. I immediately sensed a fearful tension both inside and outside the house.

"Quiet, it's a *topattumi* (night attack)," he tersely ordered.[70] "Get into your warmest clothes and be ready to leave." He told my older Akihi to get his weapons and head for the *kotan korkur*'s *porochise*. Hapo was to lead other families to the evacuation area. He put on his hunting robes, and wearing his sword and knife at his hip, he prepared his bow and arrows. We tended to our belongings in the dark, without raking the hearth. My heart was beating so hard I could hear it.

I had often heard of *topattumi*, and I knew there was an evac-

70. *Topattumi* were small wars. People, usually of a different locality such as the basin of another river, who had become bandits for economic or other reasons, assaulted and plundered, or, according to oral tradition, sometimes killed, the members of another *kotan*.

uation area for emergencies, but this was the first time I'd encountered one. Since the meeting place was a secret, only people old enough to own homes knew its location. It was said that when a *topattumi* team approached a target *kotan*, its most skilled spellcaster would pray to *wenkamui* (evil spirits) and use *wen-itak* (evil chanting) to send the villagers and their dogs into a deep, magical sleep. I suddenly realized that the dogs in the *kotan* were unusually quiet.

The *katkemat* from next door came to relay the *kotan korkur*'s orders. "Until the command, women and children should stay in their *chise* and not head for the evacuation space," she said. "They must think we're a pretty wealthy *kotan* after we put on such a grand *iyomante*, although it's not really the case," she added. Her tone was surprisingly relaxed, almost as if she were smiling. Her manner helped to calm my pounding heart. Huchi prayed without pause to our ancestral gods and the various deities of the *kotan*. When the *katkemat* went home, Acha and Akihi left for the *porochise*. I heard the busy, metallic sound of people treading on the frozen snow outside as they went this way and that.

The *katkemat* soon came back with the order: "People going to the evacuation space should meet downriver at Sarushnai Pond." Hapo went to the house on our other side to relay the message. Otasam Kotan was made up of eight households, but when retirees were included, there were quite a few more houses.

Lit up by the moon, the *kotan* floated clear blue-white in the reflection of the snow. It was almost brighter than noon on a cloudy day. Just as we were about to leave our entranceway, the *katkemat* came back with a newer command, "Hold off on assembling; stay in your *chise* and keep watch a while longer."

Dressed for battle, a group of youths swiftly headed upriver. One of them was the young man who had courted me. I had never before seen him looking so dependable.

A *menoko makiri* (knife for women and girls).

Soon after they left, the *kotan* dogs began barking all at once, as if on command. Men could be heard yelling upstream. We stiffened in an effort to hear better and offered prayers to every deity we could think of, starting with the fire god. All three of us women, including Huchi, wore knives at our hips, and my little Akihi had his bow and arrows at his side. As I thought about what would happen when the enemy attacked, my body trembled involuntarily.

"Ohohohoho—y," sounded the alarm. A youth had come back from the battlefield. Hapo and I went out to look. It was my big Akihi. Standing at the center of the *kotan*, he raised his voice and announced, "Everyone, have no fear! The enemy is fleeing! Women start the *peutanke*."

Calls of *peutanke* rose throughout the *kotan*, warning the next *kotan* of the emergency. This would also serve to alarm the *topattumi* band. Hapo's "wohh-y" was the piercing *peutanke* call I'd heard during the flood. As I mimicked it, I found my eyes tearing, maybe because of the release of all my fearful tension. *Peutanke* echoed throughout the mountains that were glistening blue-white in the moonlight. With the addition of the dogs' howling, the *kotan*, till then tensely silent, was suddenly transformed into a space of sound.

Led by the *kotan korkur*, the warriors came back. By this time several of the younger boys had been sent down as messengers to each *kotan* along the river. We gathered at the *porochise*. All the *ekashi* of our *kotan*, as well as most of the *huchi*, were present. Among them was Horpecha-huchi. At the request of the *kotan korkur*, she began to explain the situation.

She had discovered the *topattumi* when telling her grandson a *uwepeker* as she wove a mat. The child, who had been listening attentively, was by then peacefully breathing in his sleep. Even though it was much later than usual, she herself didn't feel the least bit sleepy. She was almost finished with the mat and decided to complete it before retiring for the night. It was a truly quiet night; there wasn't even a crackle from the hearth, where the firewood was turning into embers.

She finished the mat and was covering the ashes to suppress the hearth fire when she sensed a strange atmosphere building outside. It may have been some kind of sound or movement of the air, or perhaps a sensation related to *ue-inkar*. She cracked opened the sacred window behind the seat of honor and peered out. What she saw made her *chikuwakka kamka oshma pekor ku=yainu* (feel like she'd been splashed with cold water).

Beneath the glow of the half moon reflecting off the snow, strangely dressed creatures were dancing quietly in a large ring. In the middle stood a man chanting spells in a low voice, while those in the circle danced soundlessly, alternately thrusting their swords and bows up into the sky and down toward the earth. Looking around the circle, she noticed that the men ranged in age from young to old, and that women and children were also present. Horpecha instantly grasped that they were *topattumi*. The women and children were necessary because the bandits would need every possible helping hand to carry away their loot. The eerie dance and chanting were part of a pre-attack ritual. According to legend, this *kamuinomi* caused blood-red fireballs to leap from the *topattumi* band into the sky above the *kotan* and circle around until the villagers and their dogs fell into a deep sleep. Seizing that opportunity, the thieves would slit everyone's throat and steal everything from the *kotan*.

"Hmm, come to think of it, none of the dogs in the *kotan* are barking. How odd," she thought, determining that the enemy's spell must already have been cast, sending them to sleep. This meant that the *ainu* must also be fast asleep.

Horpecha quietly nudged her young grandson awake. "We're in deep trouble. The night attackers I've always told you about are here. Don't make a sound—they're out by the sacred window. Go out from the dirt floor and report to the *kotan korkur* without letting them see you. Okay? You're a boy, screw up your courage. Quickly!"

Having been disciplined on a daily basis by Huchi so that he would grow up to be a respectable *ainu*, the boy immediately understood the danger and stealthily slipped out. Practically creeping through the snow, he slipped into the large house at the center of the *kotan* and awoke the *kotan korkur*.

It was thus that the *kotan* had been able to prepare for battle. At home, Horpecha offered desperate prayers to the god of fire, and about the time her grandson would have arrived at the large house, pulled out an old *tashiro* (a sword for use in the mountains). The metalwork on this sword was loose, and when shaken it clattered. From inside the *chise*, which was pitch-dark because Horpecha had covered the embers with the ashes, only the clattering sound of the sword leaked outside.

The *topattumi* band had completed its preinvasion rites and was initiating its advance into the *kotan* that should have been deep in sleep. The *chise* approached first by the man who seemed to be the leader was Horpecha's, the closest one. But hearing the sound of the sword, he came to a terrified halt. Ordering those behind him to stop, he listened for two or three breaths, then turned around and fled, commanding the others, "We're in trouble, they've got a supernatural sword. It's an *ipetam* (sword that devours human). Run!"

His voice grew louder and louder, and by the end of his command to retreat, he was shrieking. The *topattumi* band fell apart. At this moment the dogs were released from the spell and began howling all at once. The first group of emergency fighters also leaped out of the *porochise*, raising their voices in chase.

The *topattumi* band had taken the sound of the sword as that of a magic sword. The existence of an *ipetam* was fairly well known through rumor. Once drawn, even by someone without any martial skill, this sword could not help but kill someone close to it, for the sword itself wanted to suck blood. It was said that before it killed, the *ipetam* shook with the joy of the hunt and clattered. But no one knew where this magical sword was, and Horpecha had, on a sudden inspiration, exploited the rumor.

The *kotan korkur* held back the youths who wanted to pursue the bandits, saying, "Don't follow them too far. They won't return tonight. Let's gather at the *porochise* to discuss strategy."

Everyone, other than those who were sent to relay this message to the other *kotan* along the river, soon appeared. Hearing Horpecha-huchi's story, the women wept over her bravery and resourcefulness, taking turns to press her hand in gratitude. That she had stayed awake, unaffected by the spell, was perhaps due to her *ue-inkar* or *tusu* abilities.

After listening to everyone's opinions, starting with the *ekashi*, the *kotan korkur* stood up and announced his decision. "They've got about thirty people. With elders and women among them, they can't escape so quickly. To prevent their ever coming back, we will destroy them utterly. They crossed the river and ran to

the west, but it seems they came from up north, in the direction
of Rikunpet. I'd like to consult with the chief of Nuipet and lie
in wait to cut them off in a frontal assault."

Nuipet was the *kotan* above Akpet. Our *kotan korkur* was exceptionally wise and courageous, so in times of emergency such
as war, he became the leader of the entire river branch. His messengers would soon be arriving at their destinations.

The *kotan korkur* selected four of our *kotan*'s bravest men and
headed for Nuipet with them. They were not only *rametok*
(heroic), but fleet of foot and tough as well. Just in case, a second band of nine guards was organized to protect the *kotan*. Akihi was still young, so he was in the second group. Acha was appointed the leader of this group and sent Akihi and two others
to keep watch at the *chashi* along the riverbank above and away
from the *kotan*.[71] Amid all the tension, the night sky began to
whiten and the day of the battle broke. The women were kept
busy preparing emergency rations. The five men who had departed for the chase took particularly hard dried meat with
them.[72]

Around Horpecha-huchi's house, the traces of the bandits'
footsteps in the circle could be seen in the slanted light of the
morning sun. Their retreating steps continued across the frozen
Chepkaunpet River and into the woods on the opposite bank.

71. *Chashi* is generally understood as "stronghold," but researchers agree
that the word cannot be simply defined. Besides being a fort for war purposes,
it is considered to have served as a religious site, a trading post, a market, a watch-
tower, and a negotiation hall. Its use differed from era to era. See, for example,
Hokkaidō-related articles in *Nihon jōkaku taikei* (Japanese castles) (Shin-Jin-
butsuōraisha, 1980), vol. 1; Udagawa Hiroshi, *Ainu denshō to chashi* (Ainu oral
tradition and *chashi*) (Hokkaidō Shuppan Kikaku Center, 1981); Uemura
Hideaki, *Kita no umi no kōekisha tachi* (Northern sea traders) (Dōbunkan, 1990).
Concrete facts about *chashi* are yet to be found.

72. Meat treated with hot water and dried on the rack over the hearth for
a month or so was called *sakanke kam*. It was convenient for traveling.

Most of the *kotan* along the river were on its eastern side, so they must have invaded from along the mountain ridge on the west. When I thought about how our lives had barely been saved the night before, I was filled with new affection for the *kotan* and mountain range. I prayed again to the deities of the *kotan* and our ancestral gods to express my profound thanks. If Horpecha-huchi hadn't been awake under the protection of the gods, the *kotan* might by now be ravaged and soaked in blood.

But the battle wasn't over yet. We took turns sleeping to recover from exhaustion, while the *ekashi* and *huchi* prayed continuously to the fire god for the safety and victory of the assault troops.

The results of the battle were conveyed by two youths who returned late that night. One youth from our *kotan* was seriously wounded and receiving treatment at Chichap Kotan, attended by our *kotan korkur* and another youth. The injured one was Itakshir, the youth who had tried to court me. Worried, his mother was in tears, but the poisoned arrowhead had been extracted immediately and the wound treated, so his life was not in danger. Poor Itakshir. Remembering his brave, hooded form as he went into battle the night before, I considered going the next day to Chichap Kotan to help tend him. This also happened to be Unayanke's *kotan*.

The chase of the invaders described by the two young men was a ghastly battle, even though it ended in our victory. They first assembled at Nuipet, where they worked out a battle strategy under the guidance of the commander, Menkakush.[73] He selected twelve of the best warriors from all the *kotan* along the

73. It is extremely difficult to verify wartime organization in Ainu society several centuries ago. Kaiho Mineo, discussing a later era in his *Nihon hoppō-shi no ronri* (Theory of the history of northern Japan) (Yūzankaku, 1974), defines as *taishō* (colonel) the leader who oversaw the communities along a single river, and as *sōdaishō* (general) the leader who commanded a federation

A *rum* (arrowhead). The dent is for
applying *surku* (wolfsbane poison).

river. Three were from our *kotan*. The twelve
raced up the river to cut off the enemy. Naturally, one of the twelve was Unayanke, whose
martial skill was superb.

The twelve climbed over the hardened snow
along the Chepkaunpet River at incredible
speed, circled around the pass, and came upon
the enemy's path of retreat. The thirty or so
members of the *topattumi* band were fleeing
along the range of the western bank of the river,
climbing northward as predicted. The twelve lay
in wait for them by the range until the bandits
were within arrow range, then leaped out all at
once. Their first target was the younger men. Several fell with
the first round of arrows, but those who weren't hit, or who were
only slightly wounded, returned their own arrows. The women
and children ran away screaming. While the twelve stalwarts on
our side had an overwhelming advantage, the enemy also had several skilled archers. As the battle raged on, they lost about half
of their men; we also had four wounded.

---

of communities along different rivers. For example, the seventeenth-century
hero Shakushain falls into the category of general.

The largest Ainu warfare so far hypothesized is that in which Sakhalin Ainu
forces fought against the Yuan (Mongols) in the late thirteenth century. For forty
years between 1260 and 1300, it is probable that the Sakhalin and Hokkaidō
Ainu military confederacy fought against tens of thousands of Yuan troops. See,
e.g., Hora Tomio, *Hoppō ryōdo no rekishi to shōrai* (The history and future of the
northern territories) (Shinjusha, 1973); Uemura, *Kita no umi no kōekisha tachi.*
Around that time, the Yuan were defeated in Vietnam, Okinawa, and (because
of typhoons) Kyūshū.

Treating injuries was difficult. The poison would circulate unless an arrowhead was removed immediately and the flesh around it cut out. The venomous poison came from wolfsbane, which kills even a brown bear with ease.[74] Because of the need to treat the wounded, the number on our side who could fight continuously was reduced to fewer than half of the original twelve. The enemy, on the defensive and with no time to take care of their wounded, left their fallen to die.

The captain of the assault forces was the eldest son of Commander Menkakush. On careful consideration, he decided to halt the battle temporarily and consult the will of the gods.[75] Layering two pieces of honing stone, each as thick as a finger, he sliced through them with his *tashiro*. If he could cleanly cut through both, it meant that our forces were assured complete victory even if they continued fighting, while cutting through only one meant the chance of winning was fifty-fifty, and neither meant certain defeat. The result was one and a half, for he could not cut through the second stone all the way. Based on this, and the fact that he didn't want a single death on our side, he reasoned that we had punished the enemy enough and should retreat without pursuing them any farther.

74. Some say that wolfsbane was never used, because the Ainu had a common law banning the use of poison as cowardly, but a fair number of oral transmissions mention its use.

75. The description of the night attack here draws on the "Kotan no yōtō" (The magic sword of the *Kotan*), a legend told by Kimura Kimi (1900–1988) of Penakori in Biratori town and recorded by Kawakami Yūji of the same place. See Kawakami Yūji, *Saruunkuru monogatari* (Tales of Sarunkur) (Suzusawa Shoten, 1976). Kimura Kimi learned the story from her late father Sanouk (Kawakami Yūji's grandfather). The method of divination in our story here differs from that in Kimura Kimi's tale. The use of honing stones is a method used in eastern Hokkaidō.

As in Kimura's legend, many old tales have it that all invaders, from old men to little children, were killed. Some view this as a result of exaggerating the protagonist's victory through repeated tellings.

Before ceasing battle, our captain called out to the enemy, "We have an *ipetam*. The time has come for us to draw it. On guard!" Frantically seeking any opening to flee, the moment our side halted its attack, the remaining fighters on the enemy side staggered after the women and children, who had escaped earlier. On the battlefield were left eleven corpses from the enemy side. Some were still barely alive, but by the time our men started preparing them for a proper *iyoitakkote* (ritual of sending the soul off to the spiritual world), the poison had circulated and they had breathed their last.

The assault troops returned down the incline, helping the four wounded. Because Itakshir's leg was seriously injured, they carried him on a makeshift stretcher. The other three were youths from different *kotan*. It was evening when they returned to Chichap Kotan. Aunt Monashir was looking after the wounds.

When the two youths had finished their report, everyone at the *porochise* expressed feelings of relief and happiness that the battle had ended in victory. And while Itakshir's life was not endangered, we all offered words of sympathy to his mother, showing our appreciation for his bravery. The hearth fire was rekindled and we all joined in thankful prayer to the fire god.

Itakshir's parents and younger sister were planning to leave for Chichap Kotan the next morning, so Akihi and I decided to go with them. Other families also sent along people to help with any tasks resulting from the battle.

THE DAY OF YOUNG GREENS

Following the *topattumi* attack, the *kotan* along the Chepkaunpet River realized once again the necessity for training in the arts of warfare. Even the archery games played by children assumed a new intensity. Horpecha's inspiration and, more important, the powers that enabled her to ward off the enemy's *wen-itak* were esteemed highly, and she won renewed respect from people as a *tusukur*.

The social exchange between Unayanke's family and mine continued, including a joint bear hunt by the fathers and sons. With each event, there was a provision of gifts. Because we were closer to the sea, we tended to give them things like kelp. The most heartfelt present Unayanke gave me was a jewel box.[76] He knew that he couldn't begin to compete with Petennouk's nearly divine carving skills, yet he had made this with great care, and each stroke in the pattern revealed its maker's deep sincerity.

The arrival of spring was no later than usual for a winter of abundant snow, but it did take a while for the mountain snows to melt. It was not until some time after the spring prayers for the *kotan* took place that everything melted. When the first flowers of spring were in bloom, a formal engagement ceremony was held between Unayanke's and my households.[77] From our side, a robe that I had sewn, and from their side, a wine pourer and earrings were presented. The wedding date was set for a month later. At that time, Unayanke's clan would come to our home for a six-day reception at our *kotan* that included rites such as making offerings to our ancestors and performances of *yukar*. Then our clan would go to Unayanke's *kotan* for another six-day reception, after which my family would depart without me.[78]

76. Called *matsuwop* (woman's box) or *ponsuwop* (little box), this is a personal jewel box for necklaces, earrings, and so forth. It is also used as a pillow and always kept by the owner's side

77. In the world of *yukar*, one year is divided into the *sakupa* (summer year) and *matapa* (the winter year). A ritual called *kotan nomi* is held in each of the in-between seasons, i.e., in the *paikar* (spring) and *chuk* (autumn), for the purposes of giving (1) thanks for the harvest in the last *pa* (summer or winter), (2) prayers for the harvest in the coming *pa*, and (3) offerings to the ancestors.

78. Wedding rituals such as gift giving, receptions, and living together differed widely from region to region. We cannot generalize any one form as

An *etnup*
(wine pourer).

One day shortly before the wedding, Hapo and I visited Unayanke's family, naturally staying overnight in Chichap Kotan to discuss details of the reception and help with preparations. Because their *kotan* was at the highest point upstream along our river branch, snow still remained on the mountains. I was washing wine containers out by the watering place when Unayanke came by. Somewhat hesitantly, but at the same time as if with a hidden resolve, he told me he'd like to show me around the *ponto* (small lake) the next day. This lake was the source for the Chepkaunpet River and was right beneath the ridge of the mountain range. Although I had heard about this beautiful, mysterious lake, I had never seen it. According to Unayanke, the patches of remaining snow made it easy to hike there, but it would soon become difficult. While there, we could also catch trout and gather *pukusa* and other wild plants to preserve.

Thinking over his invitation, I gazed into the current of the creek rushing by forcefully because of the melting snow. I felt inclined to accept, but answered that I'd ask Hapo first. I sought

a type in Ainu society. Wedding receptions were later simplified, but long ago they seem to have lasted six or seven days.

Hosh (leg guards). This kind, used particularly in summer, is called *sakosh*.

her permission by emphasizing our purpose of exploring the little lake on the way to get trout and mountain plants. Briefly pondering this mountain excursion that would involve two days and a night in the hills, she smiled gently and said, "You go ahead and do that. I remember such a time myself." There wasn't a trace of my strict Hapo. It was as if a smile showed not only around the little wrinkles at the corners of her eyes, but even on the white hairs sprinkling her temple.

Having completed our travel preparations the night before, we left Chichap Kotan in a valley filled with faint light. Now that we were in the season of long days, members of the *kotan* were still asleep.[79] Unayanke's family was also asleep, and only Hapo got up to send us off at the doorway. Two or three stars still remained in the western sky. It was a perfect day, without a cloud in sight.

With our legs and feet protected by leg guards and sandals, we

79. The night is brief in summer in high latitude areas of Hokkaidō. It becomes light at 2:30 A.M.

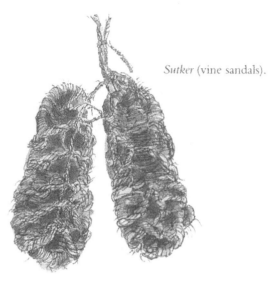

Sutker (vine sandals).

immediately headed straight upriver toward the lake.[80] The trout and vegetables would be a burden, so they would wait until the way home. Unayanke had another stop in mind as well. He wanted to show me the ridge near the lake, the site of the battlefield where they had attacked the *topattumi* band. I wasn't uninterested, but it was definitely less consequential to me than the lake. For Unayanke, however, who had played an important role at the time, the two were equally meaningful.

As the morning sun began extending its rays into the valley, there was a gradual increase in snow patches, so we changed out of our sandals into deerskin shoes.[81] As we came out of the lowest part of the valley and the climb became easier, Unayanke be-

80. Sandals were woven of grapevine skin. These are much stronger than straw sandals.

81. The soles of deerskin shoes are made so that, like seal fur on skis, the nap of the fur is directed backward, preventing slippage on the way up and helping one to slide on the way down.

gan reciting a *yukar*, though without a melody and more in the style of *uwepeker* narration. He said this was a favorite piece of the best *yukar*-telling *ekashi* in Chichap Kotan. It was one of the Ponyanpe epics, but a long one that I'd never heard before.

As usual, this Ponyanpe was without parents. He and his two brothers and younger sister were raised by an aunt. Eventually learning the reason why he had no parents, he was dragged into various intrigues and headed into battle. . . .

The little lake was in a relatively remote area, somewhat lower than the battlefield. We decided to go to the battlefield before heading for the lake. The snow was reflecting the sun's rays, and the fir forest, mixed here and there with deciduous trees, warmed from the many patches of sunlight. We removed our outermost deerskin jackets and continued climbing.

After surviving perilous situations and numerous battles, Ponyanpe finally rescued his two elder brothers, who had been imprisoned inside a large chest. In the denouement of the story, he sent his brothers back home under the protection of his guardian deity. Only Ponyanpe and his love, Princess Ishikar, remained. He escorted her to the battlefield where the fighting had been most terrible.

At this point, Unayanke switched from his *uwepeker*-style narration to the melodious singing of *yukar*. For his *repni*, he beat time against his climbing stick with a withered branch.[82]

"O my princess,
  come quickly and see.
  It is here

82. *Ekimne kuwa* (see drawing above).

An *ekimne kuwa* (walking stick
for mountain climbing).

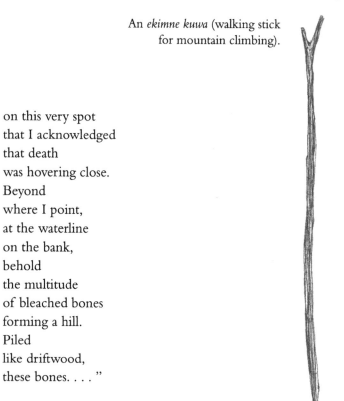

on this very spot
that I acknowledged
that death
was hovering close.
Beyond
where I point,
at the waterline
on the bank,
behold
the multitude
of bleached bones
forming a hill.
Piled
like driftwood,
these bones. . . . ”

As he sang, we arrived at the battlefield. The simultaneous progression of the *yukar* and the reality of the field made the story almost too vivid. At least there
were no bleached bones, but here and there were scattered articles of enemy clothing and shoes.

"It was in this shadow," Unayanke recalled, "that we lay in
wait and jumped them. . . . It was about here that Itakshir was
wounded. . . . I was shooting from behind this tree with my bow,
when two arrows came at me at once. One I dodged with the
tree, but I couldn't get out of the way of the other one. My
skin was grazed just lightly by the edge of the arrowhead and

feathers as the arrow flew by my neck. See, it only broke my skin. . . . "

If the arrowhead had been one fingerlength closer to his neck, Unayanke might have died in action, as it is very difficult to remove the flesh around the poison in the case of a neck wound. And what about me . . . ? Unable to stop my emotions at the mere thought, I exclaimed, "*Kuyupo* (sweetheart)!" and held tightly onto Unayanke as he continued his narration.[83] His voice muffled, he held my head to his chest. Then, laughing in a low voice, he observed, "It wasn't like this in the *yukar*," and went on.

> "Princess Ishikar
> in amazement
> pressed her nose,
> pressed her mouth,
> exclaimed in shock
> and shed
> two pure tears,
> three pure tears,
> and calling
> '*Kuyupo!*'
> prepared
> to pull me close,
> but taken aback
> by my armor,
> opened her arms,
> spread her fingers,
> and stepped away.
> At her virtuousness

83. *Kuyupo*, literally "older brother," is an eastern Hokkaidō expression, typical of *yukar*, for addressing a sweetheart (it is *yuppo* in the original *yukar* from the Iburi area). Men called their sweethearts "younger sister."

I laughed
aloud. . . . ”

Angered that Ponyanpe had laughed at her, Princess Ishikar glared at him, saying, “I so wish for us to be tender toward each other, but you keep wearing that armor. I can't get close with all that fierceness upon you. What's so amusing about that?” And so Ponyanpe removed his armor. Calling to his paternal and maternal deities in the heavens, he thanked them for lending him the armor from the land of the gods. He then proposed to return the armor as he was now returning to his home from the battlefield. Thereupon, a small breeze arose, picking up the armor and carrying it off to Kamui Moshir in a roar of thunder. Ponyanpe repeatedly prostrated himself in onkami *to the armor as it disappeared into the heavens. . . .*

Coming to our senses, we performed a simple *kamuinomi* to thank the gods for saving Unayanke and to pacify the poor young souls of the enemy who had died in battle here. A pile of silver fir pine branches lay over the place where the corpses had been gathered and buried in the snow. The snow was still there, but by midsummer the bodies would turn into skeletons.

Leaving the battlefield behind, we went down the snowy incline toward the *ponto.* Our deerskin shoes slid with ease, so we had fun gliding between the trees, using canes for balancing. Whenever the slope leveled out, Unayanke continued the *yukar* as we walked.

“Inviting
  my princess
  to my birthplace,
  I called a cloud
  and leaped high
  into the sky.
  A graceful wind

from the land of the gods,
a gently blowing wind
in my ears,
sweetly rustled
over two villages,
over three villages,
skimming two mountains,
skimming three mountains;
finally we neared
my homeland,
Tomisanpech River,
and its source,
Naruki Hill. . . . "

At that moment, we climbed over a small hill. Suddenly, a magnificent lake appeared. Speechless, I stood still.

"This is the *ponto*," Unayanke said simply. However small it was, this was the first time I'd seen such a beautiful, mysterious, dreamlike lake. More than the lake itself, the scenery around it made me imagine that this was what the land of the gods must look like. A light mist hovered over the surface, but faded away before our eyes.

According to rumor, if you left my *kotan* and headed along the seashore toward Kusur Kotan, paddled a canoe for several days along the Kusur River on the way to Kutcharo Kotan, then went deep into the forest, there was a huge *kamui-to* (lake of dead spirits) called Mashunto.[84] The lake had no entrance or exit; it was

84. Kusur, Kutcharo, and Mashunto are present-day Kushiro, Kussharo, and Lake Mashū. According to *Chiri Mashiho chosakushū* (Works of Chiri Mashiho [Heibonsha, 1973]), vol. 3, the name Mashū is considered to come from *mash-un-to* (a marsh with seagulls); this lake of dead spirits (*kamui-to*) seems to have been considered a sea that washed the shores of the spiritual world.

A *chip* (canoe).

always shrouded in mist and led to the realm of dead souls. It was said that an *ainu* who viewed the surface of the water could never return to Ainu Moshir.

This little lake, however, had no hint of a demonic character. It seemed a perfect paradise for the gods and also for the animal deities, those gods who were sent to Ainu Moshir in the form of animals. Birds were chirping and the patches of snow showed the footprints of many small animals. The *kamui* of this lake must have been a very kindhearted god. The grassland along the lakeside no longer had any snow, and although the grass hadn't grown yet, little shoots were peeking out from among the dry, withered leaves. A massive elm stood on the grassy terrain. "This is the god of the earth here," Unayanke told me and bowed ritually. It was a truly divine tree.

The sun had started to tilt now that it was noon, so we prepared for the night. We built a hut and gathered firewood. There

were no trout this high in the mountains, but we would be able
to catch any number of char on our bone hooks, and there was
an abundance of *pukusa*. As we worked, Unayanke continued
singing the *yukar*.[85]

"Like a flying bird
  swooping downward
  onto soft grass
  I landed.
  My princess
  following me
  landed
  by my side.
  So lovely
  was she
  my toughened heart that had
  led me victoriously
  through many battles
  yielded
  like green grass
  swaying
  and between my arms
  deeply

85. This *yukar* draws on a version narrated by Kannari Matsu (see glossary),
translated into Japanese by Kayano Shigeru in *Ainu minzoku bunkazai kinkyū
chōsa hōkokusho, yūkara-shiriizu* (Research reports on Ainu ethnic cultural treasures), *Yukar* series 4 (Hokkaidō Kyōiku Iinkai, 1982).
    Over one thousand *yukar* have survived, counting only those captured in
written or audio recording in Ainu. Because the researchers are few, however,
only a portion has been translated into Japanese (and a small fraction of that
into English). Kannari Matsu alone left 92 pieces, but only 16 or so have been
translated: 8 by Kindaichi Kyōsuke (published by Sanseidō); and 11 by Kayano
Shigeru (published in 18 volumes by Hokkaidō Kyōiku Iinkai). According to
Fujimura Hisakazu of Hokkai Gakuen University, these survivals amount to less
than 10 percent of those existing during the Meiji era.

deeply
I brought her close.
'My beloved,' I said,
caressing her black hair,
raising her face up,
my face close to hers,
and as my passion commanded
I kissed her.
Unmatched in bravery I may be,
but upon my face
two tears,
three tears
flowed down
moistening
my sweet princess.
Placing words in my tears,
I told her,
'Princess Ishikar,
listen closely.
I am such that
where I was born
and where I grew up
I don't know;
needless to say, I am a stranger.
Even by my kin
I was exposed
to danger of death
and spent day and night
in battle.
I endured
and withstood
and survived,
O Princess,

by taking the memory of you
as my source of strength.
Of many
beautiful maidens,
it was you alone
I cherished in my heart.
Yet I was
young in years
and without means
to convey my feelings
and so the days passed
without a kind word
from me to you,
and days passed
of agony,
fiercer than battle
this agony.'
My thoughts
I thus revealed.
My princess,
perhaps of like mind,
casting away
her maidenly pride
and modesty,
she leaned
on my arms.
'Oh my beloved,'
her voice choking,
that voice
turned into a sob,
and pure tears
she shed

while my hem
she clutched in one hand
and in appreciation of my toils
she caressed my knees
and stroked my hands.
Deeply nodding
at her gestures,
I returned to the moment
and looked about
to find from every direction
dusk settling in.
With a nod
I gazed
at my love.
'See, my princess,
these soft grasses.
Already the sun
prepares to sink;
let us cut
these grasses
for a felicitous bed
to while this night
together.
If now we return
to my castle
my siblings
will gather together
with wine and victuals
celebrating victory,
and you and I
have no hope
of time alone.

Let us talk
without restraint
of our joys
and our sufferings
over the past,
the two of us alone.'
Dreamlike
I spoke thus but
Princess Ishikar
from her tears
opened wide her eyes
and answered,
a smile of disdain
on her lips,
'What's this, Elder Brother?
Do you degrade yourself
and degrade me also?
Surely we could
talk for ten days, twenty days.
If we sleep together
will our hearts be content
from that alone?
How would we make a bed
of this grassy field?
Be patient for now, Elder Brother.'
Her words
shamed me
but I heard them through.
Her clear-cut
rejection
of the wish
I ventured to tell her
left me dishonored.

I held the sheath of my treasured sword
and about to draw it said,
'Repeat to me
those words just now.
Now of all time
when we've spoken
of our mutual feelings,
how could you,
Princess,
humiliate me thus?
When in love
what we seek,
whether god or human,
is no different,
yet you
have trodden
upon my wish
and on me and my body
heaped such shame
I wish to hide within
my wrinkles
but I too am a wisp of a stalwart
and rather than
shame myself further,
O Princess
I'll slay you,
in two and three
and with another swing
stab myself
and follow you to death.'
Her shock
greater than I'd hoped,
she gazed at me;

yet with joy,
heartfelt joy
betraying her, she replied,
'Wait now, Elder Brother.
I well know
your heart.
But are not those words
too rash?
I am just as desiring.
Listen to me
calmly.
What reason have I
to resist my beloved?
I felt this to be the time
yet being a woman
I answered
modestly.'
Speaking thus,
she stood
and letting sparkle her knife
she cropped
the tender grass,
the green grass.
In my heart
I suppressed a laugh
and watched her prepare
a bed of fresh grass,
a bed of tender grass,
and undoing my sash,
removing my hat,
wrapping them with my sword
in a belt of chain,

placed them aside.
Removing the robe
from my flesh,
I spread it open
and to that
invited my princess,
my love,
and to my chest
in my arms
closely
closely
I held her.
Her neck
on my arm,
now tenderly
I gazed up close
at the face of my beloved.
That godlike beauty
so inhuman.
I let her
turn toward me
and yet more tightly
held her close
while on her lovely lips
I pressed two kisses,
pressed three kisses.
Returning kisses
as if she'd already forgotten
her firm refusal
to prepare a bed
and in my breast
pliantly

with joy
she trembled
brimming with
two laughs and words,
three laughs and words.
In her ear
I whispered
two gentle words,
three gentle words,
and bringing together
our hearts,
bringing together our bodies,
careless of the night advancing,
be they true tales,
be they fanciful tales
we told.
I don't know when
my princess and I moved
from waking to dreaming
in blissful exhaustion
and fell into deep sleep.
What length of time
had passed I don't know;
awakening,
I raised my head
to see the sun already high
and in surprise
looked beside me
to find in my arms
my princess draped,
her breast spread open,
sweetly breathing,
sweetly sleeping.

On that godlike face
I placed two kisses,
placed three kisses,
and thus woke her. . . . "

When I woke to Unayanke's kisses, the sun was already quite high. A faint mist hung over the surface of the *ponto*. The branches of the elm tree towering high above the grassy earth were just starting to sprout young leaves.

We had been brought together, just as in Unayanke's *yukar*.

A RAINY WINTER DAY

Because Unayanke was viewed as a promising youth not only by Chichep Kotan but by the entire river branch, both of our *kotan korkur* took particular notice of our wedding. For my family, it was, therefore, an even grander occasion than when Sapo got married. And although it wasn't meant as a race, my best friend and rival in love, Umakashte, married Petennouk about a month later. Petennouk was the nephew of the *kotan korkur* of Akpet Kotan, so their ceremony was also a big affair.

Our nuptial *chise* was built by members of the *kotan* soon after I married into the community. We had our *chisenomi* a little more than two months after the wedding, at the end of summer, when the salmon season was soon to start and the *udo* berries were turning black.

Several days after the celebration, I unexpectedly encountered Aunt Monashir's famed midwifing abilities. I bumped into her near a bridge at a pond close to our *chise*. "My, it's been a while, hasn't it?" she said cheerfully as she clasped my hands. I had gotten to know her before my marriage, but we hadn't seen each other since a month after the wedding. During our celebration she had been away, tending to a birthing at a *kotan* down river.

"Let's see," she teased me, placing her left hand on my belly, "it wouldn't surprise me if you were with child by now." Reddening, I protested, "Oh, not yet." But she was already saying, "My goodness, it's no joke, you're pregnant. Take good care of yourself."

Although I thought it couldn't possibly be, I couldn't reject out of hand what this eminent midwife had said to me. I reflected that my *chuppe* did seem to be late, but I wasn't experiencing morning sickness. Half believing her, yet uncertain that even the best midwife could tell from a light touch over clothing, my doubt was stronger than my faith. When we parted, she said as if she had read my every shift in thought, "Come see me when the moon changes." She spoke as if this were as natural and inevitable as the moon returning to the same shape a month later.

She was right. My morning sickness started soon after, apparently later than usual. It was said that her *ue-inkar* ability also was powerful, so perhaps she had something beyond her touch to help her. Completely convinced of her abilities, I went to visit her. Placing a robe on my belly as I lay flat, she put her left hand below and inspected me from outside my underrobe. "Hmm, hmm. It's a healthy baby," she said. "Nothing to worry about." Then she added, "Maybe just a bit overdeveloped." Apparently her left hand was superb at diagnosis, and her right hand at treatment. "I can't say clearly yet, but I think it's a boy," she muttered almost to herself, and finished her examination.

When I went home to my parents, Hapo made me a *ponkut* (pregnancy belt).[86] Acha displayed it to the fire deity and prayed, "My second daughter, thanks to you, has grown to be a fine woman and is carrying my grandchild. I will have her wear this

---

86. *Ponkut* are worn to prevent miscarriage and, more important, as a prayer for a smooth birth. According to Aoki Aiko, *mour* (a woman's underrobe) also helped prevent miscarriage. The belt of a *ponkut*, about two inches wide, goes

ponkut, on which you have bestowed your protective powers. Please watch over her to make sure that she gives birth to a healthy child and that our descendants prosper."

My pregnancy taught me how reassuring Aunt Monashir's presence in the same *kotan* was. I now understood why Hapo was so pleased about it. Because Aunt Monashir was in the neighborhood, I could visit her easily and hear in detail how my baby was doing. Her prediction was that the baby was due around the time of the "rains that wash bear cubs" (*kimun-kamuipo hurayep*).

The salmon catch this year was not as abundant as it had been the last year or two, and while we had enough to get through the winter, we could not eat as much as we liked. But the capelin that our whole family went down to the mouth of the river to catch was plentiful, so our overall intake of fish was good.[87] Once the snows were upon us, Unayanke demonstrated what an exceptional hunter he was. Except when there were no deer in the area, he brought back just as much as we needed; it was almost as if we raised our own.

As my due date approached, my single worry increased. My baby was developing too quickly; the bear spell seemed not to have worked.[88] Aunt Monashir told me, "If things go on like this, the baby will be gigantic, so don't eat too much." But, sadly, I was unable to fight off my appetite.

One day after the cold had passed its peak and the days were lengthening, we had a day of wintry rain that seemed like a prank of the weather deity. The "rains that wash bear cubs" had finally

---

around twice and is tied in front. A piece of the dried intestine of either a bear or a dog (animals with easy births) was often placed inside.

87. Capelin do not swim to the upper reaches but stay in swarms near the rivermouth, and only for several days. During those days, families from all the *kotan* along the river gathered and made temporary sheds around the rivermouth.

88. Bear cubs are generally small and they are born easily, whether brown or polar bear. Brown bear cubs are about the size of an adult fist.

come. I went into labor that morning, after breakfast, as surely as if Aunt Monashir had been consulting with the weather deity through her *ue-inkar*. Unayanke ran to tell her, then continued on to Otasam Kotan to notify my family. His Hapo looked after me, his two younger sisters assisting her.

Aunt Monashir, who had been worried about the size of the baby, showed up immediately, but calmly reassured me, "There is no tiding yet, so there's nothing to fuss about.[89] It's your first birth, so it's going to take time." She commenced praying to Uwarikamui (the deity of childbirth). Then, removing my *ponkut* but leaving my underrobe on, she placed both hands on my belly and stroked it slowly, explaining, "I'm greeting the baby." Spreading the palms of her hands and touching her thumbs together while turning her other fingers downward, she caressed my belly from top to bottom. At my lower abdomen, she slid her left hand from left to right, then stroked first leftward with both hands, then right.

Ever since becoming pregnant, I had always asked her to explain her observations in detail, so now, before I even asked, she told me, "There's nothing to worry about, but at this rate, it'll be a breech delivery. It's a breech baby boy.[90] This isn't anything unusual, it's just a matter of whether to turn the baby around so he comes out normally, or let him come out as he is."

She examined whether the baby's legs were close together, or if they were crossed. Although it was rare for a baby's legs to be together, it made it easier to turn the infant around. Crossed legs sometimes made the task difficult enough that it was better to let the baby come out upside down. Placing her right hand where the baby's head was and her left slightly to the right side of my

89. "Tiding" means the breaking of the water.
90. In the last month, Aoki Aiko could predict with absolute accuracy the sex of a fetus.

A *mour* (female undergarment). This sample is made of cotton, but formerly *mour* were made of deerskin, which was soft and easy on the skin. The front is sewn together.

lower belly (that is, where the baby's feet were), Aunt Monashir lifted the index finger of her left hand, and, pressing with the fingertip, checked on the situation. "Whenever a baby's the least bit malformed," she commented, "I can feel pain right to the bone of my finger."

She found from her examination that the baby's legs were to-gether, and decided to turn him around for a regular birth.[91] Nat-

91. According to Aoki, the cross-legged position is more frequently seen in boy babies. For a breech birth, it is also said that the cross-legged position is easier.

urally, the question of the position of the legs was only one of the factors affecting her decision. For example, it was difficult to turn a baby around in a mother who had a short torso or a tight uterus, so in those cases, babies were allowed to come out as they were. Fortunately I had a long torso, and because I had no other complications, Aunt Monashir anticipated no problem.

She started the task of rotating him. Outwardly, it didn't look like she was using any special techniques. According to her explanation, babies moved on their own periodically, and she was just inducing the rotation by assisting the spontaneous movement. She therefore pressed with her hands only when the baby moved and never forced any kind of movement. She usually had one palm at the back of the baby's head and the other at his buttocks, and depending on the situation, turned him left or right. When the baby kicked his legs straight, she placed her hands there as support, then made sure he didn't rebound afterward.

Whenever he moved, I felt a light pain that was distinct from the pain of labor, and my breathing changed, signaling Aunt Monashir to place her hand in support. I was exhaling through my nose, sometimes moaning softly, but she told me, "Breathe with your mouth open." This was so my uterus wouldn't tighten and affect the rotation.

By this method, she said, it was not unusual for the process to take half a day; in particularly slow cases, up to three days; or in exceedingly rare cases, five days.[92] It eased the pain whenever she placed her hands on me. That day, the baby's movements started to calm down around the time that the sun moved into the western sky. My labor cramps had stopped, so Aunt Monashir left for home with the instruction, "If he starts moving again, come get me."

---

92. Time was spent on rotation so as not to cause pain to the pregnant woman.

Hapo arrived around dusk. She brought kelp and refined millet as a gift, and gave some of the kelp to two women from the neighborhood who had come to help. Hapo, who knew not only my mother-in-law but both of the neighbors, took each of their hands in greeting, hugged them, and said in a slightly teary voice, "How have you all been doing? Thank you so much for your help with my daughter."

That night, I wasn't visited by too much *maukar* (pain),[93] so I slept unexpectedly well, but from dawn the next day, the baby became quite active. Aunt Monashir, who came soon thereafter, continued her rotating technique with care. Shortly before noon, the baby turned right over with its head in the low position normally assumed at birth.

Now we just had to await the real labor pains. Perhaps because I was so anxious about the baby's overdevelopment, Auntie told me stories—whether true or false, I don't know—of other babies that she'd safely delivered, and emphasized that there was nothing to worry about.[94]

Authentic labor began as darkness set. The day had been fair after "the rains that wash bear cubs" stopped, but around evening, the chill returned; and by dark, powdery snow flurries had begun. After turning my baby over, Aunt Monashir never left my house. So when labor started, she immediately sat before me and, in a quiet voice, offered a new *inonnoitak* (chanted prayer) to the deity of childbirth.

"We have the tiding, and it should be soon, so hold onto the *nuwap tar* (birthing rope)," Aunt Monashir ordered.[95] I gripped

93. *Maukar* is labor pain in a broad sense, including that caused by the baby's kicking.

94. The largest baby Aoki delivered weighed 6,825 grams (15 lbs., 2 oz.).

95. According to Aoki, holding the birthing rope in a sitting position is inappropriate for various midwifery techniques and also harms the uterus. The

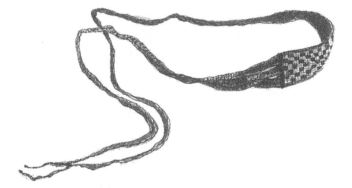

A *tar* (carrying rope), called *nuwap tar* if used for delivery.

the rope hanging from the beam, and lying on my back, I prayed earnestly to the fire deity and the ancestral gods for a safe birth.

The labor cramps came like waves, in regular intervals. The tautness in my abdomen gradually came more frequently. "Don't push yet," she instructed me, checking inside with just one finger. "Everything's okay. You've got a relaxed *mak ta apa* (birth passage)."[96] As the intervals between labor cramps shortened, each wave became longer, and the pain shifted to my hips. Aunt Monashir constantly gave me directions about how to breathe. "Don't hold your breath. Breathe through your mouth. Exhale in quick succession. . . . That's right."

The baby, who didn't move too much during the pains, tended

midwifery handed down to her prescribes lying supine. However, she encourages the pregnant woman to touch the rope right before birth, because the Ainu believe that *chise katkemat* (the mistress deity of the house) descends the rope to help with the delivery.

96. According to Aoki, a birth will be difficult if the feel is rough like the inside of the stomach of a ruminating animal (deer or cow), easy if it feels smooth and soft.

to shift about as the waves subsided. When labor became continuous and my *apa* became tautly stretched, I felt full of something hot and big. Auntie placed her foot against my buttocks.[97]

"Okay, it won't be much longer. . . . You may push. . . . Okay, push. Exhale all the way. . . . Don't rest, keep exhaling. . . . Exhale now, more. . . . "

Suddenly, the tension in my belly disappeared. Energy seemed to ebb out of me. I felt the sensation of something warm and watery flow out. "He's out!" Auntie said. I heard this as if it were a message from the heavens, and I began to drift. I remember his first cry and everyone moving busily about as if in a dream, but I apparently lost consciousness soon after.

When I came to, I was surrounded by the celebratory smiles of Unayanke, Hapo, my parents-in-law, and the two neighboring *katkemat*.

"Goodness, what a huge baby boy."

"I've never seen such a gigantic baby."

"He was a bit too big, I'm so glad you came out of it all right," Hapo's voice was wavering. With her words, my hazy consciousness suddenly returned to the real world. As Hapo clutched my hands, I found myself overwhelmed with emotion, my tears flowing like a rapids.

While I was unconscious, Aunt Monashir had taken great measures to save me from danger. Hapo's teary words of happiness had a meaning I discovered only after Aunt Monashir and the neighborhood women later described the situation to me. Even as she told me, "Don't worry," Aunt Monashir herself had been experiencing heavy stress. This was probably the second biggest baby she'd ever delivered. During the delivery, she was going to have to exercise her skills at the highest level. Not only

97. For Aoki's description of this process, see p. 73.

The technique used for the delivery of an oversized baby. The middle and index fingers press the urethra, while the thumbs work to prevent tearing the perineum.

would she have to prevent abdominal hernia and press the tail-bone up to open the pelvis, but she also had to prevent a urethral hernia and avoid or diminish the tearing of the perineum.

To prevent hernia of the urethra, she had to press closed the outer urethral meatus from the left and right with the middle fingers of both hands with the fingertips touching. At the same time, she had to press her left and right thumbs against each other and place them on the perineum. From this position, she had to spread the perineum open left and rightward, then slide her thumbs downward while separating them. At this point, the baby's head was pushing open the *apa*, so all this was helping him come out. If she pushed too far down, she would hit bone, so she had to press in, under the bone, while closing the space between her thumbs. When she pressed, the *apa* opened up completely and the baby emerged. While performing all of these actions, she was also directing my breathing. Thanks to her finger dexterity, the tear in my perineum was minimal, despite the size of my baby, and in two days it had healed.

The real danger lay in expelling the afterbirth. There was nothing unusual about the placenta itself, and she tended to me with sagebrush cotton soaked in the sap of *raspa* (a kind of deutzia). In pressing the cotton, Aunt Monashir's fingertips were also in position to hold my rectum in place. At the same time, her right hand pressed from right above my pelvic bone so as to guide the shrinkage of the uterus.

The work of her left hand stopped ordinary bleeding after birth. In my case, however, the bleeding didn't stop. It continued to flow from between the spaces in her left hand. At this rate, the abnormal loss of blood was life-threatening. Aunt Monashir yelled out directions to the women around her. "Press the blood vessels in her arms and legs!" The frantic women didn't even know how to press blood vessels. "Calm down!" she sharply scolded them. She had them straighten out my arms and legs, instructed them on the position of arteries, then had them push down hard. She slapped the cheek of one woman who panicked. The bleeding stopped in about the time that it takes two torches to burn, in twenty or thirty minutes.[98]

The baby was perfectly fine, so they cut the umbilical cord, wiped him clean with spittle, and sucked out the mucus in his mouth, all regular procedures.[99] To clean out his stomach, they soaked the juice of grated butterbur roots in sagebrush cotton, and placing it against his mouth so that he would suck induced him to spit up.[100]

Between the birth and the uproar while I bled, Unayanke's father desperately prayed to the fire and childbirth gods at the firepit in the main house. Unayanke also prayed, ready to serve

98. The torches were made of white birch bark, called *tatushpe*.

99. According to the old method Fujimura Hisakazu heard from old women in Urakawa and Shiranuka, the cord was stroked to push out the contents, then was tied at two places with thread from nettle or *ohyō*, then cut with an obsidian blade. Cleaning the baby with spittle is an old eastern Hokkaidō method Fujimura heard about. As far as Aoki Aiko heard from her mother, a tree-bark basin had long been used in Biratori for the first bathing. The umbilical cord was tied with thread from the inner skin of the staff tree, then was cut, also with obsidian.

100. This is a method in Urakawa and Shiranuka that Fujimura heard about. The techniques of preventing the tearing of perineum and stopping the flow of blood are based on what I learned either directly from Aoki or from Nagai Hiroshi, who also interviewed her. The slapping episode is also based on fact.

whenever a man's help was needed. By the time I regained consciousness, everything was over.

My tears flowed again when my mother-in-law held my big baby out to me. For a few moments, I couldn't even make out the features in his face. Aunt Monashir and the women's voices continued in conversation as they laughed cheerfully.

"Wow, Aunt Monashir, you really slapped hard!"

"Don't you tell lies. When did I slap you?"

"Ha ha ha. Look at that, she was in such a tizzy herself she doesn't even realize she hit you."

"It's true, Aunt Monashir. See, she has a bloody handprint on her cheek."

"Oh my goodness, it really is true. I'm so sorry."

The sounds from outside suggested that a blizzard was starting.

A MIDSUMMER DAY

Our first son was given the nickname Pasekur (the Heavy One). This not only indicated his size but also carried a meaning of dignity and importance. Pasekur was large, but he was also healthy. After passing two summers without experiencing anything like an illness, he arrived upon his third summer near the end of his second full year.

Around this time a few people were journeying by boat from the Chepkaunpet River for trading. Some headed for Chupka (northern Kuriles), but the usual destination was Samor-moshir ("country close by," i.e., mainland Japan).[101] Iron pots, lacquerware, and swords were usually passed from Ainu to Ainu, but lo-

---

101. Ainu trading boats appeared in Honshū over six hundred years ago, as indicated in old documents, e.g., the *Tosa ōrai* (Introduction to the Tosa Port) dating from the 1330s. In Tsugaru province, Sotogahama and Tosaminato were representative examples of ports where trade with the Ainu was conducted.

Reinforced canoes. The carved wood portions of canoes unearthed from the bank of the Yūfutsu River (Youth Center, Tomakomai city).

cals could also go on long trips to obtain articles directly. They took as exchange items the pelts of seal, sea otter, brown bear, and deer; eagle feathers for arrows; and bear innards for medicine. Sometimes the *kotan korkur* went, but often it was an adventurous man who had saved up exchange items. Usually several family members or close relatives went westward together on the summer sea, steering a reinforced canoe.[102] A group of friends could simply invite each other along, but usually there was at least one person with expertise.

Near the end of summer, smallpox suddenly broke out all over

102. A large, shallow, canoe-shaped boat reinforced by boards around the planks so as to cope with rough seas. Among the five canoes unearthed in 1961 on the outskirts of Ichinuma in Tomakomai were some boats of this type. The longest was 9 yards in length and 1 yard in width, with small holes for attaching boards. The radiocarbon dating of a pole that was unearthed with the boats suggests that the artifacts are about seven hundred years old.

the Chepkaunpet River. It was rumored that some members of Shumkari Kotan, at the mouth of the river, had gone trading and brought it back from Samor-moshir. Because interaction among all the *kotan* was heavier in summer, the infection spread extremely rapidly, and I hadn't heard the rumors yet when Pasekur caught it. I did sense some danger, however. A sudden diarrhea had spread among the infants of Shumkari Kotan, and among the several who died was Hotene's daughter. Hotene had gotten married less than a year after me, and her baby was about a year and a half old. My cousin's grief was immense.

It was the day after I heard her news. I was returning in the evening from the millet fields by the riverbank with the older of my two younger sisters-in-law. My mother-in-law, who was watching anxiously over Pasekur as he slept, blurted out the moment she saw me, "I've sent Sikosanke to get Aunt Monashir. Pasekur threw up and has a fever." He had a moistened cloth on his forehead. Around noon he had suddenly become listless, and he had had several bouts of diarrhea, which started to contain blood. I wondered if some poisonous mushrooms had gotten mixed in with his lunch, but they said they hadn't fed him any mushrooms. When I touched him, his fever was indeed very high. I immediately recalled the epidemic in Shumkari Kotan and the death of Hotene's child. Both my father-in-law and Unayanke were away, having gone close to the *ponto* at the source of the river to catch trout.

Soon, the younger of my sisters-in-law, Sikosanke, returned. "Aunt Monashir was at Chikishma's house," she said, "so I went there to get her, and she said she'd be over as soon as she finished treating Chikishma's baby." Chikishma's house was at the bottom end of the *kotan*. Her baby's symptoms apparently were very similar to Pasekur's. It seemed that this must indeed be an epidemic.

Aunt Monashir arrived after a glowing sunset and ensuing twilight. Quickly examining Pasekur, she said, "Bring me two rocks.

I'm going to grind this down, so I want a flat one and one that's easy to grip. It'd be ideal if the flat rock had a dip in the center." So saying, she pulled a small root about the size of a cowpea out of her bosom.

My mother-in-law observed, "That's *kinaraita* (agrimony)."

"Yes," Aunt Monashir responded as she washed five or six sprouting sections of the *kinaraita* root. "I want everyone to remember this. It can save lives when there's diarrhea with children's dysentery." We already had rocks for mashing, so my older sister-in-law brought them from the *pu* (storehouse). Rinsing the rocks, too, Auntie placed one root on it, pounded it flat, and wrapped it in a lightweight fabric. As she worked, she muttered, "Doesn't look good, this epidemic," and told us that Chikishma's baby almost hadn't made it.

Tying the cloth around the *kinaraita* with thread, she handed it to me, saying, "Here, give this to your little boy to suck."

Gazing at me with his vacant, feverish eyes, Pasekur extended his hands toward the cloth I held out to him. "Good boy, Pasekur. It's going to taste pretty bad, but it'll make you better, okay? Come on, suck on it, just like mama's milk." He grimaced with the first few drops, but understanding the significance of the medicine, diligently continued sucking.

Meanwhile, Aunt Monashir had placed about three stalks' worth of newly sprouting roots from the parent root of the *kinaraita* in a small pot and boiled them in the hearth. Just as they started to boil, Pasekur announced that his tummy hurt. "It hurts, eh?" she asked with a smile. "Does it feel like it scrapes against you?" Pasekur nodded, and soon wanted to go to the bathroom, so I hurriedly took him to the entranceway. His feces were muddy in texture and black. His expression relaxed somewhat.

The boiled medicine was ready, so we let it cool and gave Pasekur more to suck. Once again, he felt pain and wished to go to the bathroom. This time his feces had a bit of egglike color.

He looked even more at ease, and the sparkle in his eyes returned. His fever also seemed to have decreased a bit. To prevent dehydration, we also gave him cooled water that had been boiled. Soon after, he fell asleep. Relieved, we all had a late dinner with Aunt Monashir. On leaving, she instructed me to give Pasekur some more medicine when he awoke, whether it was late at night or early in the morning.

My mother-in-law and I went to bed after praying fervently to the fire god and ancestral deities to save Pasekur's life. Sensitive even to the slightest change in Pasekur's breathing as I slept at his side, I woke many times, but he slept deeply until the eastern skies began to whiten. From the moment he awoke, his movements showed that he had recovered. I immediately gave him some medicine. He again experienced stomach pains, but these were lighter, and his feces were close to normal.

During this epidemic at least one, and as many as three or four infants, died in every *kotan* along the river except ours. That Chichap Kotan was an exception testified to the efficacy of Aunt Monashir's emergency treatment.

My father-in-law and Unayanke, returning from trout fishing and hearing the whole story, offered prayers of thanks to the fire deity, then presented Aunt Monashir with an ample gift of trout.

HUCHI'S DAY OF REST

It was eight summers since Pasekur was born, and six years since Aunt Monashir's herbal treatment foiled the evil spirits of illness who had tried to take him away. We were soon to see the first frost of the year.

During this time my second son was born, my father-in-law was seriously wounded in a fight with a nasty brown bear, and the older of my sisters-in-law married and moved to the *kotan* downriver from us. One of the most memorable personal events for me was my older Akihi's marriage to Petennouk's younger sister. To put it another way, Petennouk's sister came into my own family home. When I heard of the engagement, I thought it must be a joke. But by the beginning of summer last year, it had become a reality, so I heard news of Petennouk every once in a while.

After his marriage to Umakashte, Petennouk withdrew into himself more and more. But Umakashte loved him no less dearly for that. Perhaps still competing with me, she also had two children. Theirs seemed to be a very happy household. Petennouk continued to be a poor hunter, but his carvings were more skilled than ever, and his name came to be known beyond the river. He sometimes received commissions, for which he was well paid in salmon and dried meat.

When I went home for my brother's wedding, Huchi seemed to have weakened dramatically. When she related *uwepeker* to Pasekur, not only was her voice without life, but she omitted details and simplified the stories she used to tell me. Her hands were uncertain at spinning thread as well. Nothing in particular was wrong with her, but she was getting far into her eighties and her body had worn out. Because we didn't want her receiving a summons from the realm of the gods, I never mentioned that possibility, but I could tell that Hapo shared the same worry. Whenever I came home, bringing with me one of her favorite foods, Huchi cried from happiness and tried to embrace me warmly the way she used to when I was a child. She was easily moved to tears.

However, Huchi's weak condition didn't worsen. That autumn I began to think that if she took it easy, perhaps she could remain in Ainu Moshir for the time being. But on the morning of the first frost my younger Akihi came to bring news that Huchi's condition was critical. It was the peak of the salmon season and the whole family was together in the salmon-fishing hut. We decided that I should go back with Akihi. Unayanke and the family would follow after finishing up.

As we ran downriver along the Chepkaunpet, the summer grass growing high on both sides of our path, I prayed to the gods for one last chance to see Huchi alive. She was always so gentle, gentler than Hapo. She was strict but kind. Huchi, who had always told us *uwepeker* and *kamui yukar* as we fell asleep, and who had raised me through maidenhood, had seemed like some kind of *kamui* sent from heaven to care for me. I couldn't imagine a day without Huchi, and she in turn poured into me all of her stories and knowledge of living. I think it must have been shortly before the day of my *chuppe* that I told my younger Akihi a tale I had learned in its entirety. Huchi, who was listening nearby, cried with joy and said, "Well, I guess that all the stories your grandma knows have been transmitted to you, Opere." In truth, the number of stories Huchi transmitted to me easily surpassed three hundred, and I have retained them all.

We traveled silently and quickly downriver; my head was filled with memories of shared moments with Huchi and, at the same time, a children's song that Pasekur and his friends had been singing about three days ago. They had no relation to each other, but no matter how I brushed the words away, I couldn't keep them out of my head. "*Emushranke tamaranke, emushranke tamaranke* (Drop your sword, drop your jewels, drop your sword, drop your jewels). . . . "

Two summers before my older Akihi's wedding, Huchi had begun living in her own retirement hut. It was a small *chise,* but hardly thirty steps from the main one. It was just far enough away that if there were a fire, it wouldn't spread.

We arrived around noon. The house was still and not a voice could be heard. My heart pounding, I burst into the entranceway. Rising in unison, cries of *raichishkar* (wail for death) and the weeping of Hapo, Sapo, and my aunt confronted me. I was too late. I pushed through the circle of family members who were stroking Huchi's body and drowning themselves in *raichishkar*. When I saw Huchi's peaceful face, I couldn't stop the welling up of *raiparpar* (lamentation). As my father shut Huchi's eyes and shifted her jaw, he softly told me, "She became a person of Kamui Moshir just now. It was truly a death provided by the gods, like an old tree falling naturally. It was a *kamui-onne* (natural death). It was a *pirka-onne* (a good death)."

I touched Huchi's face and held her still-warm hand. As I shed tears of *raichishkar*, I spoke gratefully of the love that she had given me. I spoke of my earliest memories of the firepit on the days of the blizzard, of Huchi holding a young Akihi, singing a soothing lullaby, or telling Sapo and me the tale of Pananpe and Penanpe as she spun thread. The lively expression Huchi had at such times came back to my mind's eye as clearly as the scene, just days ago, of a school of salmon as they broke the surface of the water on their way upstream. Images of how people and things were placed around the fireplace in those earlier times floated nostalgically before my eyes.

If I thought about it, this was in fact a celebratory moment. Ekashi died shortly before I was born; Huchi's life had lasted another thirty years. I was saddened by her death, but she herself had recently been half-joking that she didn't have any regrets and that the only thing left to anticipate was seeing Ekashi again in Kamui Moshir. Just as Acha had said, hers must have been a natural death. Tomorrow night, therefore, a *yukar* would be performed to celebrate her departure.[103]

Though we were all grief-stricken, we had to begin making arrangements for Huchi's safe departure to Kamui Moshir. From

103. *Yukar* were never performed in the event of early or accidental death but celebrated a natural death at the end of a long life, as in this case.

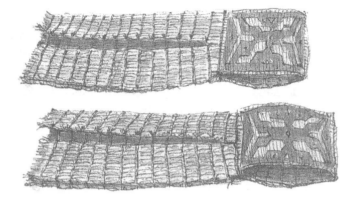

Raikur-ker (shoes for the dead).

the neighborhood, the first people to pay their last respects had begun arriving. A mat was spread near the main seats and close to the entrance. Huchi's body was laid with her head in the direction of the honored seat at the far end of the hearth. Outside, we had to prepare, first, an evening meal for the guests, then dumplings and delicacies for the deceased to take on her journey. Hapo had secretly provided for things such as hand and leg guards for Huchi's funeral dress, but we would be up all night making the *raikur-ker* (shoes for the dead) and underrobe, as well as other garments for her to take with her. We also needed to embroider her funeral clothing. Hapo took charge of assigning tasks, while young men and women among our relatives went to each *kotan* as messengers to announce the sad news. Men went to the faraway *kotan*, women to those nearby. People from the same *kotan* made their condolence calls early to help with the work.

By and by, the *kotan korkur* appeared with *kotan* members other than our relatives, who were already gathered. Actually, the *kotan korkur* was a distant relative on my mother's side. But if one were to count all those who were remotely related, it would include just about everyone along the river.

The village head, who was ten years Acha's senior, first offered prayers to the fire god. During his prayer, the others sat one by one at Huchi's bedside, each of them stroking her with one hand as they raised their voices in *raichishkar* and holding back tears with the other hand.[104] The wails of the women gradually became a melody that brought fresh tears from all of us. Having finished his prayers to the fire god, the village head chanted to the chief mourner, then approached Huchi's pillow. Shedding tears of *raichishkar,* he continued his words of condolence with a quiet refrain.

"Poor Huchi,
  until recently
  you were so well, Huchi.
  It didn't even occur to me
  that this might happen
  today.
  Poor Huchi,
  what can I say
  I have no words.
  Since the time I was young,
  always kind,
  you played with me.
  You told me
  uwepeker and
  kamui yukar.
  Even after I became an adult
  you let me confide in you.

---

104. The mourners try to avoid letting tears fall on the body.

As the chief of the *kotan*
I received endless help and
encouragement. . . . "

The genuine words of appreciation from the *kotan korkur* lasted quite a long time. Afterward, he exchanged greetings with Acha, who formally asked him to preside as leader over the funeral rites. Because the village head was an obliging and virtuous individual, they had already agreed informally about this beforehand, should the worst happen.

As evening fell, people from nearby *kotan* continued to call. Generally, each village head came first, bringing with him the people of his *kotan*.[105] The *raichishkar* of these people accumulated, one after another, and the melody of their lamentations spread continuously from the house throughout the *kotan*.

My cousin Hotene had come just before Huchi drew her last breath. Hotene's mother was Acha's younger sister, and Huchi's daughter. Hotene loved Huchi no less than I did, and her eyes were red from weeping. The death of her first child from dysentery was the deepest sadness she had experienced in her life, but Huchi's death came second. Hotene had since given birth to another daughter, who was about to turn three. She was also pregnant with her next child. We were very close but hadn't seen each other for a long time, and as we embroidered the funeral clothes, we not only reminisced about Huchi but gossiped about friends and acquaintances.

---

105. Children, even of the family lamenting a death, were normally cared for by relatives instead of attending the funeral. Children were thought to be vulnerable to the dead spirit, and contact was avoided so that they would not be affected later.

Some details of this funeral are based on what I learned from Nishijima Teru (1898–1988) of Nioi in Biratori town about her experience when her grandmother passed away.

On reflection, we realized that we were getting to a good age. Such adventures of our youth as the big *iyomante* festival were now a topic of conversation we enjoyed with a mixture of fondness and embarrassment. Itakshir, who had carried an unrequited love for me and been wounded the day of the battle, was now the father of one child. Itakshir; and of course Petennouk, whom I had rejected; Umakashte, my rival in love but also my best friend; and Unayanke, who arrived in the evening, all joined in to help with various tasks.

Mourners from relatively faraway *kotan* continued coming the following day. Those of us who had stayed up all night making the funeral clothes took turns catching a little sleep throughout the morning. During that time everything in the *chise* was done backward. The mats were laid out in reverse; robes were worn inside out; firewood, which was usually burned from the part near the root, was burned from the wrong end.[106] Relatives who lived in *kotan* far from the river continued arriving until about noon, while relatives from Huchi's maternal line cleaned and dressed the body.[107] The men took responsibility for making a burial marker, digging the grave, and cutting the grass along the path to the grave site.

When the final meal and drinking with the deceased came to an end, the main event of the formal wake was performed in the form of the *oina*, or *yukar* sung about and by a woman.[108] To mark the completion of Huchi's natural life span, Unkatuye-huchi, the

---

106. The spiritual world had landscapes and environments similar to the human world. The dead were eventually reborn in the human world as different individuals. Everything was the opposite, however, including day and night, winter and summer. This was why everything was reversed during a funeral.

107. At this time, the *ishma* (woman's inner belt; see p. 144), too, was changed to a new one for the dead. It was handled only by women of the maternal line and by the woman's husband.

108. Also called *matyukar* in eastern Hokkaidō.

best woman performer in the entire region along the river, was invited specially from Nuipet Kotan. Unkatuye-huchi was the elder sister of the Nuipet Kotan chief.

Because this female *yukar* was reserved for funerals, the tale was created only from the beginning to the middle.[109] This was the first time I had heard it, but for people of Hapo's generation and older, it was one they had heard at several funerals. The story is about a heroic single woman in search of a husband. Because there is no suitable man in the *kotan* she heads, she journeys to find one. She meets her ideal man, one with powerful supernatural powers, but though she uses every device to tempt him, his younger sister obstructs the heroine. It was truly fascinating, definitely a *yukar* that one wished to hear to the end.

The following day was the third day after Huchi's death. At last it was time for the *iyoitakkote* (requiem) and funeral procession.[110] The time for true farewells had come. Before the *iyoitakkote*, there was a final meeting between Huchi and her nearest relatives. Even though this was Huchi's celebratory journey after having lived out her natural life, Sapo, Hotene, and I felt only sadness and wept. Huchi, please take our *peker-nupe* (pure tears) and *peker-etor* (pure nose water) with you to Kamui Moshir.

First, the *kotan korkur*, acting as priest, presented a sonorous and solemn *iyoitakkote* to the fire god.

"O guardian deity of the great earth
you who descended from heaven
when you, the ancestor of this woman,

109. An unfinished *yukar* is an expression of the rebirth of the dead. In some regions (e.g., Saru), the *yukar* at a funeral was narrated until the end so that the spirit would not return wishing to hear the rest.
110. Literally, *iyoitakkote* means "to offer speech to the dead."

ascend to heaven
to be near the gods. . . . "

The *kotan korkur*'s prayer continued for some time as he requested
the god to watch over Huchi's well-being on her journey.[111] It
was now time for Acha, who was both her chief mourner and
her son, to send Huchi an *iyoitakkote*.[112]

Acha sat by Huchi's side, and although hers was a peaceful
death, there was no diminishing his feelings for his mother. For
a while, his heart was so full that he could not speak. After clearing his throat several times, he began in a voice that was a shade
weaker than usual.

"The *kotan korkur*
has just requested the aid of the fire god,
so you must also
have heard from the fire god.
You lived your life
in Ainu Moshir
worthily indeed.
As proof of this,
reminiscing of your virtue
here we have,
please note,
so many people
who have gathered,

111. The prayer is quoted from *Ainu no norito* (Ainu prayers), compiled by
Monbetsu-chō Kyōdo-shi Kenkyū-kai (Research Association of Monbetsu City
History, 1966).
112. The *iyoitakkote* for the dead was offered either by elders used to public praying or elders who were relatives. In this case, it was delivered by the oldest son. In some regions, the same person offered *iyoitakkote* to both the fire
deity and the dead.

outnumbering any crowd
ever seen in this *kotan*.
Those who await you
in the other world
too must be
grateful. . . . "

Acha continued by relating how well Huchi had nurtured him, apologized for not having duly rewarded her, and then moved on to give his words of farewell.

"For the *kotan*
    where our forebears live
    straight ahead
    without straying
    please depart.
    On the way
    evil spirits
    will try to beguile you
    and make you stop.
    They may let
    birds sing
    and flowers bloom,
    things you used to love,
    to tempt you.
    Never please
    be deceived by them
    or go astray to haunt us,
    but with this new stick
    this grave marker as your staff,
    this grave marker as your torchlight,
    only watch where it guides;
    hasten please on your journey

A *chishinaot toma* (body wrapped in a mat).

without looking aside.
For, in Kamui Moshir,
your father,
your mother,
your brothers and sisters who preceded you,
are anxiously awaiting your arrival. . . . "

Following Acha's *iyaitakkote*, a third one was offered to the grave marker by Shiratekka-ekashi. This *ekashi* from Akpet Kotan had functioned as the leader of the grand *iyomante* festival. His prayer, though short, was delivered in a solemn manner fit for communication with the gods. The essence of what he said was, "I believe you have already heard from the fire god, but please guide this person properly and quickly."

Immediately after the *iyaitakkote* were finished, the jewel necklace and other ornaments were removed and the body was reverently wrapped in a straw mat. As the sun sank, we started the procession to the grave fields. It was probably morning in the spirit world.[113]

Cut grass had been spread at the bottom of the grave, which was lined with charms of *chikupeni* (Japanese pagoda tree). The body, wrapped in straw, was placed gently into the mats that lined

113. In some areas the procession occurred during the day; but in the old days, it usually seems to have taken place at night (Fujimura Hisakazu).

A *menoko-kuwa* (female grave marker) on the left and an *okkayo-kuwa* (male grave marker) on the right.

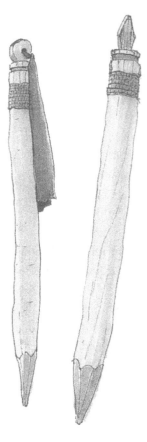

the earthen walls. When it reached the bottom, the two strings attached to the poles used to carry the body were snipped away with a scythe. As I listened to the sound of the strings being cut, I thought to myself, "Ah, Huchi has now been cut apart from us."

Everyone scooped up dirt from around the grave and tossed it in, the earth making a dry sound when it hit the mat. Next, articles beloved by Huchi were added after we damaged or broke them.[114] The burial ended with the completion of these rituals, and we finally planted the grave marker upright and sprinkled the grave with water.

Near noon on the following day, we had a *chise uhuika* (house burning). Since most of the mourners had returned home the night before, this ceremony was attended only by close relatives and neighbors. As the flames ascended to the roof of Huchi's retirement hut, the women raised their voices in the "wohh-y, wohh-y" sounds of *peutanke*, singing while they beat the ground with poles.

> "O deity who protects the house
> we send you off now,
> take care as you follow Huchi,
> already departed on her journey."[115]

THE DAY
OF THE FALLING STAR

The year after Huchi traveled to Kamui Moshir my third child was born. I secretly carried a special nostalgic fondness for this child. I somehow felt as if she, being a girl, were Huchi's reincarnation. In the ten years that followed, three more children (a girl, a boy, and another boy) were born, giving me six children in all. Aside from the daily gathering of wild plants and firewood, and the growing of millet, I spent every moment of my time raising my children, keeping house, and sometimes lending a hand in the hunting hut with the children in tow. Not one of my six

---

114. Breaking those items released their spirits so they could journey along with the owner and be of use again in the spiritual world.

115. Nishijima Teru sang this song for me from memory.

children died, thanks to the protection of the gods and the care of our excellent midwife and doctor, Aunt Monashir.

However, various changes took place along the river during these ten years. Affecting me personally were the marriages of my younger sister-in-law and brother-in-law; my younger Akihi's move to the west at the mouth of the Tokachi River to marry and live in Betcharo Kotan;[116] and the birth of seven children, two of whom died as babies, to my elder Akihi and his wife, Petennouk's younger sister.

The major event in our *kotan* was a struggle, some years earlier, with a *kotan* on the east side of the mountain (on the Shitakaropet River, east of the Chepkaunpet River) over hunting boundaries.[117] The representatives of both *kotan* participated in a grave *uko charanke* (debate) at a large hut that was built in the mountain pass for this purpose. After six entire days and nights of *charanke*, the representatives still could not come to an agreement. Finally, our two *kotan korkur* took over the debate, but neither won, and the atmosphere between the two *kotan* gradually worsened. At that point, our *kotan korkur* decided to test Unayanke.

Everyone knew that Unayanke was unsurpassed in hunting ability. He was also among the better orators, but no one knew if he could be superb. Worried that this dispute would turn ugly and end in war, Unayanke took the *charanke* seat and opened with the following:

"The mother mountain who embraces us all,
    from that same mountain,

116. Betcharo Kotan was located near the mouth of the present-day Tokachi River, where the Tokachi and the Ōtsu join.
117. A hunting area was called *iwor*. It signified not only a hunting and fishing territory but also the boundaries of the community. Differences over borders led to many fights between *kotan* and between larger river basin communities.

flowing in the same direction
are two rivers,
Shitakaropet and
Chepkaunpet.
We who live along these riverbanks
are two *ainu*,
two *utari* (fellow villagers).
We are siblings
raised by the same mother,
nursed at her breasts. . . . "[118]

In response to Unayanke's ardent delivery of these words, the tension between the antagonistic parties dissipated, as if relieved of evil spirits that had possessed it. With both sides compromising, the conflict came to a peaceful resolution. From that time forward, Unayanke's value increased even more, and the *kotan korkur*, who had no son, treated him like his own. Because the chief's *katkemat* wasn't able to have children, at her suggestion he had taken a *ponmat* (secondary wife). But she bore only girls, four in all.

What most caught my attention, however, was that Petennouk suddenly began showing signs of *tusu* ability that year. I heard secondhand about how Petennouk became a *tusukur* from my Akihi, who related what he had heard from his wife, Petennouk's younger sister. Petennouk, I realized, had lately been more and more lost in meditation. He was troubled, wondering how to respond to the voices that called from Kamui Moshir. It was like watching a dream in a state of wakefulness, so he didn't say anything to anyone, and as a result became increasingly withdrawn.

118. Unayanke's *charanke* is based on an actual speech delivered in a dispute between the Saru River and Mu River Ainu; Izumi Seiichi, "Saru Ainu no chien shūdan ni okeru IWOR" (Iwor in Saru Ainu regional groups), *Minzokugaku kenkyū* (Ethnological studies) 16 (1951).

Eventually, winter passed. One day after the season of melting snow when *pukusa*-gathering had arrived, Petennouk went bear hunting with some friends. He suddenly fell to the ground writhing. His startled companions carried him to their hut and prayed to the gods, but Petennouk's spasms continued. The words he spoke deliriously, when he finally became calm, were said to be those of remote ancestors.

Afterward, Petennouk's *tusu* powers came to be recognized as quite strong. In addition to his original protective deities, he now had a dragon deity as his *tusu* protector, but it possessed such potent powers that other *tusukur* around him couldn't detect it.

Quite unexpectedly, my oldest boy, Pasekur, began talking frequently to Petennouk. The first time occurred when Pasekur ran into Petennouk on a visit to my parental home. Apparently, something in Petennouk's words appealed to him. Because of Unayanke's training, Pasekur was among the best of the young hunters in the area, but he wasn't particularly interested in fishing. Despite this, he spent a lot of time fishing downriver that summer, so I wondered if he had found a sweetheart. Actually, he was stopping by Petennouk's house to talk on the way home. I no longer understood what Pasekur was thinking those days.

In the past year, the father-son relationship between Unayanke and Pasekur hadn't been very smooth. Until that time, Pasekur had been deeply respectful of his father, but now he became critical. Of course, they never quarreled, and I never clearly understood the reason for their tensions. But in the final analysis, I think Pasekur was rebelling against being treated like a child by Unayanke. And it couldn't have been pleasant for Unayanke to see his son growing close to an old rival, however long ago in their youth the rivalry was. Pasekur and his father talked less and less.

One night, when the capelin season was just over and it looked as if it would soon snow, we were gathered around the hearth after dinner. Pasekur, with an expression of formality, said, "I have

An *ikayop* (cylindrical arrow case).

a request." I was breast-feeding our youngest; Unayanke was making an arrow case. "I want to go away for a while on a journey," Pasekur said.

His abrupt words startled me. My heart pounded, for the tone of his voice made it clear that his "journey" was not meant for a short period of time. I asked immediately, "Where do you want to go?" Unayanke was silent. His gaze only shifted momentarily to his son before resuming work on the arrow case, but it was easy to tell by the movement of his hands that he was agitated. "I want to go to Betcharo Kotan at the mouth of the Tokachi River, where Uncle lives, and then farther in toward the mouth of the great rapids of Tokachi."

The idea of a young man traveling to different regions as a kind of rite of manhood was not unheard of in *kotan* along the river. Young men who appeared in our region on similar journeys were often invited to marry and settle here when their personal character and ability were viewed favorably. But I had never imagined that Pasekur—this had been a nickname, but it was such a fitting name that we had kept it as his real one—would say such a thing.

When I think about it now, it wasn't so far-fetched. When he was born, he was exceptionally big, and he had continued to be oversized. He had long ago outstripped his father in weight. Unayanke, who was approaching an age when he would be called *ekashi*, was himself far taller than the *kotan* average. Though not directly related to his wish to travel, I don't know how many times Pasekur had worried me by wandering deep into the forest by himself as a child, even then displaying an adventurousness that belied his untalkative nature. His ability to communicate with various animals, temporary incarnations of the gods, was stronger than other people's and he understood well their respective ways. As he grew up, he began to explore further, and he probably knew the geographical features of the area more thoroughly than did the other young men of the *kotan*.

But both Unayanke and I were convinced that the biggest influence that led Pasekur to say this must be Petennouk. Unable to decide whether to say yes, we consulted our parents and the *kotan korkur*, the wise man Shiratekka-ekashi, and even Petennouk himself.

Two days later, as Pasekur and I walked down the path along the river, I listened to him in serious conversation for the first time in a long while, trying somehow to understand what he was thinking about. Perhaps finding it easier to talk with me than with his father, he forgot his usual reticence and spoke at length. He said that while Petennouk had probably influenced him indirectly, at a deep level, the decision to make a journey was entirely his own. He said that he couldn't explain himself clearly, but it was in the natural order of things for *ainu*, who were one incarnation of the gods among many. He felt that his urge to leave might be comparable to that of the brown bear cub that leaves its parents to go on a journey after two years. Perhaps he was right. I wondered if this same natural order was the cause of the strained relations between him and his father.

Because we left late, the sky was already darkened when we arrived in Akpet Kotan. In the eastern sky, the stars were beginning to come out, and in the west the sunset at dusk was redder than usual—almost too vividly red, given that there were no clouds.[119] The sunset dyed the *kotan* a deep vermilion.

At that moment the dark vermilion suddenly brightened; for a second the entire *kotan* was wrapped in burning red light. In surprise, I looked up into the western sky to see a large star followed by a blood-red tail falling in midsky, before fading. Such a huge falling star must surely be the soul of some being. Both Pasekur and I were struck with fear, sensing that it was a bad omen. Facing the western sky where the star with its blood-red tail died out, we showed respect in *onkami* to appease the anger of the unknown *kamui*. We also prayed to the fire god and our ancestral gods for protection.

When we got to Petennouk's house, all the people of the *kotan*, surprised by the strange falling star, had just gathered there. It was no longer the time or place for personal discussion about Pasekur. The villagers had come to invite Petennouk to the village *porochise* so that they could hear the predictions of the *tusu*. After I briefly explained the reason for our visit to Umakashte, whom I hadn't seen in a while, we went to the *porochise* with everyone else.

Offerings of wine and *inau* had been laid out in the large house. The *kotan korkur* formally passed these to Petennouk and requested a *tusu*, saying, "Just now a peculiarly large, red star fell. What kind of portent is it? Please use your spiritual power and allow us to listen to the divination." Petennouk dipped the wine-offering stick in the wine and brushed his head and shoulders with it to offer it first to his protective god, saying, "*Yaiturenpe koorsutke* (I exhort my personal guardian deity)." Next, after sipping wine himself, he took the *inau* in both hands and held it in the hearthfire, and, while inhaling its fragrance, appealed in a low voice, "Although I have been welcomed to the large house this evening, and the ex-

119. Unusual redness like this was commonly regarded as an ill omen.

Chinoye-inau (*inau* just of braided shavings) and the
wine-offering chopstick used for performing the art
of *tusu* (shamanistic power).

pectations of the people of the *kotan* have been bestowed upon
me, I am only a powerless *ainu*. Dear guardian deity, please communicate your thoughts through my mouth and tell us the meaning of the wondrous falling star."

The chief's wife sat near Petennouk and waited for the beginning of the *tusu*. She was skilled at interpreting divine oracles
and asking questions. In a short while, Petennouk fell into the
special psychological state of the *tusukur*. Grasping the *inau* in one
hand, he began beating his chest with the other. At first, his words
were indistinguishable fragments, but the oracle was transmitted
in gradually clearer diction in the *tusu shinotcha* melody.[120]

"Gods and humans
    live together
    on this wonderful earth,

120. *Tusu shinotcha* is chanting at the time of divination. Words of divination are sung to a melody.

Ainu Moshir,
this bountiful earth of
Ainu Moshir.
In this Ainu Moshir
a major disaster
is coming soon.
It is one that stems not
from a natural change.
A red flame of disaster
bursts near
Repun Kotan,[121]
west of Mount Shirbesh.
It is a flame of fighting,
a flame of dispute.
How many years ahead this disaster lies
is uncertain,
but a shorter period of time
than a human life span.
It will be a large battle,
no small one
as with *topattumi*.
It will be a long war,
a painful war,
one that affects
the very existence of Ainu Moshir. . . . "

The people of the *kotan* had never heard such a dire prediction, and they glanced at each other in great unease. Even Shiratekka-ekashi, the wisest man along the river, could not con-
ceal his shock. Motionless, he stared at the fire. The chief's wife,
who was supposed to interact with Petennouk's guardian deity,

121. *Repun kotan* means "*kotan* far out in the sea." Here it refers to Matsumae.

was dumbstruck as well. With a shake of his body, Petennouk woke from his *tusu* state. He listened to the content of the oracle from the chief's wife as he drank water in exhaustion. He, too, seemed shaken as he silently stared at the fire.

The *kotan korkur* pulled himself together and, obeying proper form, gave Petennouk a token of gratitude for his *tusu*, then engaged the villagers in discussion. Although several opinions were exchanged, the scope of the matter did not allow for true solutions. Finally, at Shiratekka-ekashi's urging, it was decided that above all else, they should first offer *kamuinomi* to ward off calamity.

First, as the people's representative, the *kotan korkur* sat next to the hearth and made an especially worshipful *onkami* to the fire god and asked her to ward off the misfortune that, according to the evil omen, would be arriving. Next, representing energetic youth, Etunrachich's son Sanouk was designated by the chief to worship the guardian deity of the house, which was in the east corner. This youth's grandmother, Toitoi-huchi, had journeyed to Kamui Moshir the year following my own Huchi's day of peace. Sanouk had since come to be viewed as the young man with the brightest future in Akpet Kotan.

After the uproar over the falling star and prediction of disaster had died down somewhat and people had left the *porochise*, we asked Shiratekka-ekashi, who was already past ninety years of age, and Petennouk to remain. Along with the *kotan korkur*, we engaged them in a discussion about Pasekur's journey. After such an inauspicious incident, it was not a good time to talk, but each gave us his sincere consideration.

All three said that the trip itself, even if it were to last a few years, would be a positive experience for Pasekur. I also learned that Petennouk truly had not directly inspired the trip. On the contrary, if anything, he felt uneasy about the prospects of Pasekur's journey and had little enthusiasm for it. Petennouk's clairvoyance was gradually developing and he could see some mea-

The *chise kor kamui* (guardian god of the house).

sure of what appeared to be a future full of troubles. Though there was no fear of catastrophe or fatal illness, Pasekur would experience unexpected and onerous hardship.

We stayed in the *porochise* at Akpet Kotan that night. The next morning we went to my parental home in Otasam Kotan. Among all her grandchildren, Hapo had special affection for Pasekur and she was greatly saddened to hear of his long journey. Hapo, already more than seventy years old, had reached the years where she was telling her great-grandchildren stories. Acha's physical strength was failing these days, his spirits were low, and he grumbled often. But he showed unexpected understanding about Pasekur's journey, explaining that adventures were necessary for young men.

Having listened to the thoughts of various people, we returned along the river road to Chichap Kotan the next morning as the first snowflakes of the year began falling. Of course, talk of the ill-omened falling star and Petennouk's prediction had spread here, too, and they had offered *kamuinomi* at our *porochise* as well.

The results of the various discussions were not very pleasant, but Pasekur's mind had not changed. I was especially troubled by Petennouk's premonition of great hardship and tried to persuade my son to stay. Pasekur, on the contrary, accepted as a virtual certainty that his life would not be endangered and was completely unmoved. Of course, my father-in-law and mother-in-law, and even Unayanke, were worried and tried to persuade him not to go. But Pasekur's intentions had hardened beyond the point of changing. Rather than trying to hold him back, I could only try to teach him as much wisdom as possible for coping with troubles, and pray for his safety. We were gradually placed in the position of approving Pasekur's declaration that he would set out when spring arrived.

Once the decision was made, relations between Unayanke and Pasekur changed for the better, if anything, and they went more frequently on overnight hunting trips. Unayanke attempted to transmit to his son before the journey everything he knew about the skills and spirit needed for fighting and hunting.

That winter, we experienced more blizzards and bitter cold than usual. The "rains that wash bear cubs" caused the fallen snow to form a hard crust, but unusually good weather followed. After the two went with my father-in-law and next oldest son on a hunt to "welcome bear cubs," there was a small banquet for the *kotan*, which was combined with a celebration for the beginning of Pasekur's journey.[122] Brushing aside the suggestion my mother-in-law and I made that he at least wait until the snow melted, Pasekur left six days later.

We decided that our second son, eldest daughter, and I would go as far as Shumkari Kotan on the ocean shore to send him off. Unayanke wanted to give Pasekur, as a memento, the complete set of fire-making tools that he had used for years on hunts. The night before, he prayed earnestly to the fire god after waving the tools over the hearth, then passed them to Pasekur.

The morning of his departure, my parents-in-law, Unayanke, and the children sent off Pasekur and the three of us at the outskirts of the *kotan*. My mother-in-law had been in tears since she rose in the morning. Finally, weeping loudly, she parted from her grandson with an embrace. My father-in-law had lost an eyeball in a fight with a bear, but the tears fell even from that eye.[123]

As we descended the hardened snow of the mountain path that signaled the approaching "month when birds begin to chirp,"[124] we glided down the slope with canes and deerskin shoes, racing pleasantly along without regard for the path. It was the season when it got warmer day by day. Normally, during this time of year when we were freest to roam through the mountains and fields, my heart would be full of joy at walking about with my children, who were growing up without incident. But fragments of scenes from the time when Pasekur was a baby came and went before my eyes: that large infant my mother-in-law showed me

---

122. "Welcoming bear cubs" refers to capturing a bear cub alive for the *iyomante*.

123. This actually happened to Kayano Shigeru's father.

124. According to Fujimura Hisakazu, not only did the old names of the months differ by region but the same name could refer to different months because of the vast climatic differences between the north (Sōya at the northernmost tip of Hokkaidō and the Kuriles) and the south (e.g., Hakodate). Thus it is difficult to determine common names for the months. Given here is a list

after a difficult labor; the sounds of a blizzard and the cheerful voices of Aunt Monashir and the married women from the neighborhood talking about the weather; Pasekur, his eyes delirious with a high fever from childhood dysentery, reaching out both hands for a packet of medicine; the melody from a children's song he sang with his friends from the neighborhood; the furrows in the middle of his forehead whenever he was on the verge of tears; the morning that Unayanke took him on his first deer hunt and he waved his hand at me in the faint light of snow at dawn. . . . The various faces of Pasekur on all those days appeared one after another, superimposed on the snowy road as we speedily descended the mountain.

---

of the months by lunar calendar from *Moshiogusa* (Brine-drenched plants), an Ainu vocabulary list prepared by a Japanese about two hundred years ago. Transliteration problems make the names of some months hard to ascertain. The translation is by Kayano Shigeru. *Haprap* (February) seems to be an error for *haurap*.

1	*Enomi chup*	the month of *kamuinomi*
	or *Towetanne chup*	the month when the day begins to lengthen
2	*Haprap chup*	the month when birds begin to sing
3	*Mokiuta chup*	the month when some thatch plants are gathered (?)
4	*Sukiuta chup*	the month when thatch plants are seriously gathered (?)
5	*Momauta chup*	the month when some sweet briars are gathered
6	*Shimauta chup*	the month when sweet briars are seriously gathered
7	*Moniyora chup*	the month when some leaves fall (?)
8	*Shiniyora chup*	the month when leaves seriously fall (?)
9	*Urepoke chup*	the month when the soles of feet become cold
10	*Shunan chup*	the month when people fish salmon with torchlight
11	*Kuekai chup*	the month when even a bow snaps from the cold
12	*Churup*	the month when even river shallows freeze

At Nuipet Kotan, we greeted Menkakush, our leader during times of emergency along the river, and his son. Because of his advanced years, Menkakush-ekashi had already withdrawn from the post of *kotan korkur* and his eldest son had succeeded him.[125] As Unayanke's comrade in battle against the *topattumi*, this son also had affection for Pasekur. At Akpet Kotan, we greeted the chief, Shiratekka-ekashi; Sapo's marriage family; and, of course, Petennouk and Umakashte. Petennouk, who foresaw Pasekur's hardships, said he had nothing to give him but offered him *itaktakusa* (words used in place of purifying herbs). "The fire god of your parents' home is protecting you," he said. "You should never give up hope, no matter what hardships you face."

At my parental home in Otasam Kotan, my mother grieved with no fewer tears than my mother-in-law. Horpecha-huchi and Huisak-huchi had followed one another that very winter to Kamui Moshir, leaving Hapo feeling that she no longer had close friends of Huchi's generation in the *kotan*. Her heart now grieved at the loss of her favorite grandson. We stayed at my parents' home that night, and, joined by the chief and close relatives, we all spent the evening in festive spirits despite the pain of parting. The next morning, Acha and Hapo, as well as my elder Akihi's family, sent us off at the outskirts of the *kotan*.

We arrived at Shumkari Kotan on the ocean shore. The beach where Hotene and I used to play, drawing embroidery patterns in the sand, had not changed since my childhood. It stretched out to the west, toward the Tokachi River where Pasekur was headed. The wind was strong that day. The waves came up to the

---

125. Although the house of the patriarch who founded a *kotan* was esteemed, on his retirement it was the custom to elect a successor in consultation with other elders. The same household sometimes produced the village head for several generations.

edge of the path, washing away the sand. Hotene joined us from Shumkari Kotan to send him off at the beach.

I bade Pasekur farewell: "Wherever you go, you are not to disgrace the name of your family or your father; don't do anything to cause *kotan wente* (disgrace the *kotan*)." As I spoke, my tears became a rapids, unstoppable. When we exchanged our final embrace, my voice choked and no words came. As I looked up at Pasekur's chest and breathed in his familiar smell, I could see in the shadow of his collar the string that held the single earring I had given him as a remembrance. Pasekur embraced my second son and eldest daughter, as well as Hotene, then set off along the shore road, looking back every few steps. Once he sank onto the sand, crying; then thinking it over, continued to walk, looking back countless times as he got farther and farther away. I had a strong premonition that I would never see my son again. As I sat on the beach, scooping up and clenching the mixture of sand and ice in my hands, I wailed like a child. Each time I wiped away my tears so as to get a better view of Pasekur, he got smaller and smaller. Far in the distance where the road turned, he stood for a while, and then he was gone.

PART THREE

PASEKUR

In attempting to re-create the daily Ainu life of several hundred years ago, I borrowed the style of *uwepeker*. Because no written record remains, my only choice was to use such a method. If we consider this book as the first volume of a series titled *The Ainu People,* the sequel that I plan eventually to write should start with the first major series of conflicts between the Ainu and Shisam, the so-called Koshamain War (1456–57). Since this war is a documented incident, the second volume ought to provide a factually verifiable account of that time. To provide a link between the historical period of the planned second volume and the legendary age of part 2 in this first volume, as represented by *yukar* and *uwepeker,* I here present what subsequently happens to Pasekur, using the form of the *upashkuma* (or *uchashkuma,* factual story or precept).

The *upashkuma* transmits origins and histories of particular persons, families, and things that actually existed, while the *uwepeker* ostensibly presents a fictitious story of universal significance. (I say "ostensibly," because sometimes the *uwepeker* was used as a vehicle to relate one's own experience under the guise of fiction.) The most significant *upashkuma* are those that transmit the history of a family line. Because these contain personal details that begin with comparatively recent ancestors and end with the narrator in the present day, they are not meant for public consumption. Indeed, many were passed down as closely held family secrets, since their content could ruin relationships among people.

The story that follows is told in the form of an *upashkuma* and is about Pasekur. It is not the history of any existing person, although I have based it on a number of actual *upashkuma.* One of these is "My Grandfather's *upashkuma*" in a memoir

Kawakami Sanouk, who handed down ancestral
upashkuma (stories about rituals, place-names,
and ancestors) to his grandson, Kawakami Yūji.

by the orator Kawakami Yūji, a rancher in Penakori in Biratori
township.[1]

Because Kawakami Yūji lost his parents at a tender age, he was
raised by his grandparents. His grandfather Kawakami Sanouk died

1. Kawakami Yūji, *Saruunkuru monogatari* (The tale of Sarunkur) (Suzusawa
Shoten, 1976).

in 1952, but three months before his death, he narrated from his bed his *upashkuma* to his grandson. It explained how and why Yūji's ancestor Suneash, seven generations earlier, had left his birthplace of Tokachi, crossed the Hidaka mountain range, and come to the Saru River basin. During one harsh winter of famine, he had broken the tribal code for the sake of the family's lives. Condemned for his transgression, his entire family had been transplanted as servants to the man he had wronged. Although his child eventually became the *kotan korkur*, Suneash's fortunes never improved and he died in a tragic accident.

To return to our story, what happened to Harukor's son, Pasekur, after he left her home? Like *uwepeker*, *upashkuma* seem, in principle, to have been related in the first person, so I will follow this convention.

PASEKUR'S JOURNEY

I am Pasekur, a resident of the Shipechari River (present-day Shizunai River).

My birthplace is Chichap Kotan, in eastern Hokkaidō, at the highest reaches of the Chepkaunpet River. When I was nineteen years old, I left my birthplace and traveled to the Tokachi River. I stayed with my maternal uncle in Betcharo Kotan at the mouth of the Tokachi for about half a year, but when it was time for the salmon to migrate up the river, I went to Operperkep Kotan (present-day Obihiro) to live with the relatives of my uncle's *katkemat*. The head of the household, Shitona, was the younger brother of Katkemat's mother.

Here I helped with salmon fishing and passed the winter helping with deer hunting. I am large and strong, and because I was trained by my father, a master hunter, my hunting skills are quite good. I so pleased Shitona and his wife that they invited me to stay on, perhaps even settle down and marry into the *kotan*. They

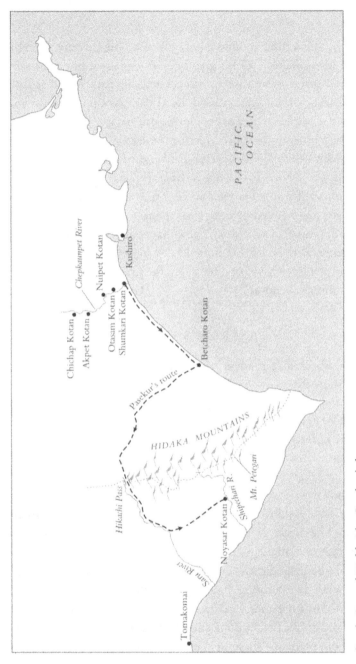

South Central Hokkaidō: Pasekur's home

had a daughter who was three or four years younger than I, and they dropped hints about my marrying her. But my adventurous spirit had not been quenched enough to make me settle down, and I parted from the family to continue my journey up the river.

When I think about it now, I didn't dislike their daughter. Had I become a resident of Operperkep Kotan at that time, I would have avoided the hardships that came later. But I was young and my yearning to travel was irrepressible. On a hot day at the height of summer, I headed for Shirtok Kotan (present-day Shintoku), where an acquaintance of Shitona's lived.

As I crossed a narrow branch river, I met a couple with a child. They were fishing for trout. We exchanged greetings and talked a little. Discovering that I was on a youthful journey and that I posed no threat to them, the husband said, "Actually, our youngest child developed a fever three days ago and has terrible diarrhea that won't stop. You wouldn't happen to be carrying some potent medicine or know of a cure, would you?"

I thought that it might, by chance, be childhood dysentery. If that were so, then Hapo had taught me in detail how Aunt Monashir had saved me, and perhaps I could use her methods. The *kotan* to which they led me had only three *chise;* it was a small community of close relatives. The sick child was a two- or three-year-old girl attended by her grandmother. Neither the grandmother's medicinal treatments nor her prayers had worked, and the child appeared to be in danger. I wasn't sure if it was childhood dysentery, but the symptoms were similar enough, so I cautiously tried the *kinaraita* treatment. The effect was immediately apparent, and she was soon better. The husband, whose name was Munkeke, and his family thanked me as if I were "some kind of *kamui* come to save them," and asked me to stay a while since they would be preparing wine for a celebratory *kamuinomi.*

This *kotan* was at the foot of the beautiful Hidaka mountain

The Hidaka mountain range in autumn, from 9,800 feet above
Niikappu. Photo by Wakabayashi Kunizō, 1962.

range, which includes Mount Poroshir.[2] It was an attractive area
that seemed to teem with deer and salmon. The people of the
kotan were also genuinely kind. Gratefully accepting their invitation, I stayed and helped with the fishing until late autumn. With
the end of the salmon season came time for the first snows.

One day I went to Munkeke's *iwor* (hunting area) and set up
amatpo (traps) in two locations.[3] That was the beginning of my
troubles.

The day after I set up the traps, the wind was very strong. That

2. Present-day Mount Poroshiri, at 6,732 feet, is the highest peak of the
Hidaka mountain range and retains glacial features.

3. *Amatpo* is also called *kuwari*. For large animals like bear, an arrow with
surk (wolfsbane) was used (see p. 114). It was equipped with variable arrowheads, and its mechanism is said to be "rare among the hunting societies of the
world." See Ishikawa Motosuke, *Dokuya no bunka* (Poison arrow culture) (Ki-
nokuniya, 1963).

A *kuitakpe* (marker)
for showing the
location of a trap
bow, the location of a
farm field, and so on.

evening, a harried messenger from the next *kotan* came to inform
Munkeke, "Something terrible has happened. An Ainu from Pipaoi Kotan has been seriously injured by the *amatpo* on your *iwor*.
A friend who was with him came for help, and five or six people
from the *kotan* have gone out."

According to the messenger, it wasn't clear whether they
would be able to save the wounded man's life. The trap markers
had been knocked over by the wind or broken by falling branches,

perhaps, and therefore had gone unnoticed by the men.[4] Pipaoi was a small *kotan* in a neighboring valley to the south, across a ridge. The *amatpo* that had caught the man was clearly the one I had set the previous day. The cross-shaped warning markers were firmly fastened with string, though, and it would take a lot for them to come loose. . . . I didn't have the details, but it was clear that this was a grave incident. After Munkeke had given it some thought, he proposed the following.

This event would cause a great uproar. It was a terrible thing even if the man survived, but if he were to die, the consequences would be unimaginable. I would have no choice but to consent to a *charanke;* and in cases like this, a stranger was at an overwhelming disadvantage. The incident might be resolved fairly simply between locals, but an outsider could be held responsible for everything. If negotiations went poorly, I might have to make amends as a servant for twenty or thirty years. And if the dispute really soured, a battle could erupt between the two *kotan.* In the worst case, the fight could develop into a conflict between the people from my native village on the Chepkaunpet River and this region. Munkeke wanted to help me, just as I had helped him. Luckily, because no one other than Munkeke and his family knew where I was from, they could pass me off as an unknown traveler. So, it was best that I escape. Afterward, Munkeke would somehow handle the *charanke.* Because it was a transgression for a Pipaoi to have entered his hunting grounds without permission, Munkeke had a defense.

I quickly made preparations for my journey, accepted a gift of dried meat from Munkeke, and left late at night by the light of the moon. Because the other side of the Tokachi was also dangerous, I planned to follow Munkeke's suggestion and cross be-

4. *Kuitakpe,* markers for the location of a trap bow, a farm field, etc., were usually cross shaped; the short horizontal portion indicated the direction of the item marked.

Utensils for making fire. From left: charcoal for lighting fire, charcoal container, lighting iron, and flint.

tween the north side of Mount Poroshir and Mount Memoro to get as far as the *kotan* of the Sarunkur (people in the Saru basin region in Hidaka). There already was snow in the mountains, and I took snow sandals and other snow gear.

This great mountain range was on a different scale than the mountains in my place of birth. The hardships I faced after this cannot be expressed in a word or two. North of Mount Memoro, there was an easily accessible pass (present-day Hikachi Pass), but my pursuers would surely catch me there. I covered my tracks by walking in the cold water of the mountain streams and crossing at waterfalls, but I finally became snowbound. A fire would have been easily detected, so I endured the cold. To hide my tracks, I walked when the snow was blowing and wore my snow sandals backward to make it appear that I was heading in the opposite direction. Since I planned to use the precious dried meat sparingly, I made it a point to catch game whenever I could. But just a short way into the mountains, rabbit and deer were already scarce. I backtracked a little and brought down a deer, then headed toward the difficult main peak. By then, however, my hands and feet were severely frostbitten from the falling snow, the bitter cold, and the long nights. It was difficult even to use my tools to make a fire.

Finally, I made it over the main peak. But one night in the middle of a snowstorm, ten days after my departure, illness and frostbite took their toll. Unable to take another step, I lost consciousness at the foot of an Ezo pine tree.

Perhaps it was a dream, but in the midst of the snowstorm, I thought I heard the most exquisite music. A young woman, divinely beautiful, appeared. She seemed to float above the deep snow. Accompanied by music, she spoke to me as if in song.

"Pasekur, be at ease, for I've hidden you from your pursuers. If you go along the stream below, you'll find a *kotan*, but don't stay there too long. Continue toward the south. Once you enter the *kotan* on the Shipechari River, you may relax. If you do as I say, your troubles will be over and your descendants will prosper. I will watch over you as you travel, so do not forget to offer me *kamuinomi*."

When I came to, the woman had disappeared. I was protected from the snowstorm, cradled by a thick branch of the silver fir. The woman, I realized, was the spirit of the tree.

SHIROMAINU

My life thereafter turned out to be largely as predicted. Now that I could make a fire and build a hut, my frostbite receded little by little, though I lost the tips of two of my toes. I entered the first *kotan*, Porosar (near present-day Furenai). It was right by the road to Tokachi, so even though it was winter I couldn't let my guard down. Fighting a desire to rest, I continued on after receiving simple medical treatment, a meal, and the night's lodging granted to any frostbitten traveler. I passed through Nupikipet Kotan and Pipok Kotan (now Nukibetsu and Niikappu). By the time I made it to the banks of the Shipechari River, through the gods' divine will, I had been traveling al-

An *echiush* (lidded
wine pourer).

most a month. One striking difference from my birthplace was
that a large number of goods were traded with the Shisam.
When I first entered Noyasar Kotan (present-day Noya), either
from the release of the stress of the last month or from exhaustion, I fell unconscious at the door of the first house on
the edge of the *kotan*. I was faintly aware of being carried in
and cared for.[5]

I told the *kotan korkur* who I was and, except for the trapping
accident, let him know everything about myself, including my
birthplace. With his permission to stay for the time being, I built
a small hut on the outskirts of the *kotan*. Until I recovered my
strength, I helped as a servant at every house and was fed in return. About a month later, a treasured wine pourer was stolen
from the chief's house. Unluckily for me, I had gone to visit the
chief just moments before. Since no one was there, I had turned
back the way I'd come, but someone witnessed this and I was instantly suspected. No matter how I denied it, I was unable to prove

5. Nukibetsu, Niikappu, and Noya are located at the western foot of the
central part of the Hidaka mountain range. It is a relatively warm area in
Hokkaidō, with less snowfall than elsewhere.

A *sutu* (punishing staff).

my innocence, and so was subjected to an investigation. In the end, I was sentenced to one hundred strokes with a punishing staff.

Just as the first blow was about to fall, a young woman in the crowd suddenly raised her voice, as if possessed by a spirit, and threw herself in front of me. She tearfully protested that I was not a criminal. I had noted this woman with curiosity since coming to the *kotan*. She was the daughter of the chief's brother and closely resembled the spirit of the silver fir. Fearing the power of some god or other, the punishment was halted, and, instead, I was tested by *saimon* (hot-water trial).[6] I was judged innocent and forgiven.

That fall, a *wen-kamui* in the form of a man-eating bear appeared and terrified the *kotan*. Six people, including the chief's child, fell victim, yet even several master hunters failed to catch the bear. Having by then completely recovered my strength, I succeeded in bringing it down by myself, using the bear-hunting secrets my father had taught me and devising my own strategy to outsmart the bear. This resulted not only in praise from several *kotan* along the river but in a confession by the criminal who had stolen the wine pourer. He was, as it turned out, the father of one of the children killed by the bear, and he confessed his crime

6. An ordeal in which a suspect was forced to put his hand in boiling water. He was determined innocent if his hand did not burn.

by way of atonement. These circumstances instantly increased people's confidence in me. The chief strongly urged me to settle permanently in this *kotan*. I, too, wished to ask for the hand of the mysterious young woman, his niece; so I entered his brother's family, and thus was formally welcomed as a member of the *kotan*.

After the grand wedding, I confided in the chief and his wife about the incident in Tokachi. The chief recommended that I change my name, saying, "Pasekur is too 'heavy' a name for you. Changing it will help you to exorcise and forget the past." Since this was a childhood nickname I had retained, I agreed and received a different name with the same meaning, "Shiromainu."

Twenty years have passed since then. My oldest son recently told me he wanted to visit my birthplace along the Chepkaunpet River, which he had never seen, and to meet his grandparents, Harukor-huchi and Unayanke-ekashi. I suddenly became nostalgic for my home and wished to go with him. But I had just recently become the chief, and my heavy responsibilities kept me from leaving the *kotan*. One morning in early spring, the same season in which I started my journey as a young man, my son set off. The above story of my life is what I told him about myself the night before he left. Just as my Hapo had cried at the beach when she saw me off, my wife, wondering whether she would ever see her son again, raised her voice and wailed as she saw him off from the top of the mountain.

I didn't have the same fear she did, but on the way home I sensed something inauspicious about the huge snowballs rolling on a snowy field. Trying to break one open, I found that the core was red snow. Shocked, I stood dumbfounded. This was an omen of a great war. A memory of a spring day returned as if it were yesterday—Petennouk's prediction on the "day of the falling star."

In the distant west at Shinori (present-day Hakodate), an Ainu was killed by a Shisam sword maker. Soon after that, we heard about the Ainu uprising and the start of the war. It was to lead to the uprising of the brave leader Koshamain in the following year.

Glossary

TERMS

All terms are in Ainu unless followed by (J.) for Japanese. Proper nouns are not italicized.

acha	short for *achapo*, uncle; may not be related to the speaker
achapo	uncle
ainu	human beings
Ainu Moshir	the homeland of the Ainu, i.e., Hokkaidō, the Kuriles, and southern Sakhalin
ainu neno an=ne p ne na ainu e	you must become a humanlike human
ainurakkur	"forefather of humans," i.e., god, also known as Okikurmi or Oinakamui
aishiroshi	family insignia used for inscription on arrowheads
akadamo (J.)	a kind of elm, also called *harunire* (J.)
akihi	younger brother
amatpo	trap
anunukehi	precious part (i.e., female genitalia)

287

apa	opening, door
apekeshkeso	literally, "many embers"; appearance of trout with red spots on their sides in August–September
ape-uchi-huchi	appellation for the female fire god in eastern Hokkaidō
asada (J.)	Japanese birch (*Astrya japonica*)
attush	cloth woven of thread made from bast fiber, usually of *ohyō*
cha	male salmon
charanke	to argue
chashi	fort
chep	fish (meaning salmon)
chepker	salmon-skin shoes
chep ohau	fish and vegetable soup
chiehe	penis
chikisani	a kind of elm
chikupeni	Japanese pagoda tree
chinoye-inau	*inau* made only of braided shavings
chinru	snow sandals
chinunukehi	precious part (i.e., male genitalia)
chip	canoe
chippo	needle cushion
chise	house or home
chise kor kamui	guardian god of the house
chisenomi	house-warming celebration

chise uhuika	house burning
chishinaot toma	body wrapped in a mat
chiurikin	flash flood
chuk	autumn
chup	moon
chuppe	moon's dew (i.e., menstruation)
echi=nu	hear me, you folks
echiush	lidded wine pourer shaped like a teapot
ekashi	elder, grandfather, male ancestor
ekimne kuwa	walking stick
emushranke tamaranke	drop your swords, drop your jewels
eniupe	pillow
E=ramatkor wa e=an pe ne na arpa	You've been prepared to do this, by heaven, now go quickly.
etnup	wine pourer
eyaipitonere eyaika-muinere	That makes you a human, makes you a god
hamu	leaf
hapo	mother
harkika-sayep	rope stand
harunire (J.)	a kind of elm, also called *akadamo* (J.)
heper-set	cage for keeping bear or owl for *iyomante*
hosh	leg guards
huchi	grandmother, grandame
Humoshirushi	first-generation ancestor of Kayano Shigeru's family

hunna	I partake, I have partaken (female speech of thanks for food)
hupcha kucha	hunting hut of fir branches
Hureshisam	red neighbors (i.e., the Russians)
ikayop	cylindrical arrow case
ikoinkar	midwife
inau	ceremonial whittled twig or pole, usually of willow, with shavings attached
inaukike	*inau* of curled shavings from whittled branches
inau kor	take the *inau* with you
inaukotchep	fish worthy of *inau* (i.e., small salmon found toward the end of the salmon season)
inonnoitak	chanting, chanted prayer
ipetam	human-devouring sword
ishma	woman's underbelt
isoitak	chatting
ita	tray
itak-kamui	spirit of word, divine speech
itako (J.)	medium; term used in northeast Honshū
iteseni	mat-weaving table
iwor	hunting or fishing area
iyairaikere	thank you
iyohaichish	improvised song of longing
iyoikir	treasure altar
iyoitakkote	requiem, ritual of sending the soul off to the spiritual world

iyomante	the festival in which an animal spirit is sent back to the world of the gods
Jōmon (J.)	prehistoric period during which a hunting and gathering way of life was followed (ca. 10,000 B.C.E.–ca. 300 B.C.E.)
kam ohau	meat (usually deer) and vegetable soup
kamui	spirit, god (male or female)
kamuichep	divine fish (i.e., salmon)
kamui moshir	the realm of the gods
kamuinomi	prayer to the gods
kamui-onne	natural death
kamui-to	lake of dead spirits
kanit	spindle stick
kaparimip	unlined appliquéd robe
karop	container for fire-making tools
katkemat	married woman, lady
kemaha pirkano monoa	the way of sitting with proper leg posture
kemonuitosayep	spindle with a needle container
kimun kamui	mountain deity, or brown bear
kimun-kamuipo hurayep	the rains that wash bear cubs (i.e., the winter rain of mid-February)
kina	grass, weeds, edible wild plants
kinaraita	agrimony
kinasut-kamui	snake deity, guardian of birth
kinasut-kamui noka	a form or image of the snake deity

kirai	comb
konchi	hood
konkani	gold
konotohewehewe	eating fast
kotan	hamlet
Kotankarkamui	the patriarchal deity that made the land of the Ainu
kotan kor kamui	the guardian deity of a village, i.e., giant striped owl
kotan korkur	village head
kotannomi	prayer for the *kotan*
kotan wente	destroying (i.e., disgracing) the *kotan*
kuitakpe	a marker for the location of a trap bow, the boundaries of a farm, etc.
kuitop	wild goose
kukorainu	my man (i.e., husband)
Kunnechup	the moon god
-kur	a suffix indicating "a person of"; as in Sarunkur, a Saru region inhabitant
kuwa	carved staff
makiri	knife
mak ta apa	passage of birth, uterine neck
marep or *marek*	fishhook for catching salmon and trout
mattepa	hygienic belt
matsuwop	woman's jewel box
matyukar	a divine *yukar* recited by a woman; also known as *oina*

maukar	labor pain in a broad sense
menoko-epeka aeham	providing a wife to stop a man's feet
menoko-kuwa	female grave marker
menoko makiri	knife for women and girls
mizunara (J.)	a kind of oak
momijigasa (J.)	a plant of the chrysanthemum family (*Cacalia delphiniifolia*)
moshir	homeland
moshirpa	the east
mour	woman's underrobe
mui	winnow
mukkuri	mouth zither
munchiro	a kind of millet
mutapa	winter
nieshike	backpack
nikar	ladder
ninkari	earrings
Noyautasap	a god appearing in the Okikurmi legends
Nukapira	the name of a rock on a hill, meaning "shaped cliff"
nusa	altar
nuwap tar	birthing rope
ohau	soup
ohyō (J.)	a kind of elm (*opiu* in Ainu)
Oinakamui	see Ainurakkur
Okikurmi	see Ainurakkur

Okikurum Chashi	Okikurmi Fort
okkayo-kuwa	male grave marker
onkami	a male greeting with ritual formality with arms raised before the chest
onturep-akam	dried wild lily-root dumplings
opere	little one (term of endearment for a young girl)
osh	female salmon
oshkur-marapto	bear's head with the entire fur still attached
paikar	spring
Pananpe-Penanpe	genre of literature for children about Pananpe, the younger brother, who lived downstream, and Penanpe, the older brother, who lived upstream
parapasui	spoon for women
pasui	or *tukipasui*; chopstick for ceremonial wine offering
pe	water
Pekerchup	the sun god
peutanke	women's shrill warning call
pirka	good, pretty
pirka-onne	good death
pito	humans, often taking on character traits of demigods
ponkut	pregnancy belt
ponmat	second wife

ponmenoko	maiden, little woman
ponsuwop	little box (same as *matsuwop*)
ponto	small lake
porochise	big house (i.e., *kotan* head's house and meeting place)
poronima	big carved bowl
poysu	small pot
pu	raised storehouse
pukusa	wild lily root with garlic fragrance, also called *kito*
pukusakina	a plant of the buttercup family
raha	liver
raichishkar	wail for death
raikur-ker	shoes for the dead
raiparpar	lamentation
rametok	heroic, courageous; one of the three most essential qualities for men along with *shiretok* (good appearance) and *pawetok* (eloquence)
raspa	a kind of deutzia shrub
ratashkep	mixture of special foods not in usual diet, especially for children
ratchako	lamp stand
raunkut	woman's underbelt
rekutunpe	neck ornament
repni	time beater used in telling stories

repun kotan	*kotan* far out to sea
repun moshir	foreign land
rimse	circle dance
ruhai	a little idiotic, dazed
rum	arrowhead
saimon	hot-water trial (i.e., a person's innocence is demonstrated when the hand is immersed in boiling water without suffering burns)
sakanke	the process of boiling and drying meat for preservation
sakanke kam	dried meat
sakekar-ontaro	vat for wine brewing
sakorpe	term used for *yukar* in eastern Hokkaidō
sakupa	summer
samor	neighboring place
Samor-moshir	country close by (i.e., mainland Japan)
sapanpe	ceremonial crown
sapo	big sister
saranip	woven bag with one strap
sarunashi (J.)	plant of the silvervine family (*Actinida arguta*)
Sarunkur	one from the Saru basin region in Hidaka
Satsumon doki (J.)	pottery that emerged in Hokkaidō and northern Honshū in the eighth to thirteenth centuries
sayokasup	ladle for gruel

sem	room with dirt floor that serves as the entrance to *chise*
Shikannakamui	the thunder god
shinkep	a bush clover
shinta or *sinta*	cradle
shirokani	silver
shisam or *sisam*	neighbor (an Ainu term for Japanese)
shishamo (J.)	capelin; said to be from the Ainu word *susam*
shitaipe	dog's eating manners
shitopera	wooden spatula used for making dumplings
su	cooking pot
suputa	lid of a pot
surku	wolfsbane poison
susam	capelin (known as *shishamo* in Japanese)
susu	willow
sutker	vine sandals
sutu	punishing staff
sutukap	grapevine skin
takusa	purifying plants
tamasai	women's necklace
tanpe pakno	That will be all.
tapkar	stomping dance
tar	carrying rope
tashiro	sword for use in the mountains

tatushpe	torch of white birch bark
tekehontomta charohontomta	arms half-done, lips half-done (referring to incomplete tattoo)
tekeinu	feeling in the hand, palpation
tekunpe	hand covers
tesh	weir for damming fish
toma	straw mat
topattumi	night attack
tuitak	another name for *uwepeker*
tuki	wine cup
tukipasui	ceremonial chopstick, used for offering wine to the gods
tulep	plant of the lily family
tunpe	a separate area of the *chise* for a daughter who has come of age
tusu	shamanistic power
tusukur	a medium
uchashkuma	see *upashkuma*
udo (J.)	a prickly shrub of the family Araliaceae (*Aralia cordata*)
ue-inkar	clairvoyance, extrasensory perception
uhuika	house burning following a death of the occupant (e.g., a grandmother's cottage that was provided for her following her husband's death)
uko-charanke	dispute resolution by debate
uko-omoinu	physical union

upashkuma	historically based legend
upopo	festival song sung seated
utar	fellow villagers, folks
utarpake	leader of fellow villagers
Uwarikamui	deity of childbirth
uwepeker	mutually pure (i.e., folktales in stylized prose)
wen-itak	chanting for evil purposes
wenkamui	evil spirits
wenkur	a bad human
wenkuripe	poor manners
wenpe	narrow-minded person
wente	destroy
yachidamo (J.)	a tree of the family Oleaceae (*Fraxinus mandshurica*)
yainikoroshima	wanting to hide in one's own wrinkles (i.e., embarrassment)
yaisama	improvisational song
yarnima	container made of tree bark
yarniyatushi	bucket made of tree bark
yuk	deer; sport
yukar	rhymed epic poetry with melodies
yukizasa (J.)	a plant of the family Liliaceae (*Smilacina japonica*)
yukker	deerskin shoes
yukur	sleeveless deerskin jacket

PEOPLE

Aoki Aiko
(1914–95)

Midwife and seer.

Bird, Isabella
(1831–1904)

British author, also known as Isabella
Bishop after marriage in 1881, noted for
her travel writings. Her travelogues from
the Far East include *Unbeaten Tracks in
Japan* (1880), *Journeys in Persia and Kurdistan*
(1891), and *Among the Tibetans* (1894).

Chiri Mashiho
(1909–61)

Ainu linguist and author of *Bunrui
Ainugo jiten* (Classified Ainu-Japanese
dictionary). His numerous writings on
the Ainu language of Hokkaidō and
Sakhalin are included in *Chiri Mashiho
chosakushū* (Works by Chiri Mashiho)
(Heibonsha, 1973–76).

Fujimura Hisakazu
(1940–)

Professor at Hokkai Gakuen University
specializing in Ainu language and culture. Among his works are *Ainu no rei no
sekai* (The Ainu spiritual world) (Shōgakkan, 1983) and *Ainu, kamigami to
ikiru hitobito* (The Ainu: People who live
with the gods) (Fukutake Shoten, 1985).

Iboshi Hokuto
(1902–29)

Ainu poet who composed in Japanese.
He left an anthology *Kotan* (Kibōsha,
1930), later republished as *Iboshi Hokuto
ikōshū: Kotan* (Kotan: A posthumous
anthology of Iboshi Hokuto) (Sōfūkan,
1984).

Kannari Matsu
(1875–1961)

Famous Ainu bard and aunt of the
linguist Chiri Mashiho. She wrote down
numerous pieces over twenty-five or so

years. Half of the materials in her more than seventy notebooks are said to have been passed down from her mother, one of the greatest bards in southern Hokkaidō.

Kayano Shigeru (1926–)
Founder and director of the Kayano Shigeru Ainu Memorial Museum, a key figure in the Ainu political and cultural revival, and the first Ainu to be elected to the Diet. Among his most recent works are *Kayano Shigeru no Ainugo jiten* (Kayano Shigeru's Ainu dictionary) (Sanseidō, 1996) and *Kayano Shigeru no Ainu shinwa shūsei* (The Kayano Shigeru collection of Ainu myths) (Bikutā Entateimento, 1988). His *Ainu no Ishibumi* is available in English translation as *Our Land Was a Forest: An Ainu Memoir* (Boulder, Colo.: Westview, 1994).

Koshamain, also spelled Kosamainu (d. 1457)
Ainu leader. He led the 1456–57 uprising against the Japanese in southern Hokkaidō. After successfully attacking ten of the twelve Japanese strongholds, he was killed by Takeda Nobuhiro (1431–94), founder of the Matsumae family.

Kubota Nezō (fl. mid-nineteenth century)
Samurai of Sakura province (presently northern Chiba) and author of *Kyōwa shieki* (A harmonious journey on a private mission), a record in five books of his 1856 travels in Hokkaidō.

Matsuura Takeshirō (1818–88)
Japanese official who explored Hokkaidō and the Kuriles in the late Edo. Ap-

pointed head of the Hokkaidō Development Office under the Meiji government, he quit in 1870 in protest against Japanese exploitation and plunder of the Ainu people and natural resources. Besides many journals and travelogues, he wrote *Kinsei Ezo jinbutsushi* (A record of modern Ainu individuals), which introduced some one hundred Ainu from all walks of life.

Shakushain, also spelled Samkusaynu (d. 1669)   Ainu leader. He led the 1669 Ainu uprising in southern Hokkaidō. It was one of the three largest organized Ainu uprisings; the other two were the Koshamain War and the 1789 uprising.

Bibliography of English-Language Books on the Ainu

Barnes, R. H., Andrew Gray, and Benedict Kingsbury, eds. *Indigenous Peoples of Asia*. Ann Arbor, Mich.: Association for Asian Studies, 1995.

Batchelor, John. *Ainu Life and Lore: Echoes of a Departing Race*. Tokyo: Kyōbunkan, 1927.

Befu, Harumi, ed. *Cultural Nationalism in East Asia*. Berkeley: University of California Press, 1993.

Bird, Isabella. *Unbeaten Tracks in Japan: An Account of Travels in the Interior Including Visits to the Aborigines of Yezo and the Shrine of Nikko*. 1880. Reprint, Rutland, Vt.: Tuttle, 1973.

Carpenter, Frances. *People from the Sky: Ainu Tales from Northern Japan*. Illustrated by Betty Fraser. Garden City, N.Y.: Doubleday, 1972.

De Vos, George. *Social Cohesion and Alienation: Minorities in the United States and Japan*. Boulder, Colo.: Westview, 1992.

Etter, Carl. *Ainu Folklore: Traditions and Culture of the Vanishing Aborigines of Japan*. Chicago: Wilcox and Follett, 1949.

Fukusawa, Yuriko. *Ainu Archaeology as Ethnohistory: Iron Technology among the Saru Ainu of Hokkaido, Japan, in the 17th Century*. Oxford: John and Erica Hedges, 1998.

Geiser, Peter, ed. *The Ainu: The Past in the Present*. Hiroshima: Bunka Hyoron Publishing, 1997.

Hanihara Kazurō, ed. *International Symposium on Japanese as a Member of the Asian and Pacific Populations*. Kyoto: International Research Center for Japanese Studies, 1992.

Hardacre, Helen, ed. *New Directions in the Study of Meiji Japan: Proceedings of the Meiji Studies Conference.* Leiden: Brill, 1997.

Hilger, Mary Inez. *Together with the Ainu: A Vanishing People.* Norman: University of Oklahoma Press, 1971.

Honda Katsuichi. *The Impoverished Spirit in Contemporary Japan: Selected Essays of Honda Katsuichi.* Edited by John Lie. Translated by Eri Fujieda, Masayuki Hamazaki, and John Lie. New York: Monthly Review Press, 1993.

Howell, David. *Capitalism from Within: Economy, Society, and the State in a Japanese Fishery.* Berkeley: University of California Press, 1995.

Kayano Shigeru. *Our Land Was a Forest: An Ainu Memoir.* Translated by Kyoko Selden and Lili Selden. Boulder, Colo.: Westview, 1994.

———. *The Romance of the Bear God: Ainu Folktales.* Translated by Iwasaki Masami et al. Tokyo: Taishūkan Publishing, 1985.

Kindaichi Kyosuke. *Ainu Life and Legends.* Tourist Library No. 36. Tokyo: Board of Tourist Industry, Japanese Government Railways, 1941.

Kreiner, Joseph, ed. *European Studies on Ainu Language and Culture.* Munich: Iudicium-Verlag, 1993.

Loos, N., and T. Osanai, eds. *Indigenous Minorities and Education: Australian and Japanese Perspectives on Their Indigenous Peoples, the Ainu, Aborigines, and Torres Straits Islanders.* Tokyo: Sanyusha, 1993.

Maher, John C., and Gaynor Macdonald, eds. *Diversity in Japanese Culture and Language.* London: Kegan Paul International, 1995.

Moes, Robert. *Japanese Folk Art from the Brooklyn Museum; Ainu Section.* New York: Universe Books, 1985.

Morris-Suzuki, Tessa. *Reinventing Japan: Time, Space, Nation.* Armonk, N.Y.: M. E. Sharpe, 1998.

Munro, Neil Gordon. *Ainu Creed and Cult.* Edited with a preface and an additional chapter by B. Z. Seligman, introduction by H. Watanabe. New York: Columbia University Press, 1963.

Nihon Seni Isho Senta. *Textile Designs of Japan.* 3 vols. Osaka: Japan Textile Color Design Center, 1959–60.

Ohnuki-Tierney, Emiko. *Sakhalin Ainu Folklore.* Washington, D.C.: American Anthropological Association, 1969.

————. *Illness and Healing among the Sakhalin Ainu: A Symbolic Interpretation.* Cambridge: Cambridge University Press, 1981.

Pearson, Richard J., ed. *Windows on the Japanese Past.* Ann Arbor: Center for Japanese Studies, University of Michigan, 1986.

Peng, Fred C. C., and Peter Geiser. *The Ainu: The Past in the Present.* Hiroshima: Bunka Hyōron, 1977.

Philippi, Donald, trans. *Songs of Gods, Songs of Humans: The Epic Tradition of the Ainu.* Princeton: Princeton University Press, 1979.

Refsing, Kirsten, ed. *Origins of the Ainu Language: The Ainu Indo-European Controversy.* 5 vols. Richmond, England: Curzon, 1998.

Roche, Judith, and Meg McHutchison, eds. *First Fish, First People: Salmon Tales of the North Pacific Rim.* Seattle: One Reel, in association with the University of Washington Press, 1988.

Shibatani Masayoshi. *The Languages of Japan.* Cambridge: Cambridge University Press, 1990.

Siddle, Richard. *Race, Resistance, and the Ainu of Japan.* London: Routledge, 1996.

Sjöberg, Katarina. *The Return of the Ainu: Cultural Mobilization and the Practice of Ethnicity in Japan.* Chur, Switzerland: Harwood Academic Publishers,1993.

Takakura Shinichiro. *The Ainu of Northern Japan: A Study in Conquest and Acculturation.* Translated and annotated by John A. Harrison. Philadelphia: American Philosophical Society, 1960.

Vovin, Alexander. *A Reconstruction of Proto-Ainu.* Leiden: E. J. Brill, 1993.

Watanabe, Hitoshi. *The Ainu Ecosystem: Environment and Group Structure.* Seattle: University of Washington, 1972.

Weiner, Michael, ed. *Japan's Minorities: The Illusion of Homogeneity.* London: Routledge, 1997.

Index

birthing rope (*nuwap tar*), 233–34,
   234
Black Power, xxxiii
bows and arrows, 43, 51
Bretons, 14n
brown bears, 22, 23, 31
Bunrui Ainugo jiten (Classified Ainu-
   Japanese dictionary) (Chiri), 22n
butterburs, *32*

Caescar, 11
canoes, *217*, 239, *239*
capelin, 26, 29–30, 229n
carving, 95, 149, 150, 243
charanke (argument), 52–53, 256,
   280
chep (fish), 26
chep ohau (fish and vegetable soup),
   97, 105, 106
Cherokees, 14
chestnuts, 31
chikisani (elm), 38
childbirth, 230–38; *see also* midwifery
China: trade with, xix; traditional
   houses in, 56
chinru (snow sandals), 196, *197*
chinunukehi (precious part; male
   genitalia), 41
chip (canoe), *217*
Chiri Mashiho, 22n, 55–56, 81, 90,
   216n, 300
chise (houses), xxii, 56–57, *58*, *59*,
   59–60, *94*; interior of, *101*; life
   inside, during snowstorm, 94–
   95, 105–9; nuptial, 228; retirement, 244, 255
chise kor kamui (guardian god of the
   house), *265*
chise uhuika (house-burning ritual),
   255
chisenomi (house-warming celebration), 134, 135, *135*

chishinaot toma (body wrapped in
   a mat), *253*
chiurikin (flash flood), 132
chopsticks, ceremonial (*pasui*), 76,
   149, *183*
Chronicle of Japan (*Nihon shoki* or
   Nihongi), 33
chuppe (menstruation), 134, 135,
   141–45, 160, 195
clairvoyance, 66, 79–82, 196–97,
   200, 202
commondity economy, 54
courtship practices, 147, 194–96, 208
cradle (*shinta*), 97
creation myths, 33–48
crown, ceremonial (*sapanpe*), *170*

dace, 27
dances, festival, 134–35, 154–56,
   155, 192–93
death, rituals surrounding, 245–55
deer, 21–24, *23*, 31
deforestation, 20–21
dispute resolution by debate (*uko-
   charanke*), 52–53, 256
divination. See *tusu*
Dun, Edwen, 108n
dysentery, treatment of, 241–42, 277

Eagle King, story of, 183–87
earrings (*ninkari*), *113*
ears, pierced, 112
Ebisu, xvii
echiush (lidded wine pourer), *283*
Edo period, 6, 13, 18, 34, 68, 102n
Egyptians, ancient, 83
ekashi (elders), xxxiv, 34, 64, 81,
   202; performance of traditional
   rituals by, 75, *76*, 152–54, 157–
   61, 253
Elm (female god), 38
embroidery, 130, 156, 187; *see also*
   tekunpe

Emishi, xvii
eniupe (pillow), *157*
Epi-Jōmon period, 4, 6
epic poetry. See *yukar*
epidemics, 239–42
Eskimo. *See* Inuit
etnup (wine pourer), *209*
Etui-huchi, 30n
Evenki, 26
Ezo, xvii, 7
Ezotō kikan (Curious sights on Ezo
    Island) (Murakami), 101

family insignia (*aishiroshi*), 50–52
family shrine (*nichineikorokamui*), *101*
family structure, 61–63
farming, 6; as subsidiary activity, 55
feeling in the hand (*tekeinu*), 64, 75
festivals. See *iyomante*
fire, creation of, 38, 43
fire-making tools, 267, *281*
firewood, gathering, 118–19
fish-hitting stick (*isapakikni*), 142
fishing, xv, *25*, 26–30, 55, 141–
    42; commercial, xx; in creation
    myth, 43
flood, 130–33
folktales. See *uwepeker*
food, 27–33, 96–97, 105–7; for
    festivals, 146
forests, 16–21, *17*
Former Hokkaido Aborigine
    Protection Act (Hokkaidō
    Kyūdojin Hogohō), xxii, xxiv
fox, 31
frog deity, tale of, 139–40
Fujimoto Hideo, 63n
Fujimura Hisakazu, 12, 67n, 99n,
    148n, 218n, 237n, 267n, 300
funerals, 245–55

gathering, 28, 31, 33, 55
genealogy, 48–53

grains: growing of, 6; *see also*
    millet
"Gratitude of the Eagle King,"
    183–87
grave markers, *254*
greetings: ritual (*onkami*), 105, 133,
    159, 264; women's, *122*, 123
guardian spirits, 81
guiding spirits, 81

Haenure (Aoki's *huchi* or grand-
    mother), 66, 68, 69, 78
Haginaka Mie, 85
hand covers (*tekunpe*), 151, 187, *188*,
    193–94
hapo (mother), 11
hare, 23; *yukar* of, 113–15
hauki (epic poetry). See *yukar*
heper-set (cage), *154*
herring, 27
Hikawa Tsuru, 129n
Hikawa Zenjirō, *76*
hito (Japanese word for human), 11
hosh (leg guards), *210*
hot-water trial (*saimon*), 284
Hotta Masaatsu, 19n
Hottentot, 10–11, 26
houses, Ainu. See *chise*
huchi (grandmother; granddame), 11,
    62
Humoshirushi, 48, 51, 54, 93
hunting, 22–23, 31, 55; in creation
    myth, 43; disputes over territory
    for, 256; family insignias and,
    51–52
hupcha kucha (hunting hut), *172*

Iboshi Hokuto, xxiii, 27, 300
ichimchimi (minute observations), 68
Ikatoshin, 53
ikayop (cylindrical arrow case), *259*
ikoinkar (midwife), 63–75, 121, 196,
    227–38

Ikorohasiw, 53
inau (ceremonial twigs or poles), 29,
    44, *44*, 48, *101*, 124, 142, *185*,
    262, *262*
inaukotchep (small salmon), 29
Inisetet (To Scoop Things), 53
inonnoitak (chanted prayer), 233
Inuit, xxxiv, 10, 56, 61
ipetam (sword that devours humans),
    202, 207
Irapekar, 53
iron tools and utensils, xviii, 3, 6
isapakikni (fish-hitting stick), 142n
ishma (woman's underbelt), *144*,
    144–45, 249n
itak-kamui (spirit of words), 166
itako (medium), 79
Iterimen, 11
Iyochiunmat, 89
iyohaichish (improvised song of
    longing), 188
iyoikir (treasure altar), *9*
iyoitakkote (ritual of sending the soul
    to the spirit world; requiem), 207,
    251–53
iyomante (spirit-sending festivals),
    xxi, xxiv, xxvi, 29, 31, 145–94,
    155, 198, 249, 267n; dancing
    at, *154*–56, 192–93; preparations
    for, 146–52; *yukar* performed
    at, 147, 160, 162–87, 189–91

Japan-Soviet Fisheries Cooperation
    Agreement (1985), 24
jewel boxes, 208
Jōmon people, 3, 6, 8, 21, 33, 55

ka (five-stringed zither), *182*
Kaizawa Seitarō, 51, 75
Kaizawa Turshino, *84*
kam ohau (meat and vegetable soup),
    97
Kamakura period, 6, 54

Kamchadahl, 11
kamui (gods), 11, 55
kamui moshir (land of the gods), 77
kamui yukar, xxxi, 26n, 123, 244; of
    bear, 124–29; of hare, 113–14
kamuichep (divine fish), 26
kamuinomi (prayer), 77, 191, *191*,
    264, 266, 282
Kanaikar, 48
kanit (spindle stick), *98*
Kannari Matsu, 63n, *86*, 218n,
    300–301
kaparimip (unlined appliquéed
    robe), *126*
katsura trees, *18*
Kawakami Sanouk, *274*, 274–75
Kawakami Yūji, 206n, 274–75
Kawasaki Steel, 60n
Kayano Shigeru, xxix, 11, 12n, 26n,
    29, 48, *49*, *50*, 51–53, 62n, 64,
    93, 94, 267n, 301
kemaha pirkano monoa (posture of
    giving birth by oneself), 69–70
kemonuitosayep (spindle with needle
    container), *107*
Khmer, 14n
kimun kamui (mountain deity), 146
kimun-kamuipo hurayep (rain that
    washes bear cubs), 22
Kimura Kimi, *87*, 206n
Kinasutkamui (snake deity), 78, 80
Kindaichi Kyōsuke, xxix, xxx
kito (lily family plant), 28
knife, women's (*menoko makiri*),
    151, *199*
Kobata Umonte, 26n
Kobuta Nezō, 301
Koin, 10–11, 26
Korea, trade with, xix
Kosamainu. See Koshamain
Koshamain, 12, 286, 301
Koshamain War, 15, 40, 273, 286
kotan (village), xxxiii, 55–57, *56*, *57*;

Indexer: Ruth Elwell
Text: 11/14 Bembo
Display: Bembo
Composition: Integrated Composition Systems

CPSIA information can be obtained
at www.ICGtesting.com
Printed in the USA
LVHW041514170519
618250LV00001B/49